Generalized
Phrase Structure
Grammar

Generalized Phrase Structure Grammar

GERALD GAZDAR, EWAN KLEIN,
GEOFFREY PULLUM, IVAN SAG

Harvard University Press
Cambridge, Massachusetts
1985

Copyright © 1985 by G. Gazdar, E. Klein, G. K. Pullum, and I. A. Sag
Printed in Great Britain
10 9 8 7 6 5 4 3 2 1

Library of Congress Cataloging in Publication Data

Main entry under title:

Generalized phrase structure grammar.

Bibliography: p.
1. Grammar, comparative and general. 2. Generative grammar.
I. Gazdar, Gerald.
P151.G45 1985   415   84-22587

ISBN 0-674-34455-3
ISBN 0-674-34456-1 (pbk.)

Contents

Preface

This book contains a fairly complete exposition of a general theory of grammar that we have worked out in detail over the past four years. Unlike much theoretical linguistics, it lays considerable stress on detailed specifications both of the theory and of the descriptions of parts of English grammar that we use to illustrate the theory. We do not believe that the working out of such details can be dismissed as 'a matter of execution', to be left to lab assistants. In serious work, one cannot 'assume some version of the X-bar theory' or conjecture that a 'suitable' set of interpretive rules will do something as desired, any more than one can evade the entire enterprise of generative grammar by announcing: 'We assume some recursive function that assigns to each grammatical and meaningful sentence of English an appropriate structure and interpretation.' One must set about constructing such a function, or one is not in the business of theoretical linguistics.

This book will not be an easy read. Parts of it – the parts most crucial to the functioning of the general theory – are formalized rather precisely. Those parts – generally the final sections of the chapters – are naturally somewhat demanding. We hope that none of the formalism is gratuitous, and although it is doubtless not as clean as it should be, we have struggled to render it conceptually clearer than when it started out, and in every case, we explain in prose what each formalized principle says and what its role is in the general scheme of things. In the semantics chapters, in particular, we have attempted to allow for the reader who has little specialized knowledge of the subject. In general, we hope that graduate or advanced undergraduate students who have had courses in some version of generative grammar, and who have at least some introductory acquaintance with logic, mathematics, or computer science, will be able to understand generalized phrase structure grammar through studying this book, and will grasp something of what a rigorous syntactic and semantic theory of language might be like.

We have numerous people to thank for their assistance in the writing of this book. Some of them will be quite surprised that we regard them as having helped; but to us, virtually every colleague who curled a lip at some ugly patch of badly worded definitions, every student who refused to shut up when told to and pressed home an embarrassing question, and every linguist who paid us the compliment of addressing our work in published or presented papers has contributed something to this book. We cannot possibly identify every one of them, but we want to mention the names of some, even at the risk of slighting the others.

Much of our work has been conducted in the intellectual community of Stanford, Palo Alto, and Menlo Park. Many people who have worked there between 1981 and 1984 have talked to us, argued with us, and contributed clever ideas. Among them are Mike Barlow, Herb Clark, Mark Cobler, Robin Cooper, Chris Culy, Murvet Enc, Elisabet Engdahl, Chuck Fillmore, Dan Flickinger, Mark Gawron, Lauri Karttunen, Martin Kay, Paul Kay, Susannah MacKaye, Geoffrey Nunberg, Kathy O'Connor, Anne Paulson, Fernando Pereira, Stanley Peters, Carl Pollard, Kelly Roach, Jane Robinson, Stuart Shieber, Susan Stucky, Henry Thompson, Hans Uszkoreit, Tom Wasow and Michael Wescoat.

The reception of our ideas have received in the British linguistics and cognitive science community has often been sympathetic and stimulating, and we have benefited from the queries and comments of Bob Borsley, Gill Brown, Keith Brown, Brian Butterworth, Ronnie Cann, Richard Coates, Grev Corbett, Connie Cullen, Anne Cutler, Roger Evans, John Foster, Alan Garnham, Steve Harlow, Geoff Horrocks, Steve Isard, Phil Johnson-Laird, Christopher Longuet-Higgins, John Lyons, Rose Maclaran, Peter Matthews, Steve Pulman, Barry Richards, Graham Russell, Aaron Sloman, Neil Smith, Larry Trask, Nigel Vincent, Anthony Warner, and Yorick Wilks.

Invitations from Harry Whitaker at the Department of Speech and Hearing, University of Maryland, in 1982 and Robert P. Stockwell at the Department of Linguistics, UCLA, in 1983 allowed us to present some of the results of our research to classes at two successive Linguistic Institutes. This was a valuable experience which taught us that we hadn't got everything as right as we thought we had. We learned a lot from Carol Anderson, Paul Chapin, Rob Chametzsky, Mary Dalrymple, Dominique Estival, Aryeh Faltz, Donka Farkas, Erhard Hinrichs, Chu-Ren Huang, Geoff Huck, Carolyn Jenkins, Mark Johnson, Ed Keenan, Michael Moortgat, Susan Mordechay, Young-Hee Na, Almerindo Ojeda, Jessie Pinkham, John Richardson, Jerry Sadock, Paul Schachter, Peter Sells, Mary Tait, and Shelley Waksler.

At longer distance, we have regularly had encouragement, support, and valuable feedback from Jan Anward, Emmon Bach, Greg Carlson, Ken

Church, Östen Dahl, David Dowty, Eva Ejerhed, Janet Fodor, Georgia Green, Takao Gunji, Lars Hellan, Pauline Jacobson, Aravind Joshi, Hans Kamp, Bill Ladusaw, Jim McCawley, Jim McCloskey, Joan Maling, Jerry Morgan, Dick Oehrle, Barbara Partee, Jeff Pelletier, Len Schubert, Frieda Steurs, Greg Stump, Rich Thomason, Mariko Udo, Annie Zaenen, and Arnold Zwicky.

Ideas are not like houseplants. They do not grow best in uniform conditions of bland comfort. They thrive when faced with opposition and counterattack. We have been greatly aided by our disputes with people who have argued that generalized phrase structure grammar is the wrong path to take in syntactic and semantic theory. We cherish particularly the challenging and stimulating critical attention our ideas have received at the hands of people like Joan Bresnan, Jean Gibson, Kris Halvorsen, Jorge Hankamer, Frank Heny, Dick Hudson, Ron Kaplan, Alec Marantz, Fritz Newmeyer, David Perlmutter, David Pesetsky, Paul Postal, Mark Steedman, Tim Stowell, and Edwin Williams. Our thanks to them are entirely sincere. We hope that if our ideas still seem wrong to them, this book will at least be valuable in making it clearer to them why they are right.

We owe a special debt to Elisabet Engdahl and Mark Gawron who made detailed comments on preliminary drafts of many of the chapters in this book (as well as several that have not been included), and to the people who have given their time to provide valuable research assistance: Mike Barlow, Mark Cobler, Dan Flickinger, Jerry Kelly, Susannah MacKaye, Karen Wallace, and Michael Wescoat.

There are several agencies and institutions without whose financial and general support the process of finishing a book with authors located in Brighton, Edinburgh, Palo Alto, and Santa Cruz would not have been possible. At Stanford University during several summers, support from the Sloan Foundation, two National Science Foundation grants (BNS-8102404, BNS-8309780), and a gift from the System Development Foundation to the Center for Study of Language and Information (CSLI) have helped support us, as has travel assistance from the British Academy (Small Grants Research Fund in the Humanities) and facilities provided by the Syntax Research Center at the University of California, Santa Cruz. Grants from the UK Social Science Research Council supported Gazdar's work at the University of Sussex. An Advanced Research Fellowship from the UK Science and Engineering Research Council (SERC) has supported Klein's work at the University of Edinburgh. A Summer Stipend from the National Endowment for the Humanities and a Faculty Research grant from the University of California, Santa Cruz, have assisted Pullum's research.

We are grateful to Hewlett-Packard Laboratories in Palo Alto for allowing access to their computing facilities after hours while we worked on an electronic typescript of this book in the fall of 1983, and to Judea Pearl of UCLA for making his computing facilities available to us during the 1983 Linguistic Institute. We would also like to record our thanks to the many computer users and consultants at CSLI, Edinburgh, Sussex, UCLA, and UCSC who have uncomplainingly wasted their own time helping us with tapes, weekend machine crashes, shell scripts, nroff macros, printer drivers, terminal emulations, and the rest of the information technology that has become a *sine qua non* of producing a book in the 1980s. And we thank our publishers, in particular Stephen Ball, Philip Carpenter and John Davey: the existence of this book is more of a testament to their tolerant persistence than it is to ours.

Finally, we express our appreciation to the Digital Equipment Corporation (DEC), whose ubiquitous machines have enabled us to collaborate in eight different locations on two continents, and to the air traffic control staffs of London and San Francisco, who have so frequently had our lives in their hands.

1

Introduction

1 Generative grammar

This book is a contribution to the discipline known as generative grammar. This approach to linguistics is characterized by its goal of investigating natural language through the construction of fully explicit descriptions of particular languages and a formalized general framework for defining the space within which to locate such descriptions. The end to which this effort is directed is the development of a general theory of the structure of natural languages. If the formal framework is restrictive enough to make nontrivial, falsifiable claims about what may and may not be a natural language, or a grammar for a natural language, then we can identify the framework itself with the traditional notion 'universal grammar', and interpret it not merely as a formal language for representing grammars of particular languages but rather as a partial characterization of what natural languages and their grammars are like.

The basic assumption made in generative grammar is that languages can be regarded as collections whose membership is definitely and precisely specifiable. The elements of such a collection are the expressions in the language. Following Montague (1970) and Brame (1981), we assume that the grammars of natural languages should define not merely the expressions corresponding to sentences but also subsentential expressions of all categories. Clearly the set of compound linguistic expressions in a natural language is not finite, so we cannot list them. An interpreted formal system defining the membership of the collection of linguistic expressions, and assigning a structure and an interpretation to each member, is required. This is what we call a grammar. The study of language is intimately bound up with the study of grammars for those who accept this basic premise of the generative approach to linguistics, and parts of this book deal in considerable detail with the precise statement of particular rules and principles of grammar. Wherever possible, we do more than just illustrate points of theory with suggestive examples or hint at what some components of the grammar might contain. There are three crucial methodological assumptions that lead us to proceed in this way:

I   A necessary precondition to 'explaining' some aspect of the organization of natural languages is a description of the relevant phenomena which is thorough enough and precise enough to make it plausible to suppose that the language under analysis really is organized in the postulated way.

II A grammatical framework can and should be construed as a formal language for specifying grammars of a particular kind. The syntax and, more importantly, the semantics of that formal language constitute the substance of the theory or theories embodied in the framework.

III The most interesting contribution that generative grammar can make to the search for universals of language is to specify formal systems that have putative universals as *consequences*, as opposed to merely providing a technical vocabulary in terms of which autonomously stipulated universals can be expressed.

These three points merit some further discussion. Consider first I, i.e. the issue of whether an explanatory account of some grammatical phenomenon can be provided without the descriptive detail having been worked out. It has regrettably become more and more common of late to find linguists suggesting that broad hypotheses about grammatical theory can be discussed in the absence both of formal work that demonstrates that certain implications follow from those hypotheses and of descriptive work showing that the putative implications are well confirmed. Our experience is that even after quite a significant amount of work has been done on a proposal for the description of some fragment of a language, it is quite difficult to see in full detail what its consequences are.

There may not even be algorithmic ways of confirming the consequences of some theories of grammar, of course: if the theory allows grammars for nonrecursive sets, then we run the risk that the claim that some string is not generated by some grammar cannot be verified in principle. Familiar statements of the type 'Thus our grammar excludes examples like (158)', in other words, may simply be untestable conjectures.[1]

This observation leads naturally to our second assumption, II, that a grammatical framework is best construed as a formal language having itself both a syntax and a semantics. A grammar characterizes a language, say Japanese, DEC10 Prolog, or the Polish postfix notation for arithmetic. A family of grammars characterize a family of languages, say the indexed languages, the natural languages, or the assembly languages for 8-bit microprocessors. Each of these object languages has a syntax and a semantics. In formal language theory, the syntaxes of a given family of object languages are themselves specified in a formal language (e.g. the Backus–Naur notation for the grammars of context-free languages). This metalanguage itself has both a syntax and a semantics. Since such a metalanguage has the grammars of the object languages as its topic, it follows that the semantics of the metalanguage has as its domain syntactic entities (strings, trees, categories, etc.) in the object languages. The syntax of the metalanguage is in many respects arbitrary, but it needs to stand in some fairly perspicuous relation to the intended semantics, and it needs to be explicit enough for one to see what can and cannot be expressed by means of it. Much of the technicality of the present work stems from an attempt, not uniformly successful, to be as explicit as possible about what our grammar formalism is, and what it means.[2]

Assumption III, that universals are most interesting when embedded as integral parts of a formal system that has some nontrivial structure, involves just as clear a break with the approaches adopted in much current work. It goes without saying that the process of searching for grammatical universals initially involves attempting to discover facts about language (as opposed to facts about some particular language or set of languages). But there is a sense in which even a precise formulation of a successful discovery of this sort will not constitute a truly interesting result in theoretical linguistics. If the fact needs a special statement, as opposed to following from the very form in which the theoretical reconstruction of the notion 'natural language' has been cast, the job is not done.

Thus, for example, one might propose that natural language grammars never exhibit direct grammatical dependencies between elements separated by more than two phrasal categories of a certain sort, or that they never permit a full category in a certain position in the clause, or whatever. But these proposed universals are not accounted for by the mere fact of their having been written down in some uninterpreted algebraic formalism. The explanatory task has not even begun when a constraint or generalization is merely stated. Only when it can be shown to be a nontrivial consequence of the definition of the notion 'possible grammar' can it be regarded as explained, because while it resides in the form of an autonomous statement it can be modified, enhanced, weakened, or even discarded with no consequences for the rest of the theory (cf. Dowty 1982b, pp. 107–8, on this important point). The penalty for failure of such a universal is effectively zero; a new universal saying something carefully hedged to avoid the last known counterexample can be constructed in a moment. Ironically, in view of the fact that such universals are often presented with a considerable fanfare of rhetoric about explanation, they have much the same status as the descriptive universals we find in the typological work that takes its lead from Greenberg (1963) – only these claims, being better researched, generally have a much longer half-life.

Our goal in the work that has led to GPSG has been to arrive at a constrained metalanguage capable of defining the grammars of natural languages, but not the grammar of, say, the set of prime numbers. (The phrase 'capable of' indicates a rather ambitious program; a somewhat less ambitious one, under which we need not require that the set of prime numbers be literally indescribable within the terms of our theory, is obtained if we replace this phrase by 'suited to'.) The universalism is, ultimately, intended to be entirely embodied in the formal system, not expressed by statements made in it. Consider, by way of illustration, the statement in (1).

(1)   [VFORM FIN] $\supset$ [$-$N, $+$V]

This states, in the terms we introduce in chapter 2 below, that having the value FIN, i.e. finite, for the feature VFORM implies being verbal and non-nominal; in other words, only a verb can have tense. We could state this in our theory of grammar as a universal feature co-occurrence restriction. But this would only amount to an admission of – hopefully temporary – defeat (an admission we may have to make at the present state of our knowledge, of course). If (1) is universal, then it should not need saying. It ought to be a consequence of the grammatical metalanguage itself – for example, by virtue of a theory of features which (unlike ours) ties tense securely to the semantic notion it expresses and simultaneously restricts its syntactic realization to verbal categories in the theory of grammar. If this were done effectively, the discovery of a language with tensed adjectives would severely compromise the theory of features as a whole and force revisions that would alter the consequences of the theory in other domains. If we simply rest content with the universal stipulation '[VFORM FIN] $\supset$ [$-$N, $+$V]', we can drop it, or modify it to say '[VFORM FIN] $\supset$ [$+$V]', at no real cost. There are, of course, languages with constructions that have been held to exhibit tensed adjectives (the so-called non-nominal adjectives in Japanese, for instance). The fact that it would be so easy to modify (1) to take account of them is precisely what we are drawing attention to.

We therefore regard universals stated within the metalanguage as inherently less interesting than those which are built into it. We exhibit in this book some claims, for example the Exhaustive Constant Partial Ordering claim about linear precedence in grammars (see chapter 3, section 2), which follow as consequences of our overall formal system. It is this sort of result that is an important goal of the GPSG approach to linguistics: the construction of theories of the structure of sentences under which significant properties of grammars and languages fall out as theorems as opposed to being stipulated as axioms.

In view of the fact that the packaging and public relations of much recent linguistic theory involves constant reference to questions of psychology, particularly in association with language acquisition, it is appropriate for us to make a few remarks about the connections between the claims we make and issues in the psychology of language. We make no claims, naturally enough, that our grammatical theory is *eo ipso* a psychological theory. Our grammar of English is not a theory of how speakers think up things to say and put them into words. Our general linguistic theory is not a theory of how a child abstracts from the surrounding hubbub of linguistic and nonlinguistic noises enough evidence to gain a mental grasp of the structure of a natural language. Nor is it a biological theory of the structure of an as-yet-unidentified mental organ. It is irresponsible to claim otherwise for theories of this general sort. It may even be incoherent, as Katz (1981) and Soames (1984) have argued.

Thus we feel it is possible, and arguably proper, for a linguist (*qua* linguist) to ignore matters of psychology. But it is hardly possible for a psycholinguist to ignore language. And since a given linguistic theory will make specific claims about the nature of languages, it may well in turn suggest specific kinds of psycholinguistic hypothesis. Stephen Crain and Janet Fodor, in a series of papers (Crain and Fodor, in press; Fodor 1980, 1983a, 1983b) have argued that GPSG does have implications for psycholinguistic concerns. Nonetheless, it seems to us that virtually all the work needed to redeem the promissory notes linguistics has issued to psychology over the past 25 years remains to be done. If linguistics is truly a branch of psychology (or even biology), as is often unilaterally asserted by linguists, it is so far the branch with the greatest pretensions and the fewest reliable results. The most useful course of action in this circumstance is probably not to engage in further programmatic posturing and self-congratulatory rhetoric of the sort that has characterized much linguistic work in recent years, but rather to attempt to fulfill some of the commitments made by generative grammar in respect of the provision of fully specified and precise theories of the nature of the languages that humans employ. Even when that is done, the psychology of language will doubtless have a vast amount of work to do before we have a scientific understanding of how the human species acquires and uses language. After all, geometrical optics long ago provided us with a fairly clear and stable means of characterizing the objects of visual perception, but the psychology of visual perception still has many problems to solve. So far, linguistics has not fulfilled its own side of the interdisciplinary bargain.

Two additional terminological points are in order about this account of our theoretical orientation. First, notice that although Langendoen and

Postal (1984) take the term 'generative grammar' to be restricted to those theories that characterize recursively enumerable sets of sentences (and not, for instance, the proper classes of finite and infinite-length strings that they claim constitute natural languages), we do not regard ourselves as committed to any such limitation. It is straightforward to interpret our grammar as admitting a proper class of structures most of which are infinite in size if that is thought desirable.[3]

And second, note that the term 'generative grammar' is sometimes used as if it referred to (even solely to) contemporary work in Chomsky's 'Revised Extended Standard Theory' (REST) such as 'Government-Binding' (GB; Chomsky 1981) but not, for example, GPSG, Lexical-Functional Grammar (LFG; Bresnan 1982b), or Arc-Pair Grammar (APG; Johnson and Postal 1980). Van Riemsdijk (1982), for example, is particularly explicit in this usage, and even critics of REST sometimes adopt it (Comrie 1984). It will be clear that our use of the term 'generative grammar' covers GPSG, LFG, APG, Montague Grammar in all its varieties, the work presented in *Syntactic Structures* (Chomsky 1957), Stockwell et al. 1973, Lasnik and Kupin 1977, and other work, but includes little of the research done under the rubric of the 'Government Binding' framework, since there are few signs of any commitment to the explicit specification of grammars or theoretical principles in this genre of linguistics.

2   Syntax and semantics

While a purely syntactic approach to a language takes it to be simply a collection of expressions or other linguistic objects, natural languages have meanings associated with their expressions. Presumably, it is only because of the meanings carried by expressions in natural languages that they exist at all. That is, regardless of whether the natural languages employed by human beings function primarily as internal representation codes in which thinking can be carried out, or media for artistic expression, or systems for inter-organism communication, or have some other rationale for their existence, there would appear to be no value in knowing a natural language if no meanings were associated with its expressions. (Compare this with the case of phonetics: to say that there is no value in knowing a natural language if one cannot vocalize and process auditory data is simply not true. Human languages subsist in other modalities than the phonetic, e.g. in private thinking, in visual, tactile and electronic codes, in hand signing, and so on.) Thus it is uncontroversial (or should be) to assume that the specification of a relation between the expressions of a language and their meanings is a central goal of linguistic theory.

Furthermore, it is now widely accepted, though not entirely uncontroversial, that the theory of meaning for natural languages falls into two subcomponents, namely pragmatics and, under a narrow construal, semantics. Under the classical definitions of these components, semantics deals with the relation between expressions and what they denote, while pragmatics deals with the relation between expressions, their denotata, and their use. A related contemporary view maintains that semantics deals with the inherent meaning of expressions, while pragmatics deals with the meanings communicated by expressions on the occasions of their use.

This book will have almost nothing to say about pragmatics, but semantics plays a crucial role in a number of places (in the treatment of agreement, for example) and the two final chapters are devoted to the technical details of the semantic theory that we adopt, which is in essence that of Montague.

The distinction between semantics and pragmatics means that semantics, as we use the term, should not be thought of as the study of meaning *simpliciter*, because there may be aspects of linguistic meaning that are not treated by semantics at all, and are not supposed to be. This raises the issue of what a semantic theory for a natural language does have to do. In this book, we adopt, without extended justification, the view of semantics that has become dominant over the past decade. We assume that, minimally, a semantic theory for a natural language has to be able to provide a recursive definition of *denotation in a model* for the linguistic expressions of the language. Denotation is a general notion, applicable in principle to sentences of imperative, interrogative, and other types, but in the case of declarative sentences (which are canonically used to make statements), it amounts to the notion of truth in arbitrary states of the world. In order to know whether a given sentence is in fact true or not, we need to know two kinds of things: what the sentence means, and what the facts of the world are. This suggests that a theory of meaning should define a function which, given an arbitrary sentence of English and a possible state of affairs, tells us whether the sentence is true or false in that state of affairs. This is done by means of a *model*. A model is an abstract 'state of affairs' in which basic expressions of the language are assigned denotations. For example, proper names might be assigned individuals as denotations, and *n*-place predicates might be assigned *n*-ary relations on the domain of individuals. The recursive clauses of the semantics will then specify how complex expressions receive a denotation in the model on the basis of the denotations of their component expressions. This sounds quite a trivial enterprise when very simple cases are considered (for example, deciding that *All swans are white* is true in a state of affairs where all the swans there are (if any) are members of the set of white objects), but it becomes nontrivial, and in fact extremely complex and challenging, when we consider an infinite domain of sentences defined by recursive application of a set of syntactic rules.

It should be clear enough that this approach does not adequately capture every aspect of our pretheoretic notion of meaning. For instance, in every state of affairs which is logically possible, circles have no corners and cubes have six faces. Hence there is no distinguishing the meanings of the sentences *No circle has corners* and *No cube has seven faces* on the basis of which models (worlds, states of affairs) they are satisfied in. Both are satisfied in every model, whether there are circles and cubes in it or not. This is a semantic problem, the problem of apparently non-synonymous necessary truths, on which current versions of model-theoretic semantics shed little light. Another thorny area involves verbs of propositional attitude such as *believe* (cf. Partee 1982). We do not hold, therefore, that the goals of a semantic theory for natural language can be attained solely by giving a recursive definition of truth in a model. What we do believe, however, is that a theory of semantics could hardly do *less* than provide such a definition of truth.

Further interest is added to the enterprise when constraints are imposed on the way in which the syntactic structure of expressions is related to their semantic interpretation. Apart from such general scientific canons as maximizing the simplicity and generality of statements in the theory, model-theoretic semanticists have attempted to adhere to a principle of compositionality, attributed to Frege, which requires that the meaning of a complex expression should be a function of the meaning of its component parts (cf. Partee, in press). Following Montague, a number of linguists have adopted what is sometimes called the *rule-to-rule hypothesis* (Bach 1976), which is not really a hypothesis but a program. The program maintains that each syntactic rule in a grammar for a natural language is associated with a semantic rule which determines the meaning of the constituent whose form the syntactic rule specifies. We adopt in this book the approach to compositionality that is inherent in the rule-to-rule program.

Again, however, there is a difference between our approach and previous ones. We do not assume that for each rule in the syntax a semantic rule must be given by stipulation. In fact, we believe that no semantic rules whatever have to be given directly by the grammar. Instead, pursuing the line initiated by Klein and Sag (forthcoming), we assume that there exists a universal mapping from syntactic rules to semantic translations (see chapter 10). We claim that the semantic type assigned to any lexical item introduced in a rule (e.g., the lexical information that *possess* denotes a function from noun phrase denotations to verb phrase denotations) and the syntactic form of the rule itself are sufficient to fully determine (i) the form of the semantic translation rule, and thus (ii) the set of logical expressions which can represent the constituent defined by the syntactic rule, and thus (iii) the model-theoretic interpretations of that constituent.

The way in which our semantic proposals will be formalized is in terms of expressions in the intensional logic that has become familiar to linguists since the work of Montague. It is impractical for us to provide a full introduction to Montague semantics here, but it is possible to gain an understanding of the relevant aspects from Dowty et al. (1981), Halvorsen and Ladusaw (1979) and Janssen (1983), especially if one has some prior acquaintance with logic. In general, it will be possible to read most of the first eight chapters of this book without taking any notice of semantic matters, since detailed discussion of the latter is postponed until the final two chapters. We note, however, that the policy of providing an explicit semantics as well as an explicit syntax entails a significant broadening of the scope of the framework in comparison with most work outside the Montague tradition.

Two further points about our position on the syntax–semantics relation must be made here. First, the intensional logic representations we shall exhibit when explicating the semantics of a linguistic expression are not intended to be a part of the linguistic description themselves. We shall adhere to the standard position in Montague semantics that intensional logic representations serve to make our semantic claims explicit, but that they could in principle be replaced by a direct mapping from expressions of English to denotations in a model. Suppose, for example, that we associate the verb phrase *saw something* with a logical expression such as $\lambda x \exists y [\text{saw}'\ (x, y)]$ (read 'is an x such that for some y, x saw y'). We could instead associate the verb phrase directly with the set of objects in the model which satisfy the condition described by the logical expression, but in general the intervening logical expression makes it much easier to see how this is done (for a reader who has mastered the notations and concepts of the logic). Nevertheless, it is not a level of linguistic description and it does not make theoretical claims of its own. A notion like 'occurs adjacent to λx in the logical representation' could not (and should not) play a role in a linguistic rule.

The second point, consequent upon the first, is that we do not intend our semantic machinery to play a role as a post-syntactic filter on well-formedness.[4] We do not assume, as some grammatical work does, that there are 'interpretive' rules which map syntactic representations into 'semantic representations', 'functional structures' or 'logical forms' and which may block the assignment of well-formedness to a sentence by refusing to assign a 'semantic', 'functional' or 'logical' representation to it or by invoking ad hoc constraints on such representations (e.g. a stipulation that logical representations must not contain vacuous quantifi-cation). Our syntactic rules generate representations which are *ipso facto* claimed to be well-formed expressions of English. There are no additional blocking devices yet to be specified, or further levels of representation with their own syntax. In a very real sense, the syntactic representations we construct are their own 'logical forms'. Insofar as there are structures defined by our syntax to which no meaning is assigned under the semantics we specify, we claim that those structures describe well-formed sentences that do not mean anything coherent, not that grammaticality is defined by reference to the overall predictions of the syntax and semantics combined. The matter is a difficult one, clearly, and there is room for much debate on particular cases, but in general the position we are taking should be familiar. We would claim, for example, that *Colorless green ideas sleep furiously* is grammatical. If the denotation of the predicate, *green* is given in terms of a function that is undefined for abstract entities like ideas, no meaning will be assigned. If the function is defined for non-physical objects but always yields falsity when applied to them, there will be a trivial but real meaning assigned (claims about green ideas will be false in every model). What cannot happen is that the matter of assigning a meaning determines grammaticality. In a natural language there can be sentences that fail to say anything, as philosophers have often pointed out; paradoxical sentences like *This statement is false* are impossible to make sense of, but that does not make them ungrammatical.

We have said that we provide sentences with syntactic descriptions that contain enough information for the provision of a direct mapping to their denotations in a model, and the intensional logic translations we associate with them are only a convenient way of making these denotations explicit. Most work in generative grammar has assumed that the description of a linguistic expression must refer to more than one level of syntactically defined structure. By contrast, we are adopting the view that grammars should be *monostratal*, i.e. referring to only a single level of representation. 'Surface structure' is the standard term that comes closest to conveying the properties of this level. As we have made clear, there are no analogs at all, in our system of description, for 'deep structure', 'initial structure', 'functional structure', 'case structure', 'Logical Form', 'shallow structure', or any 'remote structure' levels. It might prove to be the case that our assumption here is too stringent, and is not compatible with the complete explication of the general properties of natural language.[5] If this could be shown, we would have no alternative but to alter and elaborate our framework to the point where it would be an entirely different one. This, of course, we might elect to do. Our objection to additional levels of syntactic structure is not one of religious or philosophical dogma. However, our work on the topics treated in this book has convinced us that the ready acceptance of multistratal syntactic descriptions in earlier generative linguistics was thoroughly undermotivated. The existing corpus of work in GPSG shows that highly revealing systematizations of complex linguistic phenomena can be achieved within the restrictive framework that we adhere to.

If the machinery of linguistic description is to be re-enriched with distinct representational levels and mediating devices, we would hope that such moves be justified by well-supported data and careful argumentation. Nothing will be of more value to those who attempt to provide such argumentation than the availability of a fully worked out set of claims couched in terms of a seriously defended monostratal theory like the one we explore in this book. We therefore believe that our work would continue to have significant utility even if the fundamental claims of our framework should ultimately be discredited.

As things stand, however, we feel that the working hypothesis of GPSG is amply vindicated by close attention to the best known problems in the analysis of English, and by a growing body of work on languages of very different typological characteristics.[6] Moreover, our efforts to marry a linguistically interesting generative syntax with an explicitly defined semantics place our work in an arena that few have entered, since most current syntactic research is associated with no theory of semantics whatsoever.

3 Overview

The remainder of this book falls basically into three parts: the theoretical exposition of the general syntactic theory in chapters 2 to 5, the descriptive applications and analyses of chapters 6 to 8, and the introduction to the theory of semantic interpretation we assume in chapters 9 and 10.

Chapters 2 to 5 introduce the theoretical machinery of GPSG. The body of chapters 2, 3 and 4 is relatively informal, having been kept as free as possible of mathematical notation, but each chapter has a final section in which the crucial concepts are formalized with much greater precision. The reader who wishes to can skip the final sections of these chapters and return to them when or if some later passage seems to necessitate it; thus different readers may make differing decisions about the degree of detail appropriate for the understanding of a particular topic. Chapter 2 provides a theory of syntactic features, their values, their co-occurrence restrictions, their default specifications, and their role in lexical subcategorization. Chapter 3 introduces Immediate Dominance rules, Linear Precedence statements, and the notion 'head of a rule'. Chapter 4 introduces metarules, and illustrates their application to the description of two familiar domains of English syntax, namely passivization and 'subject–aux inversion'.

Chapter 5 is somewhat more technical in its content, but this is unavoidable. It presents a theory of how grammatical rules that are underspecified with respect to featural detail, together with lexical entries that are more fully specified, can determine the full structural and featural detail of a structural description for a linguistic expression. The key principles stated are the Head Feature Convention, which in the novel formulation presented here does a substantial amount of work in determining the feature specifications of the subconstituents of a phrase; the Foot Feature Principle, which distributes certain other features that relate to what is commonly called syntactic binding; and the Control Agreement Principle, which accounts in a very general way for the phenomenon of grammatical agreement. The chapter culminates in a rigorous definition of how a grammar defines a tree as admissible.

It is important that the material of chapter 5 should be grasped at least in outline if the background to the analyses in the following parts of the book is to be fully appreciated. The statements of the feature instantiation principles that the chapter presents look somewhat forbidding, but their intuitive content and their role in accounting for grammatical facts are explained and illustrated as they are introduced.

Chapter 6 begins the section of the book that shows what a GPSG analysis of the syntax of English is like. It treats the main outlines of the internal structure of verb phrases, adjective phrases, noun phrases, and prepositional phrases. Chapter 7 introduces unbounded dependency constructions of the sort that involve long-distance movement operations in classical transformational grammar, and shows how they are analysed in terms of the feature SLASH which encodes the notion of incompleteness of constituents. The initial application to Topicalization and gaps in complement object positions is followed by discussion of *wh* constructions, clefts, and parasitic gaps, together with an analysis of apparent subject gaps that does not make use of gaps in subject position at all. Then, in chapter 8 we treat the topic of coordinate conjunction, traditionally regarded as the bugbear of phrase structure approaches to syntax, and exhibit some interesting consequences of the interaction between our theories of coordination and unbounded dependencies.

Finally, chapters 9 and 10 provide an introduction to the semantic proposals that go along with our syntactic analyses. Chapter 9 treats the semantic type system for phrases and lexical items, and deals with the definition of the traditional grammatical relations such as 'subject' and 'object'. Chapter 10 covers the general theory of how interpretations are assigned to structures on the basis of the types of the lexical items they contain and the form of the syntactic rules that sanction them. It also presents some proposals concerning the semantics of unbounded dependency constructions and, lastly, idioms.

One thing we would like to stress at this point is how much of what we cover in this book is in fact general syntactic and semantic theory, of vastly broader concern than the narrow one of developing GPSG as such. Every theory of generative grammar that we know of uses syntactic features, tacitly or explicitly. Every theory that uses features needs an account of the matters we cover in chapters 2 and 5:

- What sort of formal object is a category, or a feature specification?
- Which feature specifications can co-occur with which others within a category?
- What are the default values for the features employed?
- How are the default values assigned in a manner consistent with the determination of some feature values by rules or universal principles?
- How is a classification imposed on the contents of the lexicon by the system of features?
- How is such a classification made accessible to rules?
- What principles permit and control the free assignment of feature values in categories that do not receive rule-stipulated values for some features?
- How may the feature composition of daughter categories differ from the feature composition of their mothers?
- Which constituents show grammatical agreement with which others in their feature structure, and why?

These are not GPSG-internal questions. Every syntactic theory will have to answer them in due course. The more stress is laid on stipulating as little as possible in grammatical rules themselves (cf. work in Government-Binding), the more important it becomes to have general answers to questions of this sort. What is novel about our work in this book, we believe, is not that we provide GPSG answers to the questions just listed, but that we provide the first detailed answers to them that have ever been given in any framework.

Similarly, we believe our treatment of linear precedence (constituent order) is of general import. Although many linguists have wrestled with the problems of assigning freedom of order to some pairs of constituents while assigning a grammatically specified order to others, mechanisms for doing this, and for capturing explicitly the associated generalizations, have not hitherto been spelled out with the precision found in chapter 3 of this book. The proposals found there are of very general relevance, and could readily find application within other grammatical frameworks.

Thus we do not offer this book simply as an introduction to GPSG theory. We do not believe that the right theory of syntax for natural languages will turn out to call for just the constructs developed here and no others. Rather, we think the results presented in this book will assist in providing a basis for future theories that will have wider scope and richer structure. We have dealt with some phenomena in ways that we think have sufficient merit to survive through several generations of theorizing, but there are others (for example, the theory of anaphora and ellipsis) that we have scarcely touched. Clearly GPSG, as presently formulated, is not the answer to all the questions that arise when we attempt the grammatical description of natural languages.[7] What we do believe, however, is that the answers to some of those questions can be found by improving on the analyses we offer here, not by beginning again; by increasing the level of precision in the sort of general principles we enunciate, not by retreating toward vaguer ones; by striving for better theories, not devising better rhetoric to defend the ones we already have.

Notes

1 Notice, too, how difficult it is to obtain proofs, in a mathematically respectable sense, that one description or framework of theoretical principles is exactly equivalent to another. We know what it is to see it proved that a two-tape Turing machine is equivalent to a one-tape Turing machine under a given simulation. The reader of work in syntax over the last ten years should reflect upon whether proofs in the same sense could be offered that ordering of transformations can be eliminated by appeal to surface filters, or that the principle of the strict cycle can be dispensed with given conditions of 'logical form', or that the number of 'core grammars' defined by linguistic theory is finite. Such claims are made in many contemporary linguistic works without there being any known way of demonstrating their truth. In some works we even find purported 'theorems' being stated without any proof being suggested, or theorems that are given 'proofs' that involve no definition of the underlying class of grammars and are thus empty.

2 Our thinking on this issue has been heavily influenced by Pereira and Shieber (1984) and conversations with Paul Postal and Henry Thompson. As will become evident in the chapters that follow, some parts of the GPSG metalanguage are better developed than others. The basic feature theory, the feature co-occurrence restrictions, the immediate dominance rules, and the linear precedence statements all have a straightforward syntax and a clean and apparently adequate semantics. Metarules have a fairly clear syntax and semantics, but the syntax is probably not restrictive enough (see section 5 of chapter 4) and the semantics is not general enough (in particular, it fails to interact with that of the feature co-occurrence restrictions in an appropriate way). Feature specification defaults have a simple syntax (one that is identical to that of feature co-occurrence restrictions) but the implicit semantics is of labyrinthine complexity. Finally, we fail to provide a syntax for stating the various feature principles that embody much of the empirical content of any

given version of GPSG. Instead, they end up, in effect, as clauses in the overall semantics for the metalanguage.

3 Those interested in this technical point may care to consider a simple example. The quadruple $G = \langle \{S\}, \{a, b\}, S, \{S \rightarrow aSb, S \rightarrow e\} \rangle$ which is standardly interpreted as a context-free phrase structure grammar can also be interpreted as admitting a proper class of not necessarily finite tree-like objects (dendroids, let us say) in which each nonterminal node is labeled S and dominates either, a, S, and b (in that order) or the empty string. For example, one member of the class is a dendroid with a terminal string consisting of a countable infinity of as followed by a countable infinity of bs. The class of all terminal strings of dendroids admitted by this grammar under the suggested interpretation is not, of course, recursively enumerable (since for the example just considered, the enumeration would never be completed), yet it is well-defined and it does have a property intuitively related to the familiar property of context-freeness. The reason our framework has this property is that no notion of 'derivation' enters into it.

4 As far as we know, the question of the descriptive capacity of a type of grammar similar to ours but which *does* permit grammaticality to be determined by whether a completed semantic interpretation is achieved remains to be investigated. The investigation might be rather interesting.

5 Lying near the interface between syntactic and semantic description are a number of unresolved issues involving the representation of quantifier scope and pronominal anaphora to which we will have nothing new to contribute in the present work. We have worked under the assumption that quantifier ambiguities should be handled by some variant of 'Cooper storage', cf. Cooper (1975, 1983), which represents a weakening of the strict compositionality assumed by Montague, but enables us to avoid the assumption that English has an infinite stock of pronouns distinguished from each other by abstract indices. However, work by Kamp (1980) suggests that a comprehensive treatment of these phenomena may in fact require a form of representation intermediate between syntactic representations and their model-theoretic interpretations. The development of these ideas is in its initial stages, and we have nothing to say about it in this book.

6 We are aware of GPSG work on about twenty languages, including Adyge (Vamling 1983), Arabic (Barlow 1984; Edwards 1983), Basque (Trask 1983), Catalan (Espinal i Farre 1981, 1983), Chinese (Cullen 1982; Huang 1983), Dutch (Culy 1983; Moortgat 1984), French (Finer 1981, 1982; Pinkham 1983), German (Hinrichs 1984; Johnson 1983; Nerbonne 1982, 1984; Russell 1983; Uszkoreit 1982a, 1982b, 1983; Zwicky 1984), Greek (Horrocks 1983, 1984; Horrocks and Gazdar 1981), Hindi (Dalrymple 1984), Hungarian (Farkas 1984a, 1984b), Irish (Sells 1982a, 1983a), Japanese (Gunji 1981, 1982, 1983a, 1983b, 1983c, 1983d; Ikeya 1983; Kameshima 1984; Saito 1980; Udo 1982), Korean (Kim 1984), Latin (Cann 1983a, 1983b), Makua (Stucky 1981a, 1981b, 1981c, 1982, 1983), Palauan (Georgopoulos 1983), Polish (Borsley 1983b), Scandinavian languages (Anward 1982; Greggus 1983; Maling and Zaenen 1982; Russell 1984), Spanish (Flickinger 1981; Monzon 1979; Ojeda 1984), and Welsh (Borsley 1983a, 1984a, 1984b; Sells 1983b; Harlow 1981, 1983).

7 This is especially true in the light of the fact that very recent work by Culy (forthcoming) and Shieber (forthcoming) appears to demonstrate for the first time that there can be aspects of the structure of natural languages that are beyond the power of context free systems to describe. We should make it clear that at the time of going to press we had not seen the final versions of these papers. However, the pre-publication drafts we have seen contain arguments that appear sound. Culy, confirming a conjecture related to the one made by Langendoen (1981), argues that a reduplication construction in Bambara (Mande family, West Africa) assigns to an infinite class of (arbitrarily complex) nouns a structure homomorphically equivalent to a non-context-free language, and Shieber argues that certain Swiss dialects of German show a non-context-free pattern of cross-serial syntactic dependencies. These arguments entail that there is at least one construction type in each of the two languages cited which the formal devices characterized in this book do not cover. For a theory closely related to the one outlined in this book that allows for the description of Bambara and Swiss German, see Pollard (1984). We believe that essentially all of what we accomplish in this book can carry over into such revised theories without substantial changes; but the evidence Culy and Shieber have offered, which provides surprising confirmation of conjectures that have never been validly confirmed in the past (see Pullum and Gazdar (1982) for a review), illustrate strikingly our point that we stand at the beginning of an investigation rather than at the end.

2

A theory of
syntactic features

1 Features in earlier generative syntax

In the theory of phrase structure grammars as standardly presented, category labels like 'S', 'NP', 'VP', 'N', etc. are monadic, which is to say that they have no internal structure and are not reducible to anything else.[1] Likewise, in pre-Jakobsonian phonology, phonemes like /g/, /k/, /p/, /s/, etc. were taken to be monadic and irreducible. In phonology, distinctive feature theory (Jakobson, Fant, and Halle 1951) replaced this view of the phoneme with one in which each phoneme was defined by reference to a set of features that might be specified positively or negatively. Under this conception, /g/, for example, comes to be understood as merely an abbreviation for, say,

$$
\begin{bmatrix}
+\,\text{segment} \\
+\,\text{consonantal} \\
-\,\text{sonorant} \\
-\,\text{syllabic} \\
+\,\text{high} \\
+\,\text{back} \\
-\,\text{low} \\
-\,\text{round} \\
-\,\text{anterior} \\
-\,\text{coronal} \\
-\,\text{nasal} \\
-\,\text{continuant}
\end{bmatrix}
$$

In syntax, Harris (1946, 1951) proposed that the relation between categories such as V and VP, and N and NP, was a systematic one that could be captured by breaking the monadic parts of speech labels into two components, namely a category type and a phrasal level. This insight was subsequently taken up in the 'X-bar syntax' suggested by Chomsky (1970)

17

and most fully developed in Jackendoff 1977. The fact that there was considerable descriptive potential inherent in nonterminal symbols with internal complexity was first recognized by Harman (1963). Chomsky (1965, pp. 79 ff.) developed Harman's insight further by introducing into syntax the same kind of notation for features that had already been found useful in phonology.

But at this point, development in the theory of syntactic features basically stopped. Although generative grammarians continued to assume features in their descriptive apparatus, hardly any generative grammarians attempted to give syntactic features the kind of well-defined formal underpinnings that, say, the theory of phrase structure rewriting rules had. George Lakoff's 1965 dissertation (published as Lakoff 1970) was an honorable exception, but it influenced the field more toward the development of abstract deep structures and complex transformational derivations than toward appropriate exploitation of features in phrase structure description, despite the rich proposals for feature analysis that it presented.

During the seventies, the theory of features fell gradually into a state of chaos. This is clearly illustrated in the introductory texts on transformational grammar. One might expect a theory of features to deal with, among other things, the distribution of features and feature values in rules and trees; the possibilities of co-occurrence for feature specifications within a category; and the assignment of feature values on the basis of default statements in cases where no rule or general convention has assigned a value. Introductory texts on generative grammar occasionally touch on all three of these matters, but present no coherent proposals. Thus we find Akmajian and Heny (1975, p. 163) saying:

> The Reflexivization rule has the effect of placing the feature [+ REFLEXIVE] on the NP node; we shall assume that by general convention this feature is then assigned to the head N of the NP . . .

This suggests a default assumption that NPs are not [+ REFLEXIVE], and a principle of downward copying of feature specifications from NP nodes onto their lexical N heads. But then we find on p. 199, in the context of a discussion of number agreement features, which also appear on NP, the following statement:

> We assume that these features will have been 'spread' onto the whole subject NP from the head N.

This suggests upward copying of feature specifications from the lexical head N onto other members of the NP. Which do Akmajian and Heny actually postulate: downward copying, upward copying, both, or some nondirectional principle that has the effects of both in different cases?

Akmajian and Heny are not untypical in never even raising, let alone answering, such questions.

It seems clear enough that much of what features were doing in transformational derivations was never understood by those who made reference to them, so it is not surprising that it is not explained clearly in introductory books. Consider this passage from a discussion by Stockwell et al. (1973, pp. 47–8) of a rule that is triggered by, and then erases, a feature specification involving what we would call a terminal symbol feature (see section 4):

> The ... part of the structure change which erases the exception feature that governs the rule in the first place has no purpose except to unclutter the tree somewhat. It can probably be stated in some much more general way: e.g. a convention imposed on all rules that an exception feature is erased after doing its work – i.e. after governing some rule. The difficulty with such a convention is that one would have to take care to provide that the feature was relevant in *only one* rule; in the face of that hazard, we have erased features within each rule when we were sure they were no longer needed – and we have not been consistent in erasing them even under those circumstances.

There are some evident signs of desperation here. And it is not surprising. The business of determining feature specifications in deep structure trees and then further controlling the effect of each transformational operation on feature values leads to problems in the computation of derived structure that look quite substantial. For example, the reader may like to reflect upon how an algorithm might be devised to keep track of the legality of feature manipulations in the light of the following proposed constraint due to Emonds (1976, p. 212):

> A node B introduced into a tree by a transformational insertion T (rather than by movement or copying) can never during the derivation dominate a feature that is not defined as syntactic independent of all transformations that move into B (including T).

The initially baffling aspect of this global constraint on derivations does not dissipate as one searches the literature of transformational grammar for the formal machinery in terms of which it is supposed to be interpreted. It is an inhabitant of a twilight world in which lip-service is paid to formal precision but primitives are never supplied and definitions are never stated.

It is our intention in this chapter, and in chapter 5, to lay the foundations of a formally respectable theory of syntactic features, their values, their distribution in syntactic representations, and the universal and parochial principles that govern them. This is work that any imaginable theory of syntax for human languages will ultimately have to do, so the material of this chapter should not be seen as an exercise in generalized phrase structure grammar alone. We stress in particular that most syntactic theories, including past and present transformational theory, presuppose a theory of features covering much the same ground as the one we develop here, but have left it entirely implicit and undeveloped,[2] despite the occasionally glimpsed necessity of making appeal to it as seen in the quotations above.

2   Syntactic categories

The use of a finite set of nonterminal symbols that are composed of syntactic feature specifications does not of itself increase the expressive power of the theory of phrase structure. For reasons put very nicely by Halle (1969) with respect to phonology, there is an exact equivalence between generative systems that use complex symbols (matrices of distinctive feature specifications) and those that do not. The proof is trivial. Basically, only the way the symbols are interpreted is at issue. A nonterminal symbol $[x_1, x_2, \ldots, x_n]$, where each x_i is some feature specification, can be treated as having internal structure to which statements in the grammar can refer to capture generalizations, or it can be regarded as a calligraphically ornate representation of an atomic symbol distinct from all other symbols. Moreover, anything done by a rule referring to, say, $[x_2]$ could also be done by a rule which referred to the complete list of all complex symbols in which $[x_2]$ appeared.

Illustration in more concrete terms will make this clearer. Throughout this book we shall use the traditional categories Noun (N), Verb (V), Adjective (A), and Preposition/Postposition (P), but formally we shall treat them (following Chomsky 1970) as decomposable by means of a feature system that postulates a feature specification $[+N]$ which only N and A have, and a feature specification $[+V]$ which only V and A have.[3] Thus nouns are nominal but not verbal; adjectives are nominal and verbal (capturing a traditional notion of 'substantive'); verbs are verbal but not nominal and prepositions are neither verbal nor nominal. In other words, the feature specifications $[\pm N]$ and $[\pm V]$ group the categories informally notated, N, V, A, and P into natural classes as shown in (1).

(1)

	[+N]	[−N]
[+V]	A	V
[−V]	N	P

This enables us to refer to the class of, say, nouns and prepositions/postpositions simply by writing [−V]. But any statement about [−V] items could have been made without reference to features; what is claimed about [−V] would simply be stated to true of N and also true of P.

In phonology, complex symbols for phonological units are standardly taken to be sets of ⟨*feature, feature-value*⟩ pairs. (Such a pair is what we refer to as a *feature specification*.) However, a number of phonologists have proposed that phonological units should have more internal structure than this, and some syntacticians have proposed similar enrichment for the structure of syntactic categories. Thus Chomsky (1965, p. 171) implicitly assumes a hierarchical internal structure for lexical categories, and Bresnan (1976) defines categories as ordered pairs of an integer (representing bar level) and a bundle of feature specifications. More recently, Stucky (1981c) and subsequently Horrocks (1983) have proposed that languages with object agreement be analyzed by reference to complex representations involving ordered pairs of sets of agreement feature specifications. We shall likewise be assuming that categories have a significant amount of internal structure.

One particularly useful elaboration of the theory of features, of which we adopt a special version below, involves letting features take other feature specifications, or whole categories, as their values, an idea suggested, in effect, by Anderson (1977b, 1981), Kay (1979), Evans (1982), and Pollard (1982).

In Gazdar and Pullum (1982), a theory of features was developed along these lines, using graph theory to provide the basic concepts, and reconstructing feature specifications and categories as the same sort of objects, namely directed acyclic graphs obeying the single mother and unique root conditions. The advantage Gazdar and Pullum derived from the graph-theoretic approach was that whole clusters of feature specifications could be picked out in a natural way if they shared a mother node in the graph. So, for example, suppose we take a category looking like this:

(2)

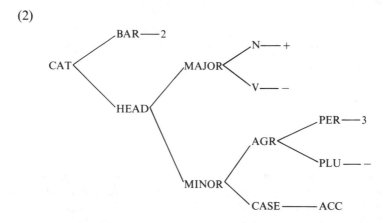

This represents (partially) the label of a 3rd person singular accusative noun phrase (NP), where an NP is theoretically reconstructed as a phrase that has the category type characterized by [+ N] and [− V] (like a noun) and the bar level 2. The 'is a value of' relation is read from the leaves on the right toward the root on the left. Thus 3 is a value of PER; PER is a value of AGR; AGR is a value of MINOR; MINOR is a value of HEAD; and HEAD is a value of CAT. If we want to say that the lexical head of an NP must have the same values for person, number, case, and the features N and V as the NP itself does (part of an important generalization we shall discuss in more detail as we proceed), we simply require that HEAD in the lexical category in question have the same graph-theoretic structure, node for node, as the NP has. HEAD, by virtue of its position in the graph, provides a way of pulling out a cluster of related feature specifications that must be referred to for a particular purpose.

We adopt a slightly different conception of feature and category in the present work.[4] We take feature specifications to be ordered pairs of the form ⟨*feature, feature-value*⟩, where a feature is an atomic symbol, and a feature-value is either an atomic symbol or a category. We take a category to be a set of feature specifications. In these terms, the category represented above would be just the set of feature specifications in (3).

(3)   {⟨BAR, 2⟩,
          ⟨N, +⟩,
          ⟨V, −⟩,
          ⟨PER, 3⟩,
          ⟨PLU, −⟩,
          ⟨CASE, ACC⟩}

We will adopt various conventions for representing categories and feature specifications, and it will be useful to mention some of them now.

Following traditional practice, feature specifications will usually be enclosed in square brackets. Thus we will use [CASE ACC], or just [ACC] (since no other feature can have ACC as a value), to stand for $\langle$CASE, ACC$\rangle$, and, in the case of Boolean features only, $[+N]$ and $[-PLU]$ to stand for $\langle$N, $+\rangle$ and $\langle$PLU, $-\rangle$, respectively. C^i stands for a category of type C having i bars, so N^2 means $\{\langle$N, $+\rangle, \langle$V, $-\rangle, \langle$BAR, $2\rangle\}$, which we shall also write as 'NP'. We add further feature detail in following square brackets, often giving just values where this makes clear what the whole feature specification must be; thus we can write NP[ACC] to stand for $\{\langle$N, $+\rangle, \langle$V, $-\rangle, \langle$BAR, $2\rangle, \langle$CASE, ACC$\rangle\}$. We will nearly always omit whatever part of the feature structure in a category has no bearing on the point at hand.

Let us return now to (3). Despite our restriction of feature values to atoms or categories, we still want to be able to refer to collections of feature specifications such as those dominated by HEAD and MAJOR in (3). The way we shall do this is by associating names such as **HEAD** with designated subsets of the set of features.

In fact, we define **HEAD** as follows:[5]

(4)   **HEAD** = {N, V, PLU, PER, VFORM, SUBJ, PFORM, AUX, INV, PAST, PRD, ADV, SLASH, AGR, SUBCAT, BAR, LOC}

Several of these features have not been introduced so far, and it may be useful if we give a preliminary introduction to some of them now. N and V distinguish major parts of speech as detailed earlier. PLU is a binary feature for representing the singular/plural distinction, while PER takes the values 1, 2, and 3 to represent person distinctions.[6]

VFORM distinguishes parts of the verb paradigm (FIN, finite; INF, infinitival; BSE, base-form, i.e. bare infinitive; PAS, passive participle; etc.), and we will normally abbreviate $\langle$VFORM, FIN$\rangle$, etc., simply as [FIN]. SUBJ distinguishes sentences from verb phrases (they have the same bar level in the present theory). PFORM is used to encode subcategorizational requirements for particular prepositions (e.g. *rely on*, and it takes *to, for, of, on*, etc., as values. Thus *rely* subcategorizes for a PP[PFORM *on*]. Throughout the book, we abbreviate PFORM specifications in an obvious way, by writing 'PP[*on*]' for 'PP[PFORM *on*]', etc. There is no ambiguity, since the appearance of a terminal symbol like *on* or *of* in a feature bundle attached to P or PP will always mean that it is a value of PFORM. AUX is a Boolean (binary) feature which identifies auxiliary verbs. Likewise, INV picks out verb-initial sentences such as direct polar interrogatives in English (see chapter 4). Another Boolean feature, PRD, distinguishes predicative complement phrases (occurring after the copula) from non-predicative phrases of similar category, and the

Boolean ADV distinguishes adverbial instances of the A^2 category from adjectival ones (see chapter 6). SLASH has to do with the theory of unbounded dependencies and is discussed extensively below, especially in chapters 5, 7 and 8. AGR, which, like SLASH, takes categories as its values, marks properties that a predicate element has by virtue of its syntactic obligation to show concord with some other element, in a way clarified in chapters 5 and 6.

Note that we have not required that the subsets we designate impose a partition on the set of features. Hence two subsets could have a non-null intersection. We shall see elsewhere in this book that this possibility is realized. **HEAD** intersects with another set called **FOOT**. For instance, we shall propose in chapter 5, following Flickinger (1983), that the feature SLASH is in the intersection of **HEAD** and **FOOT**, having the properties of both head features and foot features.

We have already seen that, on the present approach, a syntactic category C is a set of feature specifications, where each feature specification is an ordered pair consisting of a feature and a feature-value. Moreover, it should be intuitively obvious that if C has as an element a pair of the form $\langle f, v \rangle$, for some feature f, then it should not also have as an element a pair $\langle f, v' \rangle$, where v' is distinct from v. (For example, a category could not have as elements both $\langle$CASE, NOM$\rangle$ and $\langle$CASE, ACC$\rangle$.) Now it is usual in mathematics to represent functions as sets of ordered pairs which meet just the condition we mentioned above. In other words, we might well regard syntactic categories as functions. They take features as arguments, and yield what we have called feature-values as values.[7] Thus instead of saying that a pair $\langle$CASE, ACC$\rangle$ is a member of category C, we can equally well say that $C(\text{CASE}) = \text{ACC}$, i.e. C yields the value ACC for the argument CASE. Ignoring feature specifications that include categories as values for the moment, suppose we assume two finite, nonempty sets: F, the set of features, and V, the set of feature-values. Then a syntactic category is a partial function from F into V.[8] We say 'partial' because we often want to allow the possibility that a category C is undefined for some particular feature $f \in F$. A total function from F would assign a value to every element of F, but a partial function need not do so. For example, it seems sensible to suppose that prepositions do not take a value for the feature VFORM. So a preposition category which we might write as P should be such that P(VFORM) is always undefined. We will use the symbol '$\sim$' to show that a feature is undefined, thus 'prepositions are $\sim$[VFORM]' should be read as saying that prepositions do not take a value for the feature VFORM. Note that, in the case of Boolean features such as INV, the two expressions '[$-$INV]' and '$\sim$[INV]' mean different things: the former describes a category C such that $C(\text{INV}) = -$, whereas the latter means that $C(\text{INV})$ is undefined.

When a partial function C on a set F is undefined for some element $x \in F$, we say that x is not in the *domain* of C; in notation $x \notin DOM(C)$. Another way of putting it is to say that $DOM(C)$ is that subset F' of F such that C is a total function on F'. Reverting to the set theoretical representation of functions, C will be undefined for $f \in F$ if and only if no pair of the form $\langle f, v \rangle$ belongs to C. Since it is possible for a partial function to be undefined for all arguments, it follows that we admit the empty set $\{\}$ as a possible category.

The possibility of categories that are partial functions allows for a rather natural definition of the notion 'minor category'. Minor category expressions (e.g. determiners, complementizers, conjunctions, etc.) are 'minor' in that they lack a BAR specification, and thus fall outside the X-bar system altogether:

(5)   An instantiated category C is a minor category if and only if C(BAR) is undefined.

As this definition suggests, the analysis of categories that we are adopting gives us a convenient way of specifying the value that is associated with a given feature in some category. Where C is a category, '$C(f)$' can be read as 'the value which the category C assigns to the feature f' or, more simply, as 'C's value for f'. Thus 'A(PLU) $=$ B(PLU)' could be read as 'A's value for number is the same as B's value for number'.

The elements of V, the set of feature-values, will either be elements like '$+$', '$-$', or integers, or names like FIN (finite). Features that have values of this sort we will call *atom-valued features*. But a feature-value is not necessarily atomic. The other possibility is for it to be a category. Some examples will make clear the kind of roles played by the two kinds of features.

Atom-valued features include Boolean features like N, with value-set $\{+, -\}$; integer-valued features like BAR (for bar-level in the sense of X-bar theory), with value-set $\{0, 1, 2\}$; and features like VFORM, which classify verb forms in terms of values like FIN (finite), INF (infinitival), etc. The atom-valued features thus often correspond to quite traditional classifications of linguistic elements according to their grammatical properties.

Category-valued features are rather less familiar. The feature SLASH is one example. It marks constituents that would be treated in transformational terms as having had a phrase extracted by a movement rule or deleted across an unbounded context.[9] Consider the following feature specification:

(6) $\langle$SLASH, $\{\langle$N, $+\rangle$, $\langle$V, $-\rangle$, $\langle$BAR, $2\rangle$, $\langle$PER, $3\rangle$, $\langle$PLU, $-\rangle\}\rangle$

SLASH will be employed extensively in chapters 7 and 8 in connection with unbounded dependencies, and its role in the theory can only be properly understood in terms of the discussion in those chapters, but it will suffice here to say that the intuitive interpretation of the feature specification in (6) is 'lacking a third person singular noun phrase subconstituent'.

It appears to be generally assumed that grammars employing features must adopt the following stipulation:

(7)   Only a fully specified category may label a node.

However, we do not make this stipulation. In the present framework, fully specified categories have no privileged status, and something barely specified like (8)

(8) $\{\langle BAR, 2\rangle\}$

is just as much a category as any other. It is something like a Trubetzkoyan 'archicategory', having 2 as its bar level but being unspecified for all other features, even the major category features N and V. It can be read as simply 'phrase', and informally notated X^2. The availability of such underspecified categories is crucial to some of the analyses we develop in terms of our theory, as will be seen in later chapters. And although it might seem to the reader that allowing such massive underspecification in categories would lead to disastrous overgeneration of structures with vaguely labeled constituents, in fact this is not so. In the lexicon, most items are fully specified for syntactic features. This assumption interacts with the Head Feature Convention (discussed in chapter 5) to ensure that trees mostly have fully specified node labels. (What the Head Feature Convention says is basically that the head features on a mother category are the same as the head features on any daughter which is a head.)

The present theory of features makes heavy use of notions of *extension* and *unification*. These notions are defined on categories, not features. They both have relatively clear but somewhat technical definitions, which we will now present informally.

An *extension* of a category is like a superset of it, except for two details. First, the extension of a category must also be category, that is, it must be a superset which is also a function. Second, something has to be said about what it means to be a superset of a category that includes category-valued features.

In the case of atom-valued features, things are fairly clear. For example, we want $\{\langle N, +\rangle, \langle V, +\rangle, \langle PRD, +\rangle\}$ to be an extension of $\{\langle N, +\rangle, \langle V, +\rangle\}$. It simply has an additional feature specification. However, we do not want $\{\langle N, +\rangle, \langle V, +\rangle, \langle PRD, +\rangle, \langle PRD, -\rangle\}$ to be an extension of the latter, because it is not a category. Since $\langle \text{PRD}, + \rangle$ and $\langle \text{PRD}, - \rangle$ contradict each other about the value for PRD, this set does not constitute a function (even a partial one) from features to feature-values.

In the case that a category-valued feature is present in a category C, we must ensure that extensions of C preserve the details inside the value of that feature. We want extensions of a feature containing [SLASH N2[PER 3, PLU −]], for example, to preserve the third person singular information locked up inside the value of SLASH. This means that our definition has to be recursive. Informally, it goes as follows:

(9)   A category A is an *extension* of a category B ($B \sqsubseteq A$) if and only if
    (i)   the atom-valued feature specifications in B are all in A, and
    (ii) for any category-valued feature f, the value of f in A is an extension of the value of f in B.

This definition is given more precisely in section 6.

Our concept of *unification* is essentially identical to that of Kay (1979), and is closely analogous to the operation of union on sets except that, as in the case of extension, the resulting set must be a function. Unification is undefined for sets containing feature specifications that contradict each other.

(10)   Let K be a set of categories. The *unification* of K($\bigsqcup$K) is the smallest category which is an extension of every member of K, if such a category exists, otherwise, the unification of K is undefined.

For example, let $A = \{\langle \text{N}, + \rangle, \langle \text{PRD}, + \rangle\}$ and $B = \{\langle \text{N}, + \rangle, \langle \text{V}, - \rangle\}$. Then $\{\langle \text{N}, + \rangle, \langle \text{V}, - \rangle, \langle \text{PRD}, + \rangle\}$ is the unification of A and B. However, $\{\langle \text{N}, + \rangle, \langle \text{V}, - \rangle, \langle \text{PRD}, + \rangle, \langle \text{PLU}, + \rangle\}$ is not, because the gratuitous extra specification $\langle \text{PLU}, + \rangle$ is not in either A or B, and so is not in their union. Moreover, the unification of $\{\langle \text{N}, + \rangle, \langle \text{V}, + \rangle\}$ and $\{\langle \text{N}, + \rangle, \langle \text{V}, - \rangle\}$ is not defined, because of the clash regarding the value for V.

We conclude this section by noting the conventions we employ subsequently for referring to categories: α, β, C, C', C_i, ... will be used as metalanguage variables over categories. They will never occur in actual rules or metarules. X will be used to stand for the maximally underspecified category, namely {}, and is never a variable.

3 Feature co-occurrence restrictions

If a consonant is pharyngeal, then it is not nasal. Likewise, if a syntactic category exhibits a distinction in present versus past tense, then that category is not a preposition or a prepositional phrase. Restrictions of this sort are expressed in generative phonology by means of what Chomsky and Halle (1968, chapter 9) call marking conventions. Chomsky and Halle employ two kinds of marking conventions. One kind (1968, pp. 404–7) is illustrated in (11).

(11) $[+\text{voc}]$ → $[+\text{son}]$
        $[+\text{nasal}]$ → $[+\text{son}]$
        $[+\text{high}]$ → $[-\text{low}]$
        $[+\text{low}]$ → $[-\text{high}]$
        $[+\text{ant}]$ → $[+\text{cns}]$
        $[-\text{cor}]$ → $[-\text{lateral}]$

These rules can be seen to constitute part of the definition of *possible phonological segment*. Each has the potential of reducing the space of possible segments by up to 25 per cent. We will refer to absolute conditions of the type shown in (11) as *Feature Co-occurrence Restrictions* (FCRs, hereafter).

FCRs, for us, constitute part of the definition of the notion 'legal extension of a category', and thus of the notion 'fully specified syntactic category'. Some FCRs will be universal and thus be part of the definition of 'possible syntactic category in a natural language', and some will be parochial and thus be part of the definition of, for example, 'possible syntactic category in English'. Consider an analogy with phonotactics. Particular combinations of syntactic features may constitute a possible category for a language, even though the language never happens to employ the category, just as /blik/ is a possible English word, though not an actual one. Likewise, particular combinations of syntactic features may not constitute a possible category for a given language, even though the same combination would be possible for another language. Thus /dnip/ is not a possible English word, despite the fact that nothing in 'universal phonotactics' prohibits it from being a word in some other language.

FCRs are typically stated as material conditionals or biconditionals. For an example, consider the restriction in English that the feature specification $[+\text{INV}]$ implies the specifications $[+\text{AUX}]$ and $[\text{FIN}]$. $[+\text{INV}]$ is a specification that appears on sentences which include a subject but begin with a verb, and also appears on that sentence-initial verb. The FCR has as a consequence that such a verb will always be a finite auxiliary verb. It is formulated as follows:

(12)   FCR 1: $[+\text{INV}] \supset [+\text{AUX, FIN}]$

For a second example, consider the statement that the major category P cannot be associated with tense. In fact, we can make this follow as a consequence from a stronger statement: VFORM values are only associated with the major category V. This is formulated as follows:

(13)   FCR 2: [VFORM] $\supset$ [+V, −N]

(13) may be viewed as saying that the distinctions coded by the feature VFORM are only relevant to categories of type V. Unsurprisingly, our grammar also needs to contain the following FCRs in addition to (13):

(14)   a.   FCR 3: [NFORM] $\supset$ [−V, +N]
       b.   FCR 4: [PFORM] $\supset$ [−V, −N]

These three FCRs are, of course, universal in a rather uninteresting way: they amount to 'meaning postulates' which constrain the possible uses of the features VFORM, NFORM and PFORM.

There will be a substantial number of cases in the grammar where the utility of drawing some featural distinction rests on the presupposition that some other feature specification is also in force, but we shall not attempt to state all the requisite FCRs, though it would be straightforward to do so. Here are just two further examples: (i) it is only relevant to ask whether a category contains a specification for the Boolean feature PAST if it also specifies FIN as the value of VFORM. This constraint on PAST is ensured by the FCR below (see chapter 10 for some further discussion of this FCR):

(15)   FCR 5: [PAST] $\supset$ [FIN, −SUBJ]

And (ii), the only constituents that can have a phrase omitted from them are themselves phrasal constituents. It makes no sense to think of a *word* with an NP gap in it, for example. Words all have the feature SUBCAT (see section 5) and constituents with something missing are marked with the feature SLASH (see chapters 5 and 7), thus we can state the following FCR to express the fact just noted:

(16)   FCR 6: [SUBCAT] $\supset$ ~[SLASH]

4   Feature specification defaults

In English, typical consonants are not [+low], though /h/ is [+low] in the Chomsky and Halle feature system. And typical occurrences of NPs are not possessive, though possessive NPs do of course occur in English.

Chomsky and Halle (1968, pp. 405–7) introduce a notation for expressing this kind of fact in phonology, a notation which is illustrated in (17).

(17)   [*u* high]   →   [+high]
        [*u* nasal] →   [−nasal]
        [*u* low]   →   [−low]
        [*u* ant]   →   [+ant]
        [*u* cor]   →   [+cor]
        [*u* cont]   →   [+cont]

These rules tell us what the default value is for the feature in question. If nothing is said about it, then we are to assume the value specified on the right of the arrow. We will refer to markedness conventions of this kind as *Feature Specification Defaults* (FSDs, hereafter).

Our theory of syntactic categories will employ both FCRs and FSDs. In this section, we deal with the second type of marking convention, FSDs. These form an important part of the link between the highly schematic rules listed in the grammar and the fully specified structural descriptions they induce.

As the first illustration, consider rule (18).

(18)   VP → V S

Consider the rule in relation to the feature INV (mnemonic for INVerted sentence). Two of the tree fragments that we might expect to get from (18) are displayed in (19).

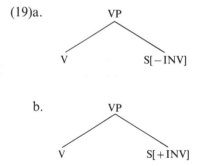

(19)a.   VP
              /   \
           V   S[−INV]

     b.   VP
              /   \
           V   S[+INV]

That is, there is no particular reason for having [−INV] rather than [+INV] on the S daughter. But if we allow the grammar to admit tree fragments like (19b), then we will end up generating examples like *Lee believes will the children be late*. So INV needs to have a default specification, namely [−INV]. We can state this default as follows:

(20)   FSD 1: [−INV]

Since there is no reason for INV not to have that specification on S, it must have it, according to the approach to defaults that we adopt in this book. There is, of course, one class of structures in which [+INV] is obliged to be present, namely those arising from rules such as (21).

(21)   S[+INV] → V[AUX] NP VP[BSE]

But, since this rule stipulates the presence of [+INV], the default will not be invoked.

For another example of the same point, let us look at the conditional FSD shown in (22):[10]

(22)   FSD 7: [BAR 0] ⊃ ~[VFORM PAS]

This says that, other things being equal, a lexical category will not get instantiated as [VFORM PAS]. Now consider the two tree fragments in (23):

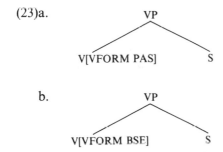

(23)a.   VP

        V[VFORM PAS]   S

   b.   VP

        V[VFORM BSE]   S

If VFORM did not have a default excluding PAS, strings like *We were believed that the earth is flat* would be permitted by the grammar. Nevertheless, there are rules which require a [VFORM PAS] specification – for example, the rules which result from the passive metarule discussed in chapter 4. For example, suppose the grammar contains rule (24):

(24)   VP[VFORM PAS] → V PP[*to*]

In this case, the [VFORM PAS] specification will be required to appear on the lexical head of the constituent admitted by this rule, and VFORM is thus relieved of the obligation to take some other value.

5   Lexical subcategorization

Any grammar of English has to provide for the ungrammaticality of such examples as (25).

(25)   *I devoured to him that the grass is green.

One approach would be to let the syntax generate strings in which (for example) verbs occur with the wrong number and type of other constituents in the VP, and use the mechanisms that associate syntactic structures with meanings to eliminate them.[11] In other words, treat strings like (25) as grammatical but not semantically interpretable. This approach, which we might call 'semantic filtering', is not appropriate to the domain under consideration. The reason is that there is fairly clear evidence that the meaning of a verb does not completely determine its subcategorization. Consider the following sets of data, in which the first two sentences in each set illustrate the (near) synonymy of two verbs, and the second two examples demonstrate a dissimilarity between them as regards subcategorization.

(26) a. The beast ate the meat (ravenously)
      b. The beast devoured the meat.
      c. The beast ate (ravenously)
      d. *The beast devoured.

(27) a. The ground sometimes shakes under your feet.
      b. The ground sometimes quakes under your feet.
      c. What is shaking the ground?
      d. *What is quaking the ground?

(28) a. He gave this to me.
      b. He donated this to me.
      c. He gave me this.
      d. *He donated me this.[12]

(29) a. It is likely that Alex will leave.
      b. It is probable that Alex will leave.
      c. Alex is likely to leave.
      d. *Alex is probable to leave.

(30) a. Aren't you even going to try to solve it?
      b. Aren't you even going to attempt to solve it?
      c. Aren't you even going to try?
      d. *Aren't you even going to attempt?

Further examples of the same sort could be given. What they suggest is that there are restrictions on contexts of occurrence for lexical items which the grammar must specify, and which cannot be reduced to facts about meaning.

Consider the following phrase structure rule:

(31)   VP → V (NP) (NP) (PP) (PP) (S)

Our problem is, for example, to ensure that V expands as *devour* only when V is immediately adjacent to NP, and not, say, PP or S as (31) would permit. Viewed in this light, one obvious strategy for coping with the facts of subcategorization is to enrich the theory of grammar by introducing context-sensitive phrase structure rules and using rules of this type for lexical insertion, along the lines exemplified in (32).

(32)   V → *bring*/_____NP
         V → *persuade*/_____NP S
         V → *decide*/_____PP
         V → *grow*/_____AP
         V → *save*/_____NP PP
         V → *trade*/_____NP PP PP

However, an approach along these lines, though initially plausible, runs into numerous difficulties. One is that these rules include a mass of statements which redundantly repeat things that the phrase structure rules have already said, e.g. that NP PP sequences are found in English VPs but PP NP sequences are not.[13] This point is made and illustrated in detail in Heny (1979). Another problem is that the rule for expanding VP will have to introduce all the different sorts of constituent that verbs can demand as their complements in some instance, and since no verbs take *all* of these (for example, *devour* takes an NP but cannot also have an indirect object or a subordinate clause, witness, **I devoured the meat to him that grass is green*) there also have to be numerous negative specifications associated with the rules in (32).[14]

In response to these problems, we adopt an alternative approach to subcategorization, one which only employs context-free phrase structure rules. Consider the set of rules in the grammar which introduce pretermi- nal symbols (such as A, COMP, Det, N, P and V). It is precisely these rules, and no others, which determine the possibilities of subcategoriza- tion for words. There is a clear sense in which these rules *are* the subcategorization frames for the language.

It is both necessary and sufficient for achieving correct subcategoriza- tion that the grammar provide a mechanism whereby the relevant subclasses of a preterminal symbol can be matched with the rules that introduce it. This can be done in a manner which is at once simple and transparent, by using integers as values for a feature SUBCAT which only appears on preterminal symbols.[15] As far as the lexicon is concerned, these integers are best seen as pointers to the rules which will allow the relevant item to be introduced.[16] We need to ensure that SUBCAT will not be defined for a category that assigns BAR a value greater than 0, and that all [BAR 0] categories are defined for SUBCAT. This is accomplished by the following FCRs:

(33)   FCR 7: [BAR 0] ≡ [N] & [V] & [SUBCAT]

(34)   FCR 8: [BAR 1] ⊃ ~[SUBCAT]

(35)   FCR 9: [BAR 2] ⊃ ~[SUBCAT]

Under this proposal, our grammar will contain rules such as those shown in (36) and (37):

(36)   VP → V[1]

(37)   VP → V[2] NP

Here, V[1] and V[2] are just an abbreviation for V[SUBCAT 1] and V[SUBCAT 2] respectively.[17] In addition, the lexicon will contain an entry which says that *weep* is a V[1], and that *devour* is a V[2]. More precisely, let us assume that a lexical entry contains at least four kinds of information: a phonological form, a category, an indication of any irregular morphology, and a meaning. Keeping to orthographical representations for convenience, we might expect entries of the following kind:

(38)   ⟨ *weep*,
        [[− N], [+ V], [BAR 0], [SUBCAT 1]],
        {*wept*},
        weep'⟩

(39)   ⟨ *devour*,
        [[− N], [+ V], [BAR 0], [SUBCAT 2]],
        {},
        devour'⟩

Now we say that a category *C* can immediately dominate a lexical item *a* just in case *C* extends the category label in the lexical entry for *a*. Consequently, V[1] can immediately dominate *weep*, but not *devour*.[18] Likewise, we ensure that V[2] will immediately dominate *abandon*, *enlighten*, *castigate*, *slap*, and so on, but not *disappear*, *elapse*, *expire*, *faint*, and so on.

Note that the interpretation of categories as feature bundles enables us to avoid the charge that totally distinct categories have to be postulated for verbs of different subcategorization types, with the result that one loses generalizations about verbs (e.g. that they all take tense). These generalizations are not lost since all verbs have at least two feature specifications in common (namely [+ V, − N]) and it is this fact which forms the basis for FCRs like (13) above.

Our proposal for subcategorization has one very specific consequence: it entails that only the items introduced by the same rule as a given preterminal category *C* can be directly relevant to the question of where *C*'s subcategorization environment is met. This is not something that is entailed by context-sensitive accounts of lexical insertion such as that of Chomsky (1965). But it is worth noting that Chomsky chooses to stipulate the very constraint that follows as a theorem from the system outlined above (see Chomsky 1965, pp. 96, 99).

There are other advantages of our context-free system for subcategorization besides the consequence just noted. One that we shall comment on briefly here concerns coordination. Consider sentence (40), involving the verb *hand*, which requires both direct and indirect objects.

(40)   We have handed or sent a copy of this letter to every student in the school.

In this example, *hand* is not in the context defined by the contextual feature specification [+ _____NP PP]. The problems for context-sensitive accounts of lexical insertion caused by the fact that coordination of lexical categories can destroy crucial adjacency relationships in this way are considerable, but have not to our knowledge been addressed by proponents of such accounts. In our system, however, there is no reference to linear adjacency in the conditions on insertion of the terminal symbol *hand*. *Hand* belongs to a category, let us say V[3], which is introduced by a rule that also specifies an accompanying NP and PP[PFORM *to*]. By the schema for coordination presented in chapter 8, section 2, any category *C* can dominate one or more *C*s, a conjunction such as *and* or *or*, and one further *C*. Thus, a V[3] can dominate two V[3]s separated by *or*. Hence a tree for (40) can be admitted. The interaction of coordination and strict subcategorization is successfully predicted by the system assumed here, in fact, whereas it has never been satisfactorily treated within the context of Chomsky's (1965) proposals.

Finally, the feature SUBCAT allows for a straightforward definition of minor lexical category: a lexical item belongs to a minor lexical category if and only if it is specified for SUBCAT, but not specified for BAR.

6   A formal theory of features

This section contains some definitions that are crucially referred to in chapter 5, but those readers who prefer to skip it on a first reading will find that much of the content of that chapter is intelligible without it.

We begin by giving a more formal account of categories. Let *A* and *F* be finite sets, of atomic feature-values and features respectively. *Atom* (the set of atomic-valued features), is a subset of *F*. Only a certain subset of *A* may be associated with any given member of *Atom*. This value-set is determined by a function ρ. Matters are straightforward as far as members of *Atom* are concerned, but become a little more complicated when we consider category-valued features. In order to define what a possible category is, we need to say what the possible values of a feature are. But, for category-valued features, this requires a definition of possible categories! To deal with this problem, we give an inductive definition of the set *K* of possible categories.

Definition 1
ρ^0 is a function from F to $POW(A)$ such that for all $f \in (F - Atom)$, $\rho^0(f) = \{\{\}\}$.

If f belongs to *Atom*, then $\rho^0(f)$ is some subset of A. If f does not belong to *Atom*, then it is a category-valued feature, and is assigned the empty category, $\{\}$, by ρ^0.

Example 1
Let $F = \{N, V, SLASH, AGR\}$, $Atom = \{N, V\}$, $A = \{+, -\}$. $\rho^0(N) = \rho^0(V) = A$, and $\rho^0(SLASH) = \rho^0(AGR) = \{\}$.

As we mentioned earlier, categories are formalized as partial functions. We use $Y^{(X)}$ to denote the set of all partial functions from a set X to a set Y.

Definition 2
The set K^0 of 0-level categories $=$
$\{C \in A^{(F)} : \forall f \in DOM(C)[C(f) \in \rho^0(f)]\}$

It follows from the preceding definition that if $\rho^0(f) = \{\{\}\}$, then $C(f)$ is undefined. Consequently, if C is a 0-level category, then $DOM(C) \subseteq Atom$.

Example 2
Continuing with the assignments in example (1), we have
$K^0 = \{\{\langle N, + \rangle, \langle V, + \rangle\},$
$\{\langle N, + \rangle, \langle V, - \rangle\},$
$\{\langle N, - \rangle, \langle V, + \rangle\},$
$\{\langle N, - \rangle, \langle V, - \rangle\},$
$\{\langle N, + \rangle\},$
$\{\langle N, - \rangle\},$
$\{\langle V, + \rangle\},$
$\{\langle V, - \rangle\},$
$\{\}\}$

We now wish to take the induction step in the definition of ρ. We shall impose an important constraint on ρ: the value-set that ρ associates with a given category-value feature f can only contain categories in which f does not already appear. That is, C can only be in the value set of f if f is not in the domain of C, or in the domain of any C' contained in C, at any level of embedding. This requires an ancillary definition.

Definition 3
Let $\in^+$ be the transitive closure of the relation $\in$. Let R be a relation.
Then $DOM^+(R) = \{x : \exists y[\langle x, y \rangle \in^+ R]\}$

Example 3

Let R be $\{\langle a, 1\rangle, \langle b, 2\rangle, \langle c, \{\langle a, 2\rangle, \langle d, 2\rangle\}\rangle\}$.

Then $DOM(R) = \{a, b, c\}$, while $DOM^+(R) = \{a, b, c, d\}$.

Definition 4

Suppose K^{n-1} and ρ^{n-1} are defined. Then we extend ρ^{n-1} to ρ^n as follows:

  (i) If $f \in Atom$, then $\rho^n(f) = \rho^{n-1}(f)$,

  (ii) otherwise, $\rho^n(f)$ is a subset of

$$\{C \in K^{n-1}: \exists C' \in \rho^{n-1}(f)[C' \subseteq C] \,\&\, f \notin DOM^+ (C)\}.$$

Thus if f is a category-valued feature, then the value-set associated with f by ρ^1 will be some subset of 0-level categories.

Example 4

Continuing with example (2), set $\rho^1(\text{SLASH}) = \{\{\langle N, -\rangle,$ $\langle V, -\rangle\}\}$ and $\rho^1(\text{AGR}) = \{\{\langle N, +\rangle, \langle V, -\rangle\}\}$. Before illustrating the values of ρ^2, we have to proceed to the next definition.

We now define higher-level categories.

Definition 5

$$K^n = \{C \in (A \cup K^{n-1})^{(F)}: \forall f \in DOM(C)[C(f) \in \rho^n(f)]\}$$

Example 5

When we reach 1-level categories, we get all the 0-level categories together with the categories formed by assigning values to the category-valued features SLASH and AGR. Thus

$$K^1 = \{\{\langle N, +\rangle, \langle V, +\rangle\},$$
$$\{\langle N, +\rangle, \langle V, -\rangle\},$$
$$\{\langle N, -\rangle, \langle V, +\rangle\},$$
$$\{\langle N, -\rangle, \langle V, -\rangle\},$$
$$\{\langle N, +\rangle\},$$
$$\{\langle N, -\rangle\},$$
$$\{\langle V, +\rangle\},$$
$$\{\langle V, -\rangle\},$$
$$\{\}$$

$\{\langle N, +\rangle, \langle V, +\rangle, \langle \text{SLASH}, \{\langle N, -\rangle,$
$\langle V, -\rangle\}\rangle\},$
$\{\langle N, +\rangle, \langle V, -\rangle, \langle \text{SLASH}, \{\langle N, -\rangle,$
$\langle V, -\rangle\}\rangle\},$
$\{\langle N, -\rangle, \langle V, +\rangle, \langle \text{SLASH}, \{\langle N, -\rangle,$
$\langle V, -\rangle\}\rangle\},$
$\{\langle N, -\rangle, \langle V, -\rangle, \langle \text{SLASH}, \{\langle N, -\rangle,$
$\langle V, -\rangle\}\rangle\},$
$\{\langle N, +\rangle, \langle \text{SLASH}, \{\langle N, -\rangle, \langle V, -\rangle\}\rangle\},$
$\{\langle N, -\rangle, \langle \text{SLASH}, \{\langle N, -\rangle, \langle V, -\rangle\}\rangle\},$
$\{\langle V, +\rangle, \langle \text{SLASH}, \{\langle N, -\rangle, \langle V, -\rangle\}\rangle\},$
$\{\langle V, -\rangle, \langle \text{SLASH}, \{\langle N, -\rangle, \langle V, -\rangle\}\rangle\},$
$\{\langle \text{SLASH}, \{\langle N, -\rangle, \langle V, -\rangle\}\rangle\},$

$\{\langle N, +\rangle, \langle V, +\rangle, \langle \text{AGR}, \{\langle N, +\rangle,$
$\langle V, -\rangle\}\rangle\},$
$\{\langle N, +\rangle, \langle V, -\rangle, \langle \text{AGR}, \{\langle N, +\rangle,$
$\langle V, -\rangle\}\rangle\},$
$\{\langle N, -\rangle, \langle V, +\rangle, \langle \text{AGR}, \{\langle N, +\rangle,$
$\langle V, -\rangle\}\rangle\},$
$\{\langle N, -\rangle, \langle V, -\rangle, \langle \text{AGR}, \{\langle N, +\rangle,$
$\langle V, -\rangle\}\rangle\},$
$\{\langle N, +\rangle, \langle \text{AGR}, \{\langle N, +\rangle, \langle V, -\rangle\}\rangle\},$
$\{\langle N, -\rangle, \langle \text{AGR}, \{\langle N, +\rangle, \langle V, -\rangle\}\rangle\},$
$\{\langle V, +\rangle, \langle \text{AGR}, \{\langle N, +\rangle, \langle V, -\rangle\}\rangle\},$
$\{\langle V, -\rangle, \langle \text{AGR}, \{\langle N, +\rangle, \langle V, -\rangle\}\rangle\},$
$\{\langle \text{AGR}, \{\langle N, +\rangle, \langle V, -\rangle\}\rangle\}\}$

Example 6
Let us now consider the value sets that ρ^2 can associate with
SLASH. According to Definition (4.ii), the following conditions must be met in order for SLASH to receive some C in K^1
as a possible value:

    a. $\exists C' \in \rho^1(\text{SLASH})]C' \subseteq C]$
    b. $\text{SLASH} \notin DOM^+(C)$

In a previous example, we had $\rho^1(\text{SLASH}) = \{\{\langle N, -\rangle,$
$\langle V, -\rangle\}\}$. Consequently, by virtue of (a) we can exclude from
consideration any C which lacks the feature specifications $\langle N,$
$-\rangle$ and $\langle V, -\rangle$. And by virtue of (b), we can exclude any C in
which SLASH is already assigned a value. As a result, we have
$\rho^2(\text{SLASH}) = \{\{\langle N, -\rangle, \langle V, -\rangle\}$
$\qquad\qquad\quad \{\langle N, -\rangle, \langle V, -\rangle, \langle \text{AGR}, \{\langle N, +\rangle,$
$\qquad\qquad\qquad \langle V, -\rangle\}\rangle\}\}$

Definition 6
The set K of all categories based on A, F and ρ is K^n, where n is the cardinality of $F - Atom$.

By virtue of the constraint we placed on ρ, $\rho^n(f)$ will only be non-empty for $f \in (F - Atom)$ if there are at least $n-1$ category-valued features distinct from f. Hence, K^n will be empty for all $n >$ cardinality of $(F - Atom)$. Since F is finite, so is K.

Example 7
If we continue the recursion from the previous example, K^2 will contain all the categories in K^1, together with categories like
$\{\langle N, + \rangle, \langle V, + \rangle, \langle SLASH, \{\langle N, - \rangle, \langle V, - \rangle,$
$\langle AGR, \{\langle N, + \rangle, \langle V, - \rangle\}\rangle\}\rangle\}$ and
$\{\langle N, - \rangle, \langle V, - \rangle, \langle SLASH, \{\langle N, - \rangle, \langle V, - \rangle,$
$\langle AGR, \{\langle N, + \rangle, \langle V, - \rangle\}\rangle\}\rangle\}$
In fact, the second of these will be the only new category in K^2 which contains the specifications $\langle N, - \rangle$, $\langle V, - \rangle$. But it cannot belong to $\rho^3(SLASH)$ because it already contains a value for SLASH. Hence $\rho^3(SLASH) = \{\}$ and similarly for $\rho^3(AGR)$.

Our next task is to define the notions of extension, identity, and unification.

Definition 7: Extension
Given two syntactic categories A and B, B is an extension of A ($A \sqsubseteq B$) if and only if
(i)   for all $f \in Atom$, if $f \in DOM(A)$ then $B(f) = A(f)$, and
(ii) for all $f \in (F - Atom)$, if $f \in DOM(A)$ then $B(f)$ is an extension of $A(f)$.

Definition 8
Given two categories A and B, $A = B$ if and only if A is an extension of B and B is an extension of A.

The relation 'is an extension of' defines a partial order on S. Our definition of unification, like that of Gazdar and Pullum (1982), is equivalent to the standard notion of least upper bound in lattice theory.

Definition 9: Unification
(i)   Let $S \subseteq K$ be a set of categories, and let $C \in K$. Then C is an *upper bound* for K if and only if for all $C' \in S$, C is an extension of C'.
(ii) C is the *unification* of S if and only if C is an upper bound for S and for all C', C' is an upper bound for S, then C' is an extension of C.

If $S = \{C_1, \ldots, C_n\}$ and C is the unification of S, then we sometimes write $\bigsqcup(C_1, \ldots, C_n) = C$.

We conclude this section by providing a formal reconstruction of our informal notation for FCRs and FSDs. These are predicates which can be either true or false of categories. Our reconstruction takes the form of a set of rules that map our FCR/FSD representations into lambda expressions of a familiar kind.

> *Definition 10*: FCR and FSD translation
> (i)   An expression of the form $[f\ v]$ translates into $C(f) = v$.
> (ii) An expression of the form $[f]$ translates into $\exists x\,[C(f) = x]$.
> (iii) An expression of the form $\sim\alpha$ translates into $\sim\alpha'$, where α' is the translation of α.
> (iv) Expressions of the form $\alpha \supset \beta$, $\alpha \equiv \beta$, $\alpha \vee \beta$, and $\alpha\ \&\ \beta$ translate into $\alpha' \supset \beta'$, $\alpha' \equiv \beta'$, $\alpha' \vee \beta'$, and $\alpha'\ \&\ \beta'$, respectively, where α' and β' are the translations of α and β respectively.
> (v)   An FCR or FSD consisting of an expression α translates as $\lambda C[\alpha']$ where α' is the translation of α.

Here are a couple of examples to show how this translation works:

> *Example 8*
> (i)   FCR 1: $[+\,\text{INV}] \supset [+\,\text{AUX, FIN}]$
>   Our abbreviating conventions, discussed above, make this equivalent to:
> (ii) FCR 1: $[\text{INV} +] \supset ([\text{AUX} +]\ \&\ [\text{VFORM FIN}])$
>   The translation rules given in Definition 10 convert this into the following lambda expression:
> (iii) FCR 1: $\lambda C[(C(\text{INV}) = +) \supset ((C(\text{AUX}) = +)\ \&\ (C(\text{VFORM}) = \text{FIN}))]$

> *Example 9*
> (i)   FSD 7: $[\text{BAR } 0] \supset \sim[\text{VFORM PAS}]$
>   translates into:
> (ii) FSD 7: $\lambda C[(C(\text{BAR}) = 0) \supset \sim(C(\text{VFORM}) = \text{PAS})]$

As can be seen, FCRs and FSDs are exactly the same kind of formal objects: functions from categories to truth values. They differ only in the role they play in the grammar, a matter which will be made explicit in chapter 5.

Notes

1 We adopt the position that, strictly speaking, a *category* is a set of expressions, while a *category label* is an object which can be used to refer to categories, and

to annotate nodes in trees. However, we will often speak of categories where strictly we mean category labels, in cases where we think no confusion will arise.

2 Hellan (1980) and Lapointe (1980) are exceptions. Note that they did not appear until about 25 years after the development of TG.

3 See Chomsky (1970) for the origins of this proposal, and Bresnan (1976) for further development. And see Jackendoff (1977) for discussion and defense of an alternative. When we need to distinguish between major class features and the lexical categories N and V, we shall simply mark the zero bar level on the latter: N^0 and V^0.

4 Although presented differently, the analysis of categories and features presented here set-theoretically has an equivalent graph-theoretic formulation. In particular, crucial graph-theoretic notions like extension and unification simply carry over into equivalent set-theoretic definitions.

5 In including SLASH among the **HEAD** features, we are adopting a proposal made by Sells (1983b) in the light of Flickinger 1983. The implications of this proposal will become apparent in chapters 7 and 8.

6 Our choice of person and number features is merely conventional here. For some serious discussion of such features, see Karttunen 1984 and Sag et al. (forthcoming).

7 In Pollard 1984 a slightly different approach is proposed: features are assigned sets of values, not just individual values. The motivation has to do with the feature representation of under-specified lexical categories (e.g. the category to which the noun *fish* belongs, which is vague rather than ambiguous on Pollard's account as regards the distinction between singular, plural, and mass nouns).

8 A more precise definition of syntactic category is presented in section 6. The definition is such that, given finite sets of features and atomic feature-values, the set of all possible categories is also finite.

9 SLASH gets its name from the informal notation used in GPSG. This notation (e.g. 'S/NP') is reminiscent of categorial grammar, which interprets the notation in a different way.

10 The need to permit conditional FSDs was first discussed explicitly by Warner in an early draft of Warner (forthcoming). As can be seen, FCRs and FSDs are notated identically and this correctly reflects their formal reconstruction (for which, see the final section of this chapter). However, they differ in the way they are invoked by the grammar, and this difference will become evident in chapter 5.

11 It might appear that Brame (1978) and Bresnan (1978) are taking this view, but in fact they postulate a level of 'functional structure', which they regard as syntactic, in the sense that linguistic rules can refer to properties of *representations* at that level. We are not sure that anyone currently espouses the 'semantic filtering' approach that we are considering (and will reject) in the text.

12 Under some transformational approaches this example and the next two could be taken to illustrate governed application of transformational rules rather than subcategorization; but in all lexicalist theories and most recent versions of

transformational grammar, subcategorization is involved.

13 Sentences like *We extend to you our sincere condolences* might look as if they refute the claim in the text, but if such structures are assigned on analysis under which the NP is in 'extracted' position outside the VP, the incompatibility dissolves.

14 Chomsky (1965, pp. 110–11, 166–7) discusses inconclusively some conventions that might supply these negative specifications.

15 Cf. Pollard (1984) for a functionally similar but technically distinct use of the feature SUBCAT.

16 As a matter of historical interest, we note that Chomsky and Halle propose a mechanism for dealing with lexical exceptions to phonological rules (1968, p. 173) which is reminiscent of our approach to subcategorization:

> Each rule of the phonology has a certain identifying number. We associate with each number n a new 'distinctive feature' $[\pm n]$. Suppose that the rule numbered n is $A \rightarrow B/C\underline{\quad\quad}D$. Then we stipulate that A must be marked $[+n]$ if the rule numbered n is to apply to it.

17 Thus V^2 and V[2] stand for different things. The former abbreviates the category V[BAR 2], whereas the latter abbreviates the category V[SUBCAT 2].

18 We have not explicitly invoked PS rules to carry out lexical insertion. To do so, we could postulate a rule schema of the form

$$C \rightarrow \alpha$$

where C and α meet the conditions specified in the text. However, this extra device is not really required, given the manner in which the grammar determines structural descriptions. For more details, see chapter 5, section 5.

3

The nature of
grammatical rules

1 Introduction

The particular class of generalized phrase structure grammars (GPSGs)
characterized in this book is weakly equivalent to a proper subset of the
context-free phrase structure grammars (CF-PSGs).[1] Two grammars are
weakly equivalent if and only if they generate the same language, i.e. set of
strings. They are strongly equivalent if they also assign equivalent
structural descriptions (under some definition of equivalence). The grammars we define here are not strongly equivalent to CF-PSGs of the
ordinary sort, being more restrictive in some ways and more expressive in
others. They are more restrictive than the general theory of CF-PSGs
because of certain restrictions they observe which CF-PSGs in general
need not observe. The central one is the Exhaustive Constant Partial
Ordering property, which will be discussed below in section 2. But they are
at the same time more expressive than the general theory of CF-PSGs
because of the use of infinite schemata in certain cases, specifically for
handling flat structure in coordination rules (e.g. describing a string like
red and yellow and green and blue in terms of an adjective node with four
subconstituents rather than two groups of two). This allows us to describe
certain tree-sets that do not have ordinary CF-PSGs, and we think that
natural languages typically instantiate this possibility. We discuss this
matter at greater length in section 4 below.

GPSGs as presented here differ from ordinary CF-PSGs in a number of
ways. Most of these have to do either with the fact that syntactic
categories are not monadic but have internal structure that rules can
access, or with another, perhaps more surprising difference: in a GPSG, as
we define the notion in this book, there are no phrase structure rules
whatsoever. The class of admissible structural descriptions is determined
jointly by a component of rule-like grammatical statements which do not
meet the definition of CF-PSG rules and a set of universal principles

governing the way in which they define structures.

We are making a break with the previous GPSG literature in taking this step. Earlier writings in this theoretical framework have couched descriptions of languages in terms of a *metagrammar*, containing statements which determined the membership of a large set of fully specified phrase structure rules, and a simple algorithm for admitting structural descriptions of sentences (i.e. trees). In the present work we eliminate the definition of fully specified phrase structure rules, and determine the admissible structural descriptions directly via a definition of well-formedness for trees. However, in the sections that follow, we will introduce the novel concepts of our theory in terms that take as their point of departure the familiar concepts of CF-PSG.

2 Immediate dominance and linear precedence

A phrase structure rule of the familiar sort specifies two distinct relations: (i) immediate dominance relations holding between a mother (i.e. left hand side) category, and (ii) linear precedence relations among daughter (i.e. right hand side) categories. Consider, for example, the rules shown in (1):

(1) $A \rightarrow B\ C\ D$ $C \rightarrow A\ B\ D$
         $B \rightarrow A\ C\ D$ $D \rightarrow A\ B\ C$

Rules such as this say firstly things like 'a node labeled A, a node labeled B, and a node labeled D can be immediately dominated by a node labeled C', and secondly things like 'where a node labeled C immediately dominates a node labeled A, a node labeled B, and a node labeled D, the node labeled A is leftmost, the node labeled D is rightmost, and the node labeled B is in the middle.' Now, in the case of this particular grammar, inspection shows that a generalization can be made about the set of trees it admits, namely that sister constituents always appear on right hand sides of rules in an order that happens to correspond to the order of the letters A, B, C, D in the Roman alphabet. This generalization is not expressed by the grammar shown in (1). It just happens to be true of it.

Suppose we adopt a different mode of characterizing the trees admitted by a CF-PSG, factoring out the immediate dominance and linear precedence relations, and stating them separately. For immediate dominance, we can use the format shown in (2), which we shall call an Immediate Dominance (ID) rule.[2]

(2) $A \rightarrow B, C, D$

This statement is not itself a CF-PSG rule. Rather, it is a statement which does part of the job of defining the set of trees that a particular CF-PSG admits.

From this point on we shall need to make occasional reference to the notion of a *local tree*. A local tree is a tree of depth one, that is, a tree in which every node other than the root is a daughter of the root. So, for example, (3a) and (3b) are local trees, while (3c) is not. However, (3c) contains two local subtrees, namely (3a) and (3b).

(3)a.

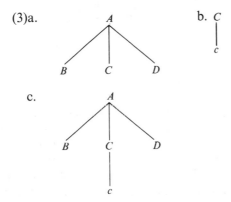

It will be convenient to have an alternative notation for local trees: we will employ the 'indented list' form often used in computer science. In this notation, the mother category appears to the left, and its daughters appear indented on succeeding lines (where top-to-bottom represents what left-to-right represents). Under this notation, the examples in (3) would appear as follows:

    a.   *A*
                B
                C
                D
    b.   *C*
                c
    c.   *A*
                B
                C
                        c
                D

However, we will only use this notation for local trees, not when we are exhibiting detailed structural analyses for constituents.

Consider what local trees the ID rule (4) admits.

(4)   *A* → *B, C, D*

This rule admits any local tree in which an A immediately and exhaustively dominates a node labeled B, a node labeled C, and a node labeled D. However, it does not say anything about the linear order in which the nodes labeled B, C and D must occur under the node labeled A. In (5) we show all the local trees admitted by (4).

(5)

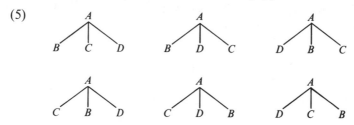

Of course, in general we will want a grammar to be able to impose some constraints on the linear precedence relations between sisters. In order to do this, we introduce a relation $\prec$, where '$A \prec B$' means that As must precede Bs. To be more precise, we intend '$A \prec B$' to be interpreted as 'a node labeled B cannot appear to the left of a node labeled A in a local tree'. Any sentence of the form '$A \prec B$' is called a linear precedence (LP) statement.[3] We intend such statements to determine an antisymmetric, transitive relation. Thus for any x, y, z, if $x \prec y$ and $y \prec x$, then $x = y$ (antisymmetry), and if $x \prec y$ and $y \prec z$ then $x \prec z$ (transitivity). A more precise formulation than this needs to refer to extensions of the categories mentioned in the LP statement rather than just the symbols of the LP statement themselves (see chapter 5, section 5).

Given what we have said so far, a grammar is defined as a pair consisting of a set of ID rules, and a set of LP statements. A grammar in such a form is said to be in Immediate Dominance/Linear Precedence (ID/LP) format. A local tree T is admitted by an ID/LP grammar G if and only if T is consistent with some ID rule in G and every LP statement in G. A (nonlocal) tree T is admitted by G if and only if (i) every local subtree in T is admitted by G, and (ii) every leaf of T is a terminal symbol. Continuing our previous example, suppose that the ID rule (4) is supplemented with the LP statement '$B \prec C$'. The set of trees admitted by this grammar (ignoring terminal symbols, for the moment) is a subset of (5), namely (6).

(6)

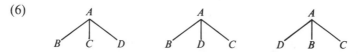

For another example, consider the grammar (7):

(7)   (i) $A \rightarrow B, C, D$ (ii) $A \prec B \prec C \prec D$
              $B \rightarrow A, C, D$
              $C \rightarrow A, B, D$
              $D \rightarrow A, B, C$

Taken together (7i) and (7ii) are extensionally equivalent to grammar (1). That is, they define exactly the same set of trees. But grammar (7) does what (1) does not: it expresses the generalization about sister constituent order.

We should make it clear at this point that treating immediate dominance and linear precedence separately in a generative grammar is an idea with a long history. Many linguists have suggested something of this sort.[4] But in fact none of the previous work does exactly what we are proposing here. We are not proposing any nonlinear levels of syntactic structure or nonlinear stages in the derivation of linearized structures. Rather, we wish to separate dominance and precedence in a set of statements that directly determine linearized structural representations. Our structural descriptions for sentences always display both dominance and precedence relations simultaneously; but the statements that determine their well-formedness deal with the two aspects of structure separately. Accordingly, we do not have rules for linearizing structures that have a prior existence in nonlinear terms. Rather, ID/LP format grammars capture generalizations by stating constituent order for the grammar as a whole, rather on a one-rule-at-a-time basis as in CF-PSGs.

Let us consider a toy grammar for part of a natural language, of a kind familiar from elementary introductions to CF-PSG (we continue to ignore terminal symbols):

(8)   S → NP VP
       S → AUX NP VP
       VP → AUX VP
       VP → V VP
       VP → V NP
       VP → V NP VP

This grammar fails to express at least two generalizations: (a) AUX and V are always initial in their constituents, and (b) NPs precede VPs. An equivalent grammar in the format just introduced, is that shown in (9):

(9)   (i)   S → NP, VP   (ii)   AUX ≺ NP
             S → AUX, NP, VP   V ≺ NP
             VP → AUX, VP   NP ≺ VP
             VP → V, VP
             VP → V, NP
             VP → V, NP, VP

This grammar expresses the two generalizations noted above, but at the cost, it seems, of additional statements.[5] This prolixity is only apparent, however, since (9i) contains much less information than (8). The greater economy of the ID/LP format becomes more obvious when we consider a grammar for the VP of a language that has much freer word order than English – like the language presupposed by the grammar in (10). Makua (Stucky (1981c)) is just such a language. We exhibit in (10) almost all the rules necessary to assign correct constituent structure to Makua VPs:[6]

(10)   VP → V   VP → V S NP
        VP → V S   VP → NP V S
        VP → V NP   VP → NP V PP
        VP → NP V   VP → PP V NP
        VP → NP V NP   VP → PP NP V
        VP → NP NP V   VP → NP PP V
        VP → V NP NP   VP → V PP NP
        VP → V NP S   VP → V NP PP

This grammar can be replaced by a much more compact ID/LP formulation:

(11)   (i)   VP → V   (ii)   V ≺ S
              VP → V, NP
              VP → V, S
              VP → V, NP, NP
              VP → V, NP, PP
              VP → V, NP, S

Now observe that ID/LP format is not just a new format for writing what are essentially CF-PSGs (though it has so far appeared that this is so). There are some PSGs that are not expressible in ID/LP format. Consider, for example, the grammars shown in (12) and (13):

(12)   S → NP VP
        S → AUX NP VP
        VP → AUX VP
        VP → V VP
        VP → V NP
        VP → V VP NP

(13)	VP → V	VP → S V NP
	VP → V S	VP → NP V S
	VP → V NP	VP → NP V PP
	VP → NP V	VP → PP V NP
	VP → NP V NP	VP → PP NP V
	VP → NP NP V	VP → NP PP V
	VP → V NP NP	VP → V PP NP
	VP → V NP S	VP → V NP PP

These two grammars are exactly as complex as (8) and (10), respectively, and yet neither can be expressed in ID/LP format.

There is a formal property that distinguishes grammars (12) and (13) from (8) and (10). It is that in (8) and (10) the set of expansions of any one category observes a partial ordering that is also observed by the expansions of all other categories. We will refer to this property as the Exhaustive Constant Partial Ordering (ECPO) property. A CF-PSG can be put into ID/LP format if and only if it has the ECPO property. Grammars (12) and (13) do not have the property. Thus (12) contains rules which exhibit NP VP order as well as VP NP order, but it restricts the former to expansions of S and the latter to expansions of VP. And (13) allows an S V order when both precede NP, but not otherwise.[7]

Exhaustive constant partial ordering is a very abstract property of grammars. As the examples above suggest, many plausible-looking sets of CF-PSG rules do not possess it. Indeed, it is a statistically unexpected property. If we consider the set of possible grammars defined on the same vocabulary as (13), with the same number of rules, and the same upper bound on the size of rules, then only a tiny proportion of this set will have the ECPO property (because from any grammar that has the ECPO property a large number of distinct grammars could be made by varying one or more orderings within specific rules in a way that destroyed the ECPO property). It would therefore be interesting and surprising if ECPO turned out to be a linguistic universal. Clearly, anyone adopting ID/LP as their format for stating grammars, as we do, is committed to the rather strong claim that it will turn out to be a universal.

ID/LP format also allows us to capture significant generalizations at a parochial level, i.e. within rules specific to a particular language. Thus, in English, a lexical item always precedes its phrasal sisters. Because of the way our theory of subcategorization works, lexical items (strictly speaking, the categories that immediately dominate them) all have a feature in common, namely SUBCAT, but nothing which is not a lexical item carries this feature.[8] So the ordering fact just noted can be expressed with a single LP statement:

(14) $[\text{SUBCAT}] \prec \sim[\text{SUBCAT}]$

From this single statement it follows that verbs will be VP-initial, that determiners are NP-initial, that English has prepositions rather than postpositions, that complementizers precede S, that coordination words are conjunct-initial, that auxiliary verbs which are daughters of S are sentence-initial, that adjectives and nouns precede their complements, that comparative and equative particles are constituent-initial, etc.

3   Heads

Consider an ID rule such as that shown in (15):

(15) $\text{VP} \rightarrow \text{V}[2], \text{NP}$

In a version of X-bar syntax, such as the one we are assuming, in which VP is a [**BAR** 2] category, (15) is more accurately expressed as (16):

(16) $\text{V}^2 \rightarrow \text{V}[2], \text{N}^2$

In a theory of categories adopted in the present work, (16) could itself be expressed more explicitly as (17):

(17) $\{\langle N, - \rangle, \langle V, + \rangle, \langle \text{BAR}, 2 \rangle\} \rightarrow$
          $\{\langle N, - \rangle, \langle V, + \rangle, \langle \text{BAR}, 0 \rangle, \langle \text{SUBCAT}, 2 \rangle\},$
          $\{\langle N, + \rangle, \langle V, - \rangle, \langle \text{BAR}, 2 \rangle\}$

Note that (17) does not, of itself, tell us that the verb is the head of the verb phrase. All versions of X-bar syntax are supplied with a definition of head which runs something like (18):

(18)   In a rule of the form:
          $\{\langle N, a \rangle, \langle V, \beta \rangle, \langle \text{BAR}, m \rangle\} \rightarrow \ldots \{\langle N, a \rangle, \langle V, \beta \rangle,$
          $\langle \text{BAR}, n \rangle\}, \ldots$
          where $n \leq m$ (sometimes: $n < m$),
          $\{\langle N, a \rangle, \langle V, \beta \rangle, \langle \text{BAR}, n \rangle\}$ is the head of
          $\{\langle N, a \rangle, \langle V, \beta \rangle, \langle \text{BAR}, m \rangle\}$

Having given such a definition of head, many accounts then go on to provide for transfer of minor features from mother to head by introducing a feature-trickling convention. This convention, called the Head Feature Convention (HFC) by Gazdar, Pullum and Sag (1982), says, in effect, that mother and head are to carry the same features.

This uncontroversial proposal has a very curious property. For example, consider some feature, say F, which can appear on verbs and (hence) verb phrases. Suppose we flesh out rule (17) to include this feature.

(19)   a. $\{\langle N, - \rangle, \langle V, + \rangle, \langle F, + \rangle, \langle BAR, 2 \rangle\} \rightarrow$
       b. $\{\langle N, - \rangle, \langle V, + \rangle, \langle F, + \rangle, \langle BAR, 0 \rangle,$
            $\langle SUBCAT\ 2 \rangle\},$
       c. $\{\langle N, + \rangle, \langle V, - \rangle, \langle BAR, 2 \rangle\}$

In this rule, category (a) and category (b) instantiate the same values for all their component features. Intuitively this should simply follow from the feature convention for heads. But it does not follow in formulations of the sort alluded to above. Instead, the correspondence of the $[+V, -N]$ values is used to define the head, and the correspondence of the $[+F]$ value then follows from the head feature convention. So feature correspondence is used to define the 'head of' relation, and then the latter is used to account for feature correspondence via a convention. The only thing that prevents the enterprise being circular is that different classes of features are involved in the two cases. Notice also that the definition of head, though it may look impressively general, actually only works thanks to a set of rule-stipulated feature correspondences of the kind illustrated in (17).

Our solution to this problem is as follows. Our theory of categories allows minimally specified categories like $\{\langle BAR, 2 \rangle\}$ or $\{\langle N, - \rangle,$ $\langle V, + \rangle\}$. Even the empty set $\{\}$ is a category in our terms (it is just that set of feature specifications with zero members). We propose to allow ID rules to contain in their right hand sides the symbol H, where this is a metagrammatical place-holder standing for a largely unspecified category which has the status of head in that rule. The exact formal character of this place-holder symbol is spelled out in the following section. Here, it will suffice to note that:

(20)   In a rule of the form $C \rightarrow \dots H \dots$
       H is a *head*.

The job of the HFC will be to determine the feature composition of the head category or categories thus identified, essentially by requiring the set of **HEAD** features that get instantiated on heads to be identical to (or a superset of) the **HEAD** features instantiated on the mother category (see chapter 5, section 4 for precise details of the HFC).

Rule (16) can now be written as follows:

(21) $V^2 \rightarrow H[2], N^2$

Under this approach, the grammar stipulates the heads in a rule directly (instead of indirectly via feature correspondences), but it does not need to stipulate any feature identities in respect of heads. All the work of ensuring featural identity between mother and head is now done by the HFC.

To indicate the bar level of a head, we will use H^2 for value 2, H^1 for value 1, and H^0 for value 0. Since a category bearing the feature [SUBCAT n] must be [BAR 0] if it has a bar at all (see 2.3), we can simply write $H[n]$ for lexical heads. And, for cases where the bar level of a head is neither implicitly nor explicitly indicated, we will henceforth adopt the convention of taking the value for BAR in an H category to be that of the mother. As it happens, this convention will turn out to be simply a consequence of the HFC, as defined in chapter 5, and of our decision to treat **BAR** as a **HEAD** feature, a decision motivated by facts about coordination (see chapter 8).[9]

4   A formal theory of ID rules

The mathematical characterization of PS rules is well known. If V is a vocabulary (for convenience, we draw no distinction between terminal and nonterminal vocabulary) and V^* is the Kleene closure of V, then a PS rule is a member of the set of pairs

(22) $V \times V^*$

Thus, (23a) is conventional notation for the pair (23b), where *BCD* is simply a string drawn from V^*.

(23)   a. $A \rightarrow B\,C\,D$
        b. $\langle A,\ BCD \rangle$

By contrast, we have not yet made clear what the formal properties of ID rules are. Consider, for example, a schematic ID rule containing a metavariable W:

(24) $A \rightarrow B,\ W$

One would like (24) to be a schema whose instances include ID rules like the following.

(25) $A \rightarrow B$
        $A \rightarrow B,\ C$
        $A \rightarrow B,\ C$
        $A \rightarrow B,\ B,\ D$

W obviously is not a metavariable over strings of elements of V, since the righthand side of an ID rule is not a string. On the other hand, without a clearer statement of the formal properties of ID rules, we cannot say what W is a metavariable over.

One possibility would be to regard the material to the right of an ID arrow as a set of categories. Yet this is not quite adequate, since it would make the last two ID rules in (25) equivalent. The reason, of course, is that two sets are identical if they have the same members, so $\{B, B, D\}$ is identical to $\{B, D\}$. However, there is an alternative mathematical construct available, namely a *multiset*. A multiset (sometimes called a bag, or a set with repetitions) is like a set, except that it may contain identical elements repeated a finite number of times. In order to make explicit that we are talking about a multiset rather than a standard set, we can add an 'm' subscript to a right curly bracket. Thus, the multisets $\{B, B, D\}_m$ and $\{B, D\}_m$ are distinct objects.

Following Knuth (1969, p. 412), we use $\uplus$ to denote combination of multisets, or 'multi-union' for short. It is defined as follows: if A and B are multisets, and an element belongs a times to A and b times to B, then it belongs exactly $a + b$ times to $A \uplus B$. We can also define an m-subset relation: if A and B are multisets, then A is an m-subset of B if and only if every element belonging a times to A belongs b times to B, $b \geq a$.

If X is any set, and M is a multiset, let us say that M *is drawn from* X, in symbols $M \leq^+ X$, if and only if every element that occurs at least once in M also belongs to X. So $M \leq^+ X$ is like set inclusion, except that it holds between a multiset and a set. Moreover, even if X is finite, there will be an infinite number of multisets M such that $M \leq^+ X$, for there is no upper bound on the number of times that a given element of X can belong to a multiset drawn from X. We use $POW_m(X)$ to denote the set of all multisets drawn from X; this is the multiset analog of the power set of X.

It is also possible to look at $POW_m(X)$ in a way which more closely parallels operations on sets of strings. Again, let X be any finite set, and let L, L_1 and L_2 be finite sets of multisets drawn from X.[10] The multi-union of L_1 and L_2, denoted $L_1 \uplus L_2$, is defined as the set of $\{M_1 \uplus M_2 : M_1 \in L_1$ and $M_2 \in L_2\}$. That is, the multisets in $L_1 \uplus L_2$ are formed by constructing the multi-union of any multiset in L_1 with any multiset in L_2. Define $L^{[0]} = \{\{\}_m\}$, where $\{\}_m$ is just the empty multiset, and $L^{[i]} = L \uplus L^{[i-1]}$, for $i \geq 1$. For example, let $L = \{\{a\}_m, \{b\}_m\}$. Then $L^{[1]} = L$, and $L^{[2]} = \{\{a, a\}_m, \{a, b\}_m, \{b, b\}_m\}$. The closure of L under multi-union, denoted $L^{[*]}$, is the set

$$L^{[*]} = \bigcup_{i=0}^{\infty} L^{[i]}$$

Now let $L = \{M \leq^+ X : \exists x \in X[M = \{x\}_m]\}$. Then $L^{[*]} = POW_m(X)$.

We return now to the considerations of ID rules. We propose that an ID rule be defined as a member of the set of pairs given below (where K is the set of categories defined by the grammar):

(26) $K \times POW_m(K)$

So, for example, the formal version of the ID rule (27a) can be represented as (27b).

(27)   a. $A \rightarrow B, B, D$
       b. $\langle A, \{B, B, D\}_m \rangle$

We can use multisets to give a precise reconstruction of our H notation for heads. A headed ID rule is to be understood as an ordered pair whose first member is an ID rule, and whose second member is an m-subset of the second member of the ID rule (intuitively, this is the multiset of heads in the rule). Thus a headed ID rule is an object of the following kind:

(28) $\langle \langle C_0, \{C_1, \ldots, C_n\}_m \rangle, \{C_1, \ldots, C_i\}_m \rangle$
       where i is less than or equal to n.

Such objects are less cumbersomely represented by means of our H notation: (28) can be rewritten as (29).

(29) $\langle C_0, \{H_1, \ldots, H_i, C_{i+1}, \ldots, C_n\}_m \rangle$

Thus (30a) stands for (30b)

(30)   a. $V^2 \rightarrow H[2], N^2$
       b. $\langle \langle V^2, \{\{\langle SUBCAT, 2 \rangle\}, N^2\}_m \rangle,$
            $\{\{\langle SUBCAT, 2 \rangle\}\}_m \rangle$

The rule in (30) is an exemplar of an important class of rules, namely those rules that introduce a lexical head: we will refer to this class of rules as 'the lexical ID rules'. A rule is a lexical ID rule if and only if it has a head which is an extension of a SUBCAT category. Note that the only bit of information about a lexical head that has to be stipulated in a rule like (30) is its subcategory – everything else about it will follow from other components of the grammar (in particular, the HFC and the FCRs found in chapter 2, section 3).

Next, consider the schematic ID rule in (31), where the C_i are categories in K and W is a metavariable.

(31) $C_0 \rightarrow C_1, \ldots, C_n, W$

Then W is interpreted as a multiset of elements of K, and the rule as a whole interpreted as the pair in (32).

(32) $\langle C_0, \{C_1, \ldots, C_n\}_m \uplus W \rangle$

Consider now the regular expression a^*, where a is an element of V. This denotes the set $\{a\}^*$, i.e. the result of closing $\{a\}$ under concatenation. The corresponding object in an ID rule is $POW_m(\{a\})$, the set of all multisets which contain zero or more repetitions of a. Notice that this is equivalent to $\{a\}^{[*]}$, according to our earlier definitions. Similarly, corresponding to the positive closure a^+ of a regular expression a is $POW_m(\{a\}) - \{\}_m$. Clearly, we could have also defined $\{a\}^{[+]}$ in the obvious way. In practice, we will simply use the notation C^* and C^+ on the right-hand side of ID rules. However, these are interpreted as the multiset analogs of Kleene closure and positive closure in the manner just indicated.

As a final point, note that we restrict the use of these closure operations to single categories. As Shieber et al. (1983) point out, the grammar $S \rightarrow \{a, b, c\}^{[*]}$ with the LP statement $a \prec b \prec c$ generates the context-sensitive language $a^n b^n c^n$. See Culy 1983, 6–8, 59–69, for some relevant formal results on the use of Kleene operations in ID/LP grammars.

Notes

1 For an introduction to these formal systems, see Aho and Ullman 1972, Hopcroft and Ullman 1979, Wall 1972, or other texts on mathematical linguistics or theoretical computer science.

2 This ID rule has six different typographical forms: A → C, D, B; A → C, B, D; A → D, C, B; A → B, D, C; A → C, D, B; A → D, B, C. However, these six versions of the rule all make exactly the same claim. They are not different rules, but merely different orthographic representations of the same rule.

3 An LP statement of the form '$A \prec A$' has the effect of preventing two nodes labeled A from occurring as sisters, in view of its interpretation as 'a node labeled A cannot appear to the left of a node labeled A in a local tree.'

4 Early suggestions by Curry (1961) and Šaumjan and Soboleva (1963) were criticized by Chomsky (1965, pp. 124 ff.), though in retrospect his criticisms can be seen to have little substance. Dahl (1974) and Dowty (1982b) have since taken up some of the ideas of Curry's paper. Several other linguists worked during the late 1960s and early 1970s on types of transformational grammar that had unlinearized trees as syntactic representations at early stages of derivations (see e.g. Hudson 1972, Peterson 1971, Sanders 1970, Staal 1967), and the idea has surfaced again recently in transformational work (Zubizaretta and Vergnaud 1981) and elsewhere (Flynn 1983). Falk (1983) presents a proposal very similar to that presented here and in Gazdar and Pullum 1981, but developed independently.

5 Note that neither (8) nor (9) captures a relevant generalization about AUX and V, namely that they share the same ordering constraint.

6 Two points should be made here. First, the list in (10) is *not* Stucky's analysis. Stucky deals with the freedom of order in Makua by defining a small set of basic rules and a set of metarules that operate on them. We have closed part of her grammar under the operation of her metarules to obtain the set of PS rules that *would* have to be listed if metarules were not employed. Second, we have omitted some VP rules that introduce infinitives and unbounded dependency-containing constituents, because these rules raise issues irrelevant to our concerns here. The rules we omit do not, however, raise any problems for the type of analysis we are presenting.

7 In each case, the addition or subtraction of rules suffices to achieve a closure under the relevant partial ordering which ECPO requires. These examples show that an ECPO grammar can have a proper subgrammar that is not ECPO. It is in fact the case that all CF-PSGs have ECPO subgrammars (albeit only trivially in some cases) and ECPO supergrammars. This means that if we are interested in the ECPO property, we must be careful not to limit our attention to some proper subset of constructions in the language that, uncharacteristically for the overall grammar, has the property or lacks it.

8 Note that ID/LP format interacts with our theory of subcategorization to predict that subcategorization is necessarily insensitive to linear order: Hendrick (1981) and Grimshaw (1982) have argued that this is indeed the case.

9 Our position on X-bar syntax in this book is similar to that of Emonds (1976, pp. 12–20), except that we differ from Emonds in taking the category S to be a maximal projection of V, and in taking P to be a lexical category. Traditionally, a lexical item is often spoken of as being the head of a whole phrase. We too will sometimes speak loosely of, e.g., *loves* being the head of a given VP, when formally it is not a head at all under our account, but rather the terminal symbol immediately and exhaustively dominated by the head.

10 The following exposition is modeled on the discussion of regular expressions in Hopcroft and Ullman 1979, p. 28.

4

Metarules
and their properties

---

1 Introduction

In the previous chapter, we introduced ID/LP format. As we saw, a grammar in this format characterizes a set of local trees in a way that makes it possible to capture generalizations that are not expressed by the extensionally equivalent CF-PSG. In this chapter we introduce a further technique for capturing generalizations, that of metarules, that is, statements that define a principled enlargement of a set of ID rules by providing a systematic way of defining new ones on the basis of those already included in the grammar.

As a way of introducing metarules, we shall present illustrative analyses of two familiar constructions in English: the passive, and the auxiliary-initial sentence type used for the polar interrogatives ('subject–aux inversion').

2 Passive

Consider the ID/LP grammar fragment in (1):

(1) (i) ID rules
       a. VP → H[2], NP
       b. VP → H[3], NP, PP[*to*]
  (ii) LP statements
       a. [SUBCAT] $\prec$ ~[SUBCAT]
       b. $N^2 \prec P^2 \prec V^2$

This fragment is responsible for English verb phrases such as those shown in (2a) and (2b), respectively.

(2)   a.   devoured the carcass
         b.   handed the sword to Tracy

Suppose we wished now to extend our grammar to permit verb phrases such as those in (3).

(3)   a.   (i)   eaten
              (ii) eaten by Felix
         b.   (i)   given to Sandy
              (ii) given to Sandy by Lee

An obvious way to do this would be to add to our grammar two more ID rules which define passive verb phrases; for example, those in (4):

(4)   a.   VP[PAS] → H[2′], (PP[*by*])
         b.   VP[PAS] → H[3′], PP[*to*], (PP[*by*])

But if we did this, our grammar would fail to express a number of significant generalizations. Notice first that the membership of the sub-categories of V defined by rules (4a) and (4b) would be identical to those defined by rules (1a) and (1b): *devour* and *eat* would both be in the subcategory V[2] as well as V[2′]; *hand* and *give* would both be in the subcategory V[3] as well as V[3′]. Except with respect to the morphological form of the verb in (3a), there are no distinctions between these subcategories, yet this would be represented as an accident. Furthermore, the form of the rules in (4) stands in a systematic relation to that of those in (1). This relation is not expressed if all four rules are merely listed.

To deal with this sort of situation, we introduce the notion of a *metarule*. A metarule should be regarded intuitively as a definition of some of the rules in the grammar on the basis of the properties of others. Metarules will be stated in the following form, where the α_i, β_i are either categories or the multiset variable W (discussed below):

$$\alpha_0 \to \alpha_1, \ldots, \alpha_n$$
$$\Downarrow$$
$$\beta_0 \to \beta_1, \ldots, \beta_k$$

The reader might like to think of the downward double arrow as meaning 'gets you'. Thus, the above schema can be read as 'any rule of the form $\alpha_0 \to \alpha_1, \ldots, \alpha_n$ gets you a rule of the form $\beta_0 \to \beta_1, \ldots, \beta_k$' (where β_0 can be derived from α_0, and $\beta_1, \ldots, \beta_k$ from $\alpha_1, \ldots, \alpha_n$, in specific ways that we clarify below). The idea is that by employing metarules we will only need to list rules like those in (1i) – we can get those in (4), not by listing, but by the application of a metarule to (1ia) and (1ib).

Earlier work in GPSG has assumed, implicitly or explicitly, that metarules can apply to any phrase structure rule in the grammar that meets their input specifications. Most, and perhaps all, of the motivation for permitting this unrestricted use of metarules came either from facts about linear precedence or from facts about the distribution of feature specifications. In the present framework, the first class of facts can no longer provide that motivation, since metarules must apply to ID rules and cannot, therefore, have any direct bearing on linear precedence. Furthermore, given the very general approach to feature instantiation that will be elaborated in chapter 5, it does not seem appropriate to also express grammar-wide generalizations about feature-passing by means of metarules, and thus the second class of facts mentioned no longer provides a motivation for an unrestricted domain of application for metarules.

The most compelling instances of metarule analyses that we know of concern metarules whose input specification picks out a class of what we have called lexical ID rules (i.e. ID rules that introduce lexical heads; see chapter 3, section 4). Following Flickinger (1983), we propose, in the present work, to adopt the following restriction on metarule application:

(5)   Metarules map from lexical ID rules to lexical ID rules.

This revised conception of the role of metarules embodies a very strong claim, one that may prove to be incompatible with the descriptive work one needs to do in the grammars of natural languages.[1] It is tantamount to saying that metarules serve solely to express generalizations about the subcategorization possibilities of lexical heads. Thus, although metarules operate on syntactic and not lexical structure, Flickinger's restriction makes them so closely tied to the lexically determined subcategorization domains of particular lexical items that they offer a compromise between lexical and syntactic statements of relatedness between construction types – a compromise that we believe may be the correct one.

The passive metarule will look something like this:

(6)   Passive Metarule
$$\text{VP} \rightarrow W, \text{NP}$$
$$\Downarrow$$
$$\text{VP[PAS]} \rightarrow W, (\text{PP}[by])$$

What this says is: for every ID rule in the grammar which permits VP to dominate NP and some other material, there is also a rule in the grammar which permits the passive category VP[PAS] to dominate just the other material from the original rule, together (optionally) with a PP containing the specification [PFORM *by*]. Notice that there is no need to specify that part of W is the head verb in the VP. Every rule that meets the input description of (6) expands the category VP, and every lexical ID rule that expands VP will introduce a V. Moreover, the head verb plays no role in the mapping performed by the metarule, and hence it would be otiose to mention the category V. Any features mentioned on categories in the input rule are assumed to be retained on those categories in the output rule, unless the metarule itself changes them. This means, in particular, that the subcategorization feature [SUBCAT i] on a lexical category will remain unchanged under the application of metarules.

Thus (6) will apply to (1ia) and (1ib) to give us (7a) and (7b) respectively.

(7)　　a.　VP[PAS] → H[2], (PP[*by*])
　　　　b.　VP[PAS] → H[3], PP[*to*], (PP[*by*])

Our conventions ensure that exactly the same class of lexical items will be permissible in the contexts defined by rules (1ia) and (7a), and likewise in the case of rules (1ib) and (7b). The generalizations about passive marking on the verb, absence of the direct object, and optional presence of a *by*-phrase, all follow from the form of the metarule in (6) as well.

Our passive metarule has further advantages. Consider the following grammatical verb phrase.

(8)　　given by Lee to Sandy.

This case simply follows from the absence of any LP rules stipulating precedence relations between subtypes of PP. Consequently, (7b) will admit trees with the *by*-phase before the *to*-phrase as well as the other way around. Furthermore, (6) cannot affect the linear order of categories in the output rule. That is, it cannot stipulate that the order is mirror image of the order of categories in the input rule, but nor does it have to stipulate that V is phrase-initial in a VP[PAS]. This restriction follows instead from the much more general LP rule shown in (1iia).[2]

3　'Subject–aux inversion' without subject, aux, or inversion

As a further example of the kind of descriptive power we achieve through the use of metarules, we will take a detailed look at English sentences with auxiliary-initial constituent order. This topic is usually discussed in terms of the notion of 'subject–aux inversion', but this is a total misnomer when applied to the account we will offer. As will be shown, our account does not mention subjects, does not refer to the auxiliary verb at all, and involves nothing that could be called inversion.

The paradigm set out in (9) indicates the essential insight of our approach: what follows the subject NP in an auxiliary-initial sentence is whatever would have been able to occur as the complement of the

(9)	a.	will do it	a'.	Will you do it?
	b.	has gone away	b'.	Has she gone away?
	c.	should leave	c'.	Should we leave?
	d.	doesn't care	d'.	Doesn't he care?
	e.	are swimming	e'.	Are they swimming?

auxiliary verb if it had occurred in a VP instead. We capture this relationship by relating two sets of rules with a metarule.

The metarule given in (10) is both elegant and parsimonious in form and contains nothing that is particular to English. Indeed, it is essentially identical to proposals made for several other languages in which VSO is a permissible order of constituents; see e.g. Gazdar and Sag (1981) on Breton, Harlow (1983) on Welsh, Horrocks (1983) on Greek, Sells (1982b) on Irish, and Uszkoreit (1982a) and Russell (1983) on German.

(10) $VP \rightarrow W$
$$\Downarrow$$
$$S[+INV] \rightarrow W, NP$$

Intuitively, (10) says that every lexical ID rule licencing verb phrases that contain material W is paralleled by another rule licencing a special type of clause that contains W plus a noun phrase.[3] The following FCR is associated with the feature INV:

(11)   FCR 10: $[+INV, BAR\ 2] \supset [+SUBJ]$

Although INV is a head feature, this FCR prevents it from ever dripping through VP (which, by definition, is $[-SUBJ]$).

In interpreting the metarule we will employ a theoretical reconstruction of the notions 'verb phrase' and 'sentence' that we use later throughout the book. Following Borsley (1983a, 1984a), we analyze both the verb phrase (VP) and the clause or sentence (S) as projections of V with bar level 2 (i.e. $\{\langle N, -\rangle, \langle V, +\rangle, \langle BAR, 2\rangle\}$). They are distinguished from each other by a feature SUBJ which intuitively indicates whether the constituent has a subject NP: VP is $V^2[-SUBJ]$, and S is $V^2[+SUBJ]$. Thus 'VP' and 'S' are to be understood henceforth as reading abbreviations ('aliases' in the sense of Evans and Gazdar (1984) and Thompson and Phillips (1984)) for these two categories, respectively. We assume that the following FCR applies to SUBJ:[4]

(12)   FCR 11: $[+SUBJ] \supset [+V, -N, BAR\ 2]$

Borsley gives some interesting arguments from Welsh syntax for the $[\pm SUBJ]$ analysis of S and VP. We shall just assume it for the time being, and demonstrate its utility in chapter 6 where we discuss the distribution of S and VP complements.

Given the abbreviatory conventions just noted, our metarule above can now be understood as amounting to the following:

(13)   'Subject–Aux Inversion' (SAI) Metarule

$$V^2[-\text{SUBJ}] \rightarrow W$$
$$\Downarrow$$
$$V^2[+\text{INV}, +\text{SUBJ}] \rightarrow W, \text{NP}$$

As mentioned above, every lexical ID rule which expands VP also introduces a H^0, so there will always be an H^0 in W. Suppose then that the output of the metarule is an ID rule of the form

(14) $S[+\text{INV}] \rightarrow H[n], \text{NP}, \text{VP}$

The LP statements for English presented in the previous section guarantee that the verb will be leftmost daughter in the linearized local trees that (14) yields. They also ensure that the NP will precede the complement VP. These LP statements can be motivated entirely on the basis of the internal syntax of VPs in English (in which verbs precede NPs which in turn precede VPs – e.g. *made me eat*). Thus the linear precedence relations that hold between the constituents in the sentential SAI construction are fully accounted for, without anything special about order or inversion needing to be said. The 'inversion' is simply just another consequence of the extremely general LP rule for English shown in (1iia). As an illustration of the application of the metarule in (13), consider the following ID rule:

(15)   a. $VP[+\text{AUX}] \rightarrow H[46], VP[-\text{AUX}, \text{BSE}]$
        b   do
        c.   did see Laurie

Applied to (15a), (13) will produce the output rule (16).

(16) $V^2[+\text{AUX}, +\text{INV}, +\text{SUBJ}] \rightarrow$
        $H^0[46], V^2[-\text{AUX}, -\text{SUBJ}, \text{BSE}], N^2$

Given the LP statements just alluded to, this in turn will admit local trees of the form shown below.

(17) $V^2[+\text{AUX}, +\text{INV}, +\text{SUBJ}]$
        $V^0[46, +\text{AUX}, +\text{INV}]$
        N^2
        $V^2[-\text{AUX}, \text{BSE}, -\text{SUBJ}]$

The motivation for the feature INV comes from the need to be able to identify auxiliary-initial sentences in order to handle facts like the following:

(18)   a.   Max always asks whether there are any problems.
        b   *Max always asks whether are there any problems.
        c.   Often (*Never) we have found ourselves alone on the beach.
        d.   Never (*Often) have we found ourselves alone on the beach.

Subordinate clauses with *whether* and positive adverbs like *often* demand clauses of the ordinary sort (not auxiliary-initial), while negative adverbs like *never* demand clauses derived via the metarule. The binary feature INV, mnemonic for 'inverted sentence' (though 'verb-initial' would be a more sensible description), allows the facts to be captured. An auxiliary-initial sentence will be introduced by a rule just in case the rule mentions the category S[| INV] since the default for the feature is [−INV].

The reader will notice that the metarule does not mention the [+AUX] property or the [VFORM FIN] (tensed) property. One might think that the metarule would therefore operate on rules of the sort that induce the VPs in (19).

(19)   a.   read my term paper
        b.   being a nuisance
        c.   written by a lunatic
        d.   to be a pilgrim
        e.   broken the rules

If so, the output rules would generate ill-formed strings like those in (20).

(20)   a.   *Read you my term paper?
        b.   *Being Kim a nuisance?
        c.   *Written the letter by a lunatic?
        d.   *To Sandy be a pilgrim?
        e.   *Broken the prisoners the rules?

But recall the FCR mentioned for exemplification in chapter 2, which we repeat here:

(21)   FCR 1:[+INV] ⊃ [+AUX, FIN]

This guarantees that rules specifying [+INV] on any category will only admit local trees in which that category is also [+AUX] and [VFORM FIN]. This excludes all the ungrammatical examples just cited. Of course, the FCR in (21) represents a fact about English: grammars for languages that have the metarule but lack the FCR, or which have a weaker FCR (e.g. '[+INV] ⊃ [+AUX]' or '[+INV] ⊃ [VFORM FIN]') would make different predictions about the languages' counterparts to the examples in (20).

The usual accounts of auxiliary-initial sentences, couched in terms of inverting the order of subject and auxiliary to form yes/no questions, differ from our account in a subtle way that might not immediately be noticed. They predict that the subject-auxiliary combinations found in interrogatives or other inverted structures will be exactly those found in noninverted sentences. But we predict this only given the following assumption: 'no verb mentions the feature value [+INV] in its lexical entry'. Since INV is a head feature, it will appear on verbs, given the Head Feature Convention, discussed in detail in the next chapter. So, if (21) is not assumed, we predict that it is possible for there to be a verb form that demands in its lexical entry the presence of the [+INV] feature specification. Such a verb will be able to appear only in clauses whose description involves outputs of the metarule. Interestingly, there are some generally overlooked facts that favor our account.

First, there are some semantic differences between inverted and non-inverted sentences. Speakers who have the item *shall* report a meaning difference between *I shall go downtown* and *Shall I go downtown?* over and above the difference between statements and questions, as was noticed by Emonds (cited by Chomsky 1981, p. 209). The *shall* in the declarative example simply conveys futurity, whereas the *shall* in the question has a deontic sense comparable to that of *should*. Notice also the following facts (due to John Payne): *Kim mightn't go* has negation within the scope of the *might* (i.e. meaning 'possibly Kim will not go'), while *Mightn't Kim go?* suggests the reverse scope (i.e. meaning 'is it not the case that possibly Kim will go?'). We do not offer an analysis of these semantic differences, but it seems unlikely that they could be described correctly without reference to whether a particular auxiliary verb was inverted or not.

Less subtly, consider the following paradigm from British English:

(22)   a.   *I amn't going.
         b.   *Amn't I going?
         c.   *I aren't going.
         d.   Aren't I going?

These facts are noted by Hudson (1977). We are aware of no analysis of the auxiliary system of English that provides an explicit account of them, with the exception of that in Gazdar, Pullum and Sag 1982, which we follow here. *Aren't* has an entry in the lexicon with the features $\{\langle N, -\rangle,$ $\langle V, +\rangle, \langle AUX, +\rangle, \langle NEG, +\rangle, \langle PER, 1\rangle, \langle PLU, -\rangle, \langle INV, +\rangle\}$, but no element in the paradigm of *be* is listed with the entry $\{\langle N, -\rangle,$ $\langle V, +\rangle, \langle AUX, +\rangle, \langle NEG, +\rangle, \langle PER, 1\rangle, \langle PLU, -\rangle, \langle INV, -\rangle\}$. In other words, the INV feature has to be present if the agreement features on a negative form are first person singular. The $\langle INV, -\rangle$ version of *aren't* is never first singular.

Just as we predict the possibility of auxiliary verb forms which only appear inverted, so we also predict that it is possible for there to be an auxiliary verb that cannot invert. We understand that in many varieties of American English there are certain modals (*might* and *ought*, for example) which have clear auxiliary properties (e.g. having a negative form in *n't*, providing a context for VP ellipsis, etc.) but which do not occur in inverted position. However, we have not investigated this systematically.

4 Metarules and expressive power

The idea of using a grammar to generate one's grammar, which is what we are doing when we employ metarules, originates, as far as we know, with van Wijngaarden (1969), who used the technique to give a perspicuous syntax for a computer programming language, ALGOL 68. A good introduction to his work can be found in Cleaveland and Uzgalis 1975. Janssen (1980) later employed a van Wijngaarden-style two-level grammar to define a generalization of Montague's PTQ syntax. Linguists in general did not pick up the idea until GPSG work started being circulated in 1979, though in a little-known semi-published paper, D. T. Langendoen (1976) published some useful mathematical results on the generative capacity of systems employing grammar-generating grammars.

What Langendoen did was to identify the conditions under which infinite grammars with rules of a certain type could generate languages that would not be generable by finite grammars with that type of rule. For example, one of his results is that an infinite set of context-free (Type 2) rules generated by a metagrammar with only right linear (Type 3) rules can only yield a context-free language. However, another is that an infinite set of context-free rules generated by a context-sensitive (Type 1) metagrammar can generate a non-context-free language. Clearly, then, it can be important to understand the character of the metagrammar if one wants to correctly assess the expressive power of the grammar it induces. This is not an unimportant point in the context of considering the expressive power of metagrammatically induced phrase structure grammars. Langendoen's results cited above suggest that if the members of a set of metarules are permitted to interact in such a way as to recursively define an infinite set of rules, it is possible for the language generated by the grammar to be non-context-free. There has been some interesting recent work of a mathematical nature directed at further elucidation of this point.

Gazdar (1982, p. 180, n. 28) mentions a conjecture of Aravind Joshi's to the effect that if no more than one essential variable is permitted in a metarule that applies to CF PS rules (as opposed to ID rules), then only context-free languages can result, regardless of whether the induced grammar is finite or not. This conjecture is now known to be false. Hans Uszkoreit proved in 1982 that a metagrammar using metarules limited to a single essential variable, and applying them to CF PS rules, can define an infinite grammar capable of generating a non-CF language. A brief and elegant demonstration of this, constructed later by Christopher Culy, can be found in Gazdar and Pullum 1982, p. 45.

Subsequently it has been shown by Peters and Uszkoreit (1982) that the use of such metarules can induce (infinite) grammars for any recursively enumerable set.

These are surprising results, but it needs to be emphasized that their consequences for linguistic practice are completely different from the consequences for transformational linguistic practice that follow from the results of Peters and Ritchie (1973) on transformational grammars. Peters and Ritchie demonstrated that an ordinary *finite* transformational grammar can be provided for any recursively enumerable set. This means that no set of sentences that has any kind of recursive definition of membership could fail to be transformationally describable. No such results hold for GPSG as developed in this book. The definition of finite closure (see Definition 8 in section 5, below) guarantees finiteness for the sets of rules induced by our metarules.[5] Thus the Peters and Uszkoreit result has no direct consequences for the kind of theory we are exploring, though it does perhaps have some indirect ones (see Shieber et al. 1983).

Since the analogy between metarules and transformations is perhaps a tempting one, and since it is also a very misleading one, we will conclude this section with some brief comments on the contrast between the two devices. A transformation maps derivational strings into derivational strings (or in some formalizations, trees into trees). A metarule maps rules into rules – in the current GPSG theory, ID rules into ID rules. If one adds transformations to the theory of CF-PSG, there are two consequences. First, by the Peters and Ritchie results, one completely changes the expressive power of the theory. Second, the structures get assigned to sentences at at least two distinct significant levels: 'deep structure', generated by the phrase structure rules and 'surface structure', the output of the transformational deformations applied to the deep structure representation and its intermediate-stage successors.

By contrast, if one adds metarules in the way that we do here, where they amount to nothing more than a novel type of rule-collapsing convention for rules, then one merely enlarges, in a systematic and well-defined way, the set of rules in the overall grammar. That overall grammar itself still comprises a finite set of ID rules. As such, it is CFL-inducing.[6] Thus neither of the consequences mentioned in the previous paragraph obtain. The expressive power of the theory is not changed, because the grammar definition is provided under the terms of finite closure. And there is only one level of representation in the syntax. The metarules do not define a level of representation, because they do not characterize any structures at all; they characterize a set of additional rules.

The sorts of generalizations directly capturable by metarules and by transformations are not in an equivalence relation or even a subset relation. The most one can say is that they intersect. Transformations scan trees (strictly, phrase markers) globally, so that elements that are not sisters can be accessed: a transformation looking for the sequence *AB* can find it in a configuration [*A* [*BCD*]] or [*A* [[*BC*]*D*]]. A metarule cannot directly mimic such global scanning. Given the theory developed here, where metarules operate on ID statements, a sequence *AB* cannot be identified in the configurations just cited by a metarule. A metarule could operate on all the rules that introduce *A* and *B* as daughters, and define some new rules corresponding partially to them, but metarules in our sense are unable to mimic even extremely simple transformational operations such as permuting the order of two adjacent elements (metarules cannot tamper with linear order) or raising some constituent into a higher clause (metarules cannot operate across constituent boundaries). Thus a familiar problem with the passive transformation is illustrated in (23).

' (23)   a.   Someone believed Sandy had left.
         b.   *Sandy was believed had left.

No analog of this problem can arise in a metarule analysis of passive since the latter only has access to categories that are daughters of VP – a granddaughter, such as the subject of a complement, simply is not there to be tampered with. As Brame (1978, pp. 101–2) has pointed out, both the problem that (23) poses for the passive transformation (or, more generally, NP-movement), and the constraints needed to avoid the problem, are simply artifacts of the transformational apparatus itself.

We have offered these remarks in an effort to forestall the confusion that arises from making intuitively-based attempts to comprehend the effects of metarules by loosely analogizing from transformations. But the only fully effective way to avoid such confusion is to resist the temptation to think in terms of this analogy at all. Metarules are not similar to transformational operations on structural representations in any relevant way.

5   A formal theory of metarules

In this section, we try to spell out in more detail the way in which metarules determine a mapping on the class of lexical ID rules.[7] A mastery of these details will not be crucial to understanding later developments in the book, though many readers may benefit from a quick skim through the definitions.

We start by trying to pin down more closely what a possible metarule can look like. A metarule consists of a *pattern* and a *target*. The pattern matches certain input rules, and the input rules together with the target determine certain output rules. The pattern and target of a metarule are schematic lexical ID rules. They are schematic in that while the terms of a lexical ID rule consist only of categories, metarule patterns and targets can also contain a variable *W* to the right of the ID arrow. *W* is a variable over a multiset of categories, and is used in metarules. It is an object language variable. From now on, we will use α, β (i.e. Greek lower case letters from the beginning of the alphabet) as metalanguage variables that range over categories and *W*.

Intuitively, some of the categories mentioned in a metarule target correspond to categories in the pattern. Consider, for example, the SAI metarule, repeated here.

(24) $V^2[-SUBJ] \rightarrow W$

                               $\Downarrow$

                    $V^2[+INV, +SUBJ] \rightarrow W, NP$

The category $V^2[+INV, +SUBJ]$ in the target corresponds to the category $V^2[-SUBJ]$ in the pattern. We now try to spell out what this correspondence involves. What seems to be important is that the two categories agree with respect to the major class features N and V, and that the target category has at least as many feature specifications as the pattern category to which it corresponds. Before formulating a definition along these lines, it will be useful to introduce the notion of restricting a function to a certain domain. If g is a function from A to B we write $g : A \rightarrow B$. If $g : A \rightarrow B$ and $X \subseteq A$, then the *restriction* $g|X : X \rightarrow B$ is defined as

$$(g|X)(x) = g(x) \text{ for all } x \in X.$$

We can now capture the idea that two categories C_1 and C_2 agree with respect to a certain set X of features by requiring that their restrictions $C_1|X$ and $C_2|X$ are identical. Then the required notion of correspondence goes as follows:[8]

> *Definition 1*: Correspondence
> If C_1 and C_2 are categories, then C_2 *corresponds to* C_1 if and only if
> (i) $C_1|\{N, V\} = C_2|\{N, V\}$, and
> (ii) $DOM^+(C_1) \subseteq DOM^+(C_2)$.

We tentatively adopt the hypothesis that the form of a metarule pattern is more constrained than our remarks earlier suggested. We shall suppose that no more than two terms can occur to the right of the ID arrow, and that one of them must be the variable W. Thus, there can be at most one category in the right-hand side of the pattern. It happens that none of our subsequent definitions make crucial use of this assumption. Note, however, that if we maintain it, the binary branching SAI metarule of Gazdar, Pullum and Sag (1982) is illegitimate, since its pattern contains two categories on the right-hand side.

If the assumption just mentioned turns out to be tenable, then it will be worth exploring the possibility of an alternative notation for metarules. One that suggests itself would make use of a 'possible-daughters-of' operator D, where $D(S)$, for example, stands for any member of the set of multisets that are possible 'right-hand sides' (RHSs henceforth) for ID rules expanding S. A VSO-inducing metarule, such as SAI, could then appear as

$$S \rightarrow NP + D(VP)$$

where this is to be interpreted as saying that a RHS for expanding S may consist of the multiset union of (a multiset containing) an NP with a multiset identical to the RHS of any VP rule. Likewise, passive might appear thus

$$VP[PAS] \rightarrow D(VP) - NP$$

where this is to be interpreted as saying that a RHS for expanding a passive VP can consist of the RHS for any VP less one NP. A version of the slash termination metarule discussed in chapter 7 could appear like this:

$$a/\beta \rightarrow D(a) - \beta$$

Our definitions of *pattern* and *target*, then, are as follows:

> *Definition 2*
> A metarule *pattern* is of the following form, where P_0 and P_m are categories, $m = 0$ or 1, and W is a variable over multisets:
> $$P_0 \rightarrow W, P_m$$
> A metarule *target* is of the form
> $$a_0 \rightarrow a_1, \ldots, a_k$$
>
> where
> (i) a_0 corresponds to P_0, and for $1 \leq i \leq k$
> (ii)   at most one of the a_i is the variable W, and
> (iii) at most one of the a_i corresponds to P_m (if present).

Metarules and their properties

We use α as a metavariable ranging over terms in a rule, where by 'term' we mean either a category or the variable W.

We remarked earlier that the pattern of a metarule is intended to match an input rule. We first need to detail the conditions under which the terms of a pattern match the terms of an ID rule.

> *Definition 3*: Category and variable matching
> (i) A category P *matches* a category C if and only if C is an extension of P.
> (ii) The variable W *matches* any multiset of categories.

This means, in effect, that in order to specify some category in the input rule of a metarule, we do not have to be concerned with arbitrary details of that category; we will match any category that is an extension of the relevant category in the pattern.

> *Definition 4*: Pattern matching
> A pattern $P_0 \rightarrow W, P_m$ *matches* an ID rule $C_0 \rightarrow C_1, \ldots, C_n$ if and only if
> (i) P_0 matches C_0, and
> (ii) if P_m is present, there is some C_i, $1 \le i \le n$, such that P_m matches C_i.
> (iii) In addition, W matches and *is bound to* the multiset consisting of $C_1, \ldots, C_n$ minus the occurrence of C_i that was matched by P_m.

For example, consider the metarule pattern $V^2 \rightarrow W, P^2$. this matches a rule like $V^2 \rightarrow H[3], N^2, P^2[\text{PFORM } to]$ because V^2 (trivially) matches V^2 and P^2 matches $P^2[\text{PFORM } to]$. W matches and is bound to $\{H[3], N^2\}_m$.

Next, we need to consider how a metarule, given an input rule, determines an output rule. We proceed by specifying the way in which triples (α, m, r) consisting of a term α in the target, the rest of the metarule m, and the input rule r, determine some term or terms in the output.

> *Definition 5*: Category and variable determination
> Let r be an input rule of the form $C_0 \rightarrow C_1, \ldots, C_n$, and let m be a metarule with a target of the form $a_0 \rightarrow a_1, \ldots, a_k$.
> (i) Suppose α in the target is a category, α corresponds to P in the pattern of m, and P matches the category C in rule r. Then (α, m, r) determines the category
> $$C' = \alpha \cup C|(DOM^+(C) - DOM^+(\alpha))$$
> (ii) Suppose α in the target is a category which corresponds to no P in the pattern of m. Then (α, m, r) determines category α.

(iii) Suppose a is the variable W, and W in the pattern of m is bound to $C_i, \ldots C_l$. Then (a, m, r) determines the multiset $C_i, \ldots C_l$.

The most important of the clauses in the preceding definition is (i). What it says is the following. Suppose we have a situation in which P in the pattern matches an input category C, and category a in the target corresponds to P. In order to compute the output category C', we in effect unify a with C, except that whenever a and C disagree over the value of some feature, a always wins. That is, C' contains all the feature specifications in a plus any that are contained in C but not in a. For example, set C, P, and a as follows:

(25) $C = \{\langle N, - \rangle, \langle V, + \rangle, \langle BAR, 2 \rangle, \langle SUBJ, - \rangle, \langle AUX, + \rangle\}$
       $P = \{\langle N, - \rangle, \langle V, + \rangle, \langle BAR, 2 \rangle\}$
       $a = \{\langle N, - \rangle, \langle V, + \rangle, \langle BAR, 2 \rangle, \langle SUBJ, + \rangle\}$

Notice that P matches C, and that a corresponds to P. To arrive at C', we first ensure that every specification in a belongs to C'. Second, C' must contain every feature specification which we get when C is restricted to those features in its domain which are not also in the domain of a; i.e. those features in $(\{N, V, BAR, SUBJ, AUX\} - \{N, V, BAR, SUBJ\}) = \{AUX\}$. Consequently,

(26) $C' = a \cup \{\langle AUX, + \rangle\}$
       $= \{\langle N, - \rangle, \langle V, + \rangle, \langle BAR, 2 \rangle, \langle SUBJ, + \rangle, \langle AUX, + \rangle\}.$

Definition 6: Rule determination
Given a metarule m with input r, and a target of the form $a_0 \to a_1, \ldots, a_k$, then (m, r) determines a rule $r' = C_0 \to C_1, \ldots, C_n$ if and only if
(i) C_0 is determined by a_0, and
(ii) for each C_i, $1 \le i \le n$, C_i is present if and only if it is determined by (a_j, m, r) for some j, $1 \le j \le k$.

To illustrate this, let us return to our earlier example of the SAI metarule, whose pattern was

$V^2[-SUBJ] \to W,$

and whose target was

$V^2[+INV, +SUBJ] \to W, N^2.$

Among the rules matched by the pattern is the following:

(27) $V^2[+AUX, -SUBJ] \to H^0[46], V^2[-AUX, BSE]$

Taking (27) as input, the metarule determines an output rule as follows.

The left-hand category of the output is $V^2[+\text{AUX}, +\text{INV}, +\text{SUBJ}]$, since this is determined by the left-hand category of the target in the manner described above. The N^2 in the target requires there to be a category N^2 in the output rule (by clause (ii) of Definition 5). The variable W in the target requires there to be $H^0[46]$ and $V^2[-\text{AUX}, \text{BSE}]$ in the output, since W in the pattern matched and was bound to these categories (by clause (iii) of Definition 5).

Finally, we can define the function that is associated with a metarule.

> *Definition 7*: The metarule relation
> Let m be a metarule with pattern p and target t. Then m induces the relation f_m where $f_m = \{\langle R, R' \rangle : R \text{ and } R' \text{ are sets of lexical ID rules and } R' = \{r' : \exists\, r \in R, p \text{ matches } r \text{ and } (m, r) \text{ determines } r'\}\}$.

When, as in our exemplification above, one is only dealing with a single metarule m, it is easy to see what grammar results from its application: it will consist of all the original rules R plus the rules resulting from the application of f_m to R. Matters become slightly more complicated when we consider closing a grammar under the application of a set of metarules. Essentially, the complete set of rules in the grammar will be the maximal set that can be arrived at by taking each metarule and applying it to the set of rules that have not themselves arisen as a result of the application of that metarule. We call this maximal set the *finite closure* of the basic rules under the set of metarules.

Following Thompson (1982), we provide below a recursive definition of the finite closure (FC) of a set R of rules under a set of M of metarules.

> *Definition 8*: Finite closure
> i. $FC(R, \{\}) = R$
> ii. $FC(R, M) = \bigcup_{m \in M} f_m(R \cup FC(R, M - \{m\}))$

By clause (i), the finite closure of R under the empty set of metarules is just R; by clause (ii), the finite closure of R under an nonempty set M is found by computing, for each metarule $m \in M$, the set which results from applying f_m to R plus all the rules that resulted from taking the finite closure of R under M minus m, and then forming the union of all those sets. It should be clear that (as the name implies) the finite closure of a finite set of rules R will itself be finite.

Notes

1 See Anderson 1984 for an explicit argument to this effect, and Gunji 1983b for a compelling analysis of Japanese reflexives which is inconsistent with Flickinger's restriction.

2 Note that the grammar will admit (ii) given (i):

(i) $S \rightarrow X^2$, H[−SUBJ]

(ii) S[VFORM PAS]

  NP

  VP[VFORM PAS]

This in turn will give rise to strings like *Lee kissed by Jo*. We assume that this is a well-formed S[VFORM PAS], but that the latter category plays no role in the grammar of English (i.e., no rule of English that introduces S either invokes it or permits it, and thus it cannot be introduced). Note that the analysis of auxiliary-initial sentences given in Gazdar, Pullum, and Sag 1982 *did* invoke such a category in the analysis of sentences such as *Was Lee kissed by Jo*?

3 There is an empirical issue about the constituent structure of sentences like (9a′) through (9e′). Our metarule ends up assigning them a ternary branching structure, i.e. [V NP VP]. There are two conceivable alternatives: the sentences could have either [V [NP VP]] or [[V NP] VP] as their top-level bracketing structure. All three bracketings seem to be attested in the literature, in fact, though the third, in which the auxiliary verb and the subject form a constituent, is defended only by Ades and Steedman (1982) as far as we know, and we will not discuss it further here. The other two have often been defended in both transformationalist and GPSG works. The ternary branching structure is induced by the metarule given in passing by Gazdar (1981b). The second, with the subject and the rest of the clause in a subconstituent that excludes the auxiliary, is advocated in Gazdar, Pullum, and Sag 1982. However, we now reject the analysis of SAI found therein on empirical grounds: it exacerbates the problem of correctly assigning nominative case, it entails a very artificial analysis of copula constructions, and it provides no way at all of handling such British English examples as *Have you a match*?

4 This FCR will allow us to treat S simply as an abbreviation for the category {⟨SUBJ, +⟩} (or {⟨COMP, NIL⟩}) if we want, since the other necessary featural components of an S will be obligatorily added during feature instantiation if the grammar contains the FCR (see also FCR 15 on p. 112 below).

5 The only infinite set of rules that we do admit in our grammar, the set induced by the schema for coordination, has the Type-3-generable property that guarantees context-freeness for the resultant language under the Langendoen results.

6 To see this, at least in abstraction from the matter of feature instantiation dealt with in the next chapter, note that a finite set of ID rules can be used to induce a finite set of CF-PSG rules if a linear order is imposed on the daughters of each

ID rule in some way. The maximum number of CF-PSG rules results if all possible orders of daughters are allowed. In that case, each ID statement yields at most *d!* CF-PSG rules where *d* is its number of daughters. The size of the whole CF-PSG will be the sum of all the *d!* values for the different ID rules. This will still be finite, and any finite set of CF-PSG rules generates a CFL by definition. Hence a finite set of ID rules can only generate a CFL, no matter what assignment of linear order is employed.

7 We are grateful to Roger Evans and Henry Thompson for emphasizing the importance of this task to us. Our approach owes much to the definitions proposed in Thompson and Phillips 1984. See also the important discussion of formalizing metarules in Kay 1983 and Stucky 1983.

8 As in chapter 2, section 6, DOM^+ is the transitive closure of the 'in the domain of' relation. This is required because we may need to pay attention to feature specifications inside category-valued features in a given category.

5

Universal feature
instantiation principles

---

1 Introduction

We have discussed in the previous chapters the formulation of rules and metarules. But none of the ID rules stated or derived by metarule so far are specific enough to characterize anything like the class of structures we require for English. Consider, for example, the main S expansion rule and relevant LP statement.[1]

(1)   (i) $S \rightarrow NP, VP$
        (ii) $NP \prec VP$

According to what we have said so far, (1i), by itself, will admit both the local trees in (2), since in each of them a node labeled S immediately and exhaustively dominates nodes labeled NP and VP.

(2)   a.   S
               NP
               VP
    b.   S
               VP
               NP

If we also specify that LP statements must be taken into account when admitting local trees, then it might seem that the grammar fragment (1) will only admit (2a). This is clearly too restrictive an interpretation of tree admissibility, since we want to be able to let further features appear on the categories in (2a). In order to generate a string like *It is good*, feature specifications for singular number and finiteness (tense) have to be present:

(3)   S[FIN]
            NP[−PLU]
            VP[FIN, −PLU]

Let us consider an alternative formulation of the conditions under which an ID rule admits with a local tree:

(4)   An ID rule $C_0 \rightarrow C_1, \ldots, C_n$ admits a local tree t if and only if the root of t is labeled C_0', and C_0' immediately and exhaustively dominates nodes labeled $C_1', \ldots, C_n'$, and for each i, $1 \leq i \leq n$, C_i' is an extension of C_i.

This is an important step in the right direction. It says, in effect, that an ID rule like (1i) will admit any local tree which meets the immediate dominance conditions and in which feature specifications have been freely added to the categories mentioned in the rule. According to (4), therefore, (1i) does admit the tree in (3), and in this case we say that the extra feature specifications on categories in the tree − [VFORM FIN] and [+PLU] − have been *instantiated* on those categories. By contrast, those feature specifications whose presence on categories in the tree is directly determined by the ID rule are said to be *inherited* by those categories. Moreover, the category C_i in an ID rule from which a category C_j inherits feature specifications is said to be C_j's *licencing* category.

However, the regime for tree admissibility that we have just sketched is too liberal. For example, the local tree in (5) would also be admitted by (1i):

(5)   S[FIN]
            NP[−PLU]
            VP[BSE, +PLU]

A mismatch in number specifications on NP and VP would give rise to strings like *It are good*; and the mismatch in VFORM values between S and VP would give rise to strings in which the subcategorization requirements of a verb like *say* are violated: *I said that they be here* (cf. *I require that they be here*).

Notice the strategy we adopted in determining the interaction between ID rules and LP statements. By themselves, ID rules are permissive. They say nothing about linear precedence, and anything that is not forbidden is allowed. LP statements are restrictive. They exclude some of the local trees compatible with ID rules and thus narrow down the class of objects admitted by the grammar as a whole. We will follow a restrictive, rather than permissive, strategy with respect to feature instantiation. By themselves, ID rules typically place little restriction on the categories that label the trees they admit. The only condition is that the feature specifications mentioned in the ID rule must be inherited by the corresponding categories in the tree. But apart from this constraint, no limit is placed by an ID rule on the ways in which the categories in the tree extend the categories in the rule. Thus, by itself, rule (1i) is compatible with a large set of local trees, one for each different way of extending the categories mentioned in the rule. The task that confronts us now is to narrow down the set of possible category extensions.

In fact, we have already discussed some devices which exclude certain of these extensions, namely FCRs and FSDs. The first, as their name suggests, limit the feature specifications that can co-occur within any given category. An FCR like (6), which we repeat from chapter 2, precludes (7) from being a possible category:

(6)   FCR 2: [VFORM] $\supset$ [+V, −N]

(7)   NP[VFORM FIN]

Since (7) is not a possible category (with respect to (6)) it cannot be a possible extension of the category NP mentioned in rule (1i), and hence cannot label a node in any tree admitted by that rule. It is important to note, however, that FCRs determine *properties* of categories in a tree, on a one by one basis. They do not say anything about the *relations* that hold between different categories. Yet, in order to exclude local trees like (5) above, we need to invoke conditions that are irreducibly relational. For instance, we need to say that if category C_0 has certain **HEAD** feature specifications, then some other category C_i also has those **HEAD** feature specifications. And if category C_j has some specification for PLU, then an agreeing category C_k must also have that specification. Consequently, in the following sections, we will elaborate conditions on feature instantiation which have precisely this relational character.

Before we turn to these further conditions on feature instantiation in admissible trees, however, it will be useful to give a more rigorous account of the space over which they are defined. The definition below formalizes the idea presented in (4), namely that an ID rule admits all the local trees arrived at by mapping categories in the rule into legal extensions of those categories in the tree. Each of these trees is said to be *projected* by the rule.[2]

Before we give the definition, we need to clarify the role played by FCRs in defining the notion of a legal extension of a category. In chapter 2, we defined an FCR to be something that is either true or false of a category. We will say that a category C is *legal* if and only if every FCR is true of C. So C will be a legal extension of C' if and only if C is legal and C is an extension of C'.

Definition 1

Let $r = \langle\langle C_0, \{C_1, \ldots, C_n\}_m\rangle, W_H\rangle$ be an ID rule and let t be a labeled local tree:

$$t = \quad C_0'$$
$$C_1'$$
$$.$$
$$.$$
$$.$$
$$C_n'$$

We say that ϕ is a *projection function* if and only if ϕ is a one–one, onto function whose domain is $\{C_0, C_1, \ldots, C_n\}_m$, whose range is $\{C_0', C_1', \ldots, C_n'\}_m$, and which meets the following conditions:

(i) $\phi(C_0) = C_0'$, and
(ii) for all i, $0 \le i \le n$, $\phi(C_i)$ is a legal extension of C_i.

Whenever r is a rule, and ϕ is a projection function, we use $\phi(r)$ to denote the local tree which is determined by ϕ.

We will normally refer to these projection functions simply as *projections*. As a point of detail, notice that ϕ need not map, say, C_2 in a rule into C_2' in the tree. More generally, the 'less than' relation on the numerical subscripts on categories is not preserved under ϕ. The indexing of daughter categories in the schematic ID rule in this definition is quite arbitrary and reflects nothing more than the fact that we have to write ID rules down in some order or other, even though this order has no systematic significance. By contrast, the indexing of categories in the local tree is highly significant: it reflects the linear precedence relations that hold between daughters in the tree. The way the mapping ϕ has been defined, the linear order of the daughter categories $\phi(C_i)$ can be any permutation of the order in which the C_i appear on the right-hand side of the rule, which is exactly what we want.[3]

Finally, let us remind the reader that the notation '$C \mid F$', where C is a category and F is a set of features, means 'the restriction of C to F'. It is that category which is just like C except that it is undefined for every feature not in F. So $\phi(C_0)|\textbf{HEAD}$ is the category that consists of all and only the **HEAD** feature specifications of $\phi(C_0)$. In what follows, we will also make use of the notation $F \sim C$, where C is a category and F is a set of features. We use this as an abbreviation for '$F - DOM(C)$', i.e. the set of all those features which are in the set F but which are not in the domain of the function C. For example, $\phi(C_i)|\textbf{FOOT} \sim C_i$ is the category you get when you restrict $\phi(C_i)$ to all those **FOOT** features that are not specified on C_i. Recall that C_i is the category in the ID rule that licences the occurrence of $\phi(C_i)$ in the tree. Any feature which is in $DOM(C_i)$ is a feature which received a value in the ID rule. So anything in $\phi(C_i)|\textbf{FOOT} \sim C_i$ is a **FOOT** feature specification that has been instantiated on $\phi(C_i)$ but was not present on the licencing category C_i.

2 The Foot Feature Principle

In preceding chapters, we have mentioned a class of features called 'foot' features, formally picked out as the members of a set called **FOOT**.[4]

Consider the example in (8).

(8)   These reports, the wording on the covers of which has caused so much controversy, are to be destroyed.

The word *which* is not the head of the NP *the wording on the covers of which* in anybody's theory of grammar. And yet *which* is indubitably responsible for that NP's being a *wh*-phrase, and its consequent ability to appear in the position which it occupies in the example. If, as in many analyses, we postulate a WH feature specification on this NP, then we are faced with the problem of relating it to the non-head lexical item that is, in some intuitive sense, responsible for it.

The same issue arises in feature-driven theories of reflexives, such as that of Gazdar and Sag (1981). Such theories need to be able to account for the fact that a PP which contains a reflexive NP must be marked as containing a reflexive, even though the reflexive NP is not the head of the PP, and cannot be.[5]

Finally, we note that the issue also arises if, following Bear (1981), one construes the 'slash categories' of Gazdar (1981b) as being categories that carry a feature encoding all relevant syntactic information about the category that is missing from the slash category; that is, if we assume that the category 'VP/NP', intuitively interpreted as 'a VP with an NP missing from within it', should be formally reconstructed as VP[SLASH NP], where SLASH is a category-valued feature. We will assume that this is indeed the correct theory of the 'slash' device. SLASH appears not to obey the Head Feature Convention (see section 4, below). Consider the example in (9).

(9)   Who did you want to seem to like?

Under a slash category analysis employing SLASH features, we must claim, among other things, that *to like* carries the SLASH feature in *seem to like* and that *to seem to like* carries the slash feature in *want to seem to like*. And yet in neither case is the infinitival VP the head of the constituent that introduces it.

At first sight, it seems that we have three very different phenomena here, phenomena whose only common property is a negative one, namely the property of appearing to violate the provisions of the Head Feature Convention. However, we are going to claim that the same feature instantiation principle governs all three cases, and that the differences between the phenomena all follow from other aspects of the grammar.

We assume that **FOOT** picks out the following set of features:[6]

(10)   **FOOT** = {SLASH, WH, RE}

All the **FOOT** features are category-valued. In the case of RE, the value is a category containing the agreement details of the reciprocal or reflexive anaphoric element that the feature marks, and thus of its required antecedent. So, for example, a reflexive pronoun like *himself* will have the feature specification [RE NP[PER 3, −PLU, REMOR REFL]], where the value of REMOR indicates whether the pronoun is a reflexive ([REMOR REFL]) or a reciprocal ([REMOR RECP]). Likewise, WH takes as its value an NP category that has agreement features, and, in addition, this NP value is also defined for the feature WHMOR. So, for example, an interrogative pronoun like *what* will have the feature specification [WH NP[PER 3, WHMOR Q]]. And SLASH, as we have just seen, takes as value a category incorporating the details of a 'gap' or missing constituent. The feature WHMOR takes values that mark the lexical distinctions that exist between relative pronouns ([WHMOR R]), interrogative pronouns ([WHMOR Q]), free relatives ([WHMOR FR]), and exclamatives ([WHMOR EX]). There are slight differences in the sets of *wh* items that can appear in the various *wh* constructions. Thus, for example, in standard varieties of British and American English, *what* cannot be used in relative clauses (**This is the thing what I do*) but is used in interrogatives (*What do you do?*). There are also possibilities for relative *wh*-words that are not shared by interrogative ones; for example, *whose* can be used for non-humans if it is a relative pronoun (*the dog whose leg was hurt*) but not if it is an interrogative one (*Whose leg is that?* can only mean 'Which human being's leg is that ?').

We shall not deal with the use of **FOOT** features in full detail here, since we return to it in more detail in the chapters that make most use of them (chapter 7 for SLASH and WH). What we shall discuss here is the principle governing their distribution. We will call that principle the Foot Feature Principle (FFP). The intuitive idea underlying the FFP is a rather straightforward one. The behavior of **FOOT** features that are explicitly specified in ID rules, or which have arisen through the operation of metarules, is not regulated by the FFP. Such specifications are simply inherited by the corresponding categories in the admitted trees. However, **FOOT** feature specifications can also be instantiated on categories in trees, and the FFP constrains the distribution of these specifications in the following manner: any **FOOT** feature specification which is instantiated on a daughter category in a local tree must also be instantiated on the mother category in that tree.

The motivation is simple. **FOOT** features record grammatically significant information, such as the fact that a constituent is missing somewhere or that it has to be syntactically bound to some antecedent. If they are to be instantiated on daughters in local trees, it is crucial that their presence also be manifested on the mothers of those daughters, lest they be admitted in trees in places where there is no licence for them. Provided the **FOOT** feature information is written into the mother category in each local tree in which it is instantiated on a daughter, the presence of the special syntactic property they represent cannot be lost – i.e. buried inside a constituent that looks normal as far as its root node is concerned. So consider a hypothetical case of an ID rule introducing three daughters, where neither mother nor daughters have any **FOOT** features specified. Then feature instantiation might lead to one daughter getting SLASH, another WH, and the third RE. The FFP will simply require the instantiated mother in the local tree to carry all three.

This renders some kinds of local tree impermissible. Suppose we try to derive via feature instantiation a tree with the category PP as the value for SLASH on one daughter, and the category NP as the value for SLASH on another. The FFP will require the mother to have both as the value of SLASH. But this is impossible under the theory we present here. NP and PP are distinct, and the feature SLASH can only be assigned one value by a given category.

It is worth pointing out at that, in saying this, we are characterizing a general theory that has desirable chacteristics for application to English and many other languages, but is probably too strong. In some languages, the Scandinavian languages, for example, there can indeed be a PP gap and an NP gap in the same constituent – indeed, more than two gaps in one domain must be postulated for some examples (see Engdahl 1980). If the interpretation of these facts in our terms is that SLASH must code multiple dependencies simultaneously, then clearly a modification (and weakening) of the theory is needed. Either SLASH must take a finite sequence (or stack) of categories as its value, or values of SLASH must be allowed to contain values of SLASH, or some other modification must be introduced. We are well aware that the restriction to single gaps may be a parochial restriction. Indeed, the restriction may exclude full coverage of some dialects of English; the matter turns on the acceptability of strings like *Which computer is this program likely to be easy to excecute on?*, which we do not treat. There has been interesting work in GPSG devoted to exploring these issues (cf. Maling and Zaenen 1982). But it is beyond the scope of this book to enter upon a discussion of Scandinavian unbounded dependency constructions. We therefore set out the theory in terms that permit only one gap per constituent. This lends clarity to the theory of **FOOT** features, and it probably helps rather than hinders the business of seeing exactly what needs to be done to cover multiple gaps, since it localizes the problem and sets up a context within which attempted solutions can be formulated.

We now give our statement of the FFP

> *Definition 2*: Foot Feature Principle (FFP)
> Let Φ_r be the set of projections from r, where $r = C_0 \rightarrow C_1, \ldots, C_n$.
> Then $\phi \in \Phi_r$ *meets the FFP on r* if and only if
> $$\phi(C_0)|\mathbf{FOOT} \sim C_0 = \bigsqcup_{1 \leq i \leq n} \phi \ (C_i)|\mathbf{FOOT} \sim C_i$$

Recall that any feature (specification) which is in **FOOT** $\sim C$ is a **FOOT** feature which is not assigned a value in the category C. Thus, if $\phi(C)$ specifies a value for such a feature, the specification is instantiated rather than inherited from the licencing category C. So definition 2 says that the **FOOT** feature specifications that are instantiated on a mother category in a tree must be identical to the unification of the instantiated **FOOT** feature specifications in all of its daughter categories.

We will illustrate the operation of the FFP by reference to SLASH. As before, we use C/C' as an abbreviation for $C[\text{SLASH } C']$. Consider the three ID rules shown (11).[7]

(11) a. $A^1 \rightarrow H[42]$, V^2/NP
      b. $VP/NP \rightarrow H[40]$, $VP[FIN]$
      c. $VP \rightarrow H[47]$, PP, PP

Here, (11a) is the rule responsible for expressions like *easy to solve*, (11b) for expressions like *believe solves the problems*, as in *who do you believe solves the problems*, and (11c) for expressions like *talk to Kim about Sandy*.

Of the local trees compatible with rule (11c), (12a) and (12b), among others, meet the FFP:

(12) a. VP/NP
          V[47]
          PP
          PP/NP
      b. VP/NP
          V[47]
          PP/NP
          PP

But though the trees in (13) and (14) are projections of rules (11a) and (11b), respectively, they do not meet the FFP on those rules:

(13)   A^1/NP
            A[42]
            VP/NP

(14)   VP/NP
            V[40]
            VP[FIN]/NP

(13) is in violation of the FFP because there is an instantiated SLASH specification on the mother but no corresponding *instantiated* SLASH specification on any daughter; the SLASH specification on the VP daughter is inherited from the licencing category VP/NP in rule (11a). Similarly, (14) violates the FFP because there is an instantiated SLASH specification on a daughter but no corresponding *instantiated* SLASH specification on the mother; the feature specification [SLASH NP] on the VP is inherited from the licencing category in rule (11b). Since the local trees in (12) are admitted by the FFP, and those in (13) and (14) are excluded, the grammar will generate examples like those in (15a) and (15b) but not those in (16a) and (16b):

(15)   a.   Who did you talk to Kim about?
          b.   Who did you talk to about Sandy?

(16)   a.   *What was the problem easy to solve?
          b.   *Which problems do you believe solves?

3   The Control Agreement Principle

We now address the question of what is traditionally called agreement. Agreement has often been used in textbooks of generative linguistics to illustrate the inadequacy of context-free phrase structure grammars. For example, Grinder and Elgin (1973, pp. 57–9) summarize the facts of English verb phrase agreement and assert that 'The grammatical phenomenon of Subject–Predicate agreement is sufficient to guarantee [that] English is not a CF-PSG language'. The phenomenon in question does not, of course, determine non-CFL status for English; indeed, Lyons (1968, pp. 239–46) provides a detailed discussion of government and concord in the course of which he gives (pp. 242–3) a CF-PSG for English subject–verb agreement. And our own analysis, outlined below, is equivalent to one stated in terms of context-free rules, in the sense that from our analysis a context-free rule analysis could be immediately constructed.

Until recently, generative accounts of agreement phenomena, including all transformational accounts that we know of, have provided no basis for thinking that distribution of agreement features is other than arbitrary.[8] That is, they have provided no basis for predicting which constituents will agree in a given language and which will not. An important step toward explaining agreement phenomena was taken by Keenan (1974) and Keenan and Faltz (1978, 1984). Starting from a conception of semantic structure rather similar to our own, Keenan (1974, p. 302) offers the following universal principle governing agreement processes:

(17)   Function symbols may present a morpheme whose form is determined by the noun class of the argument expression.

A more succinct formulation of (17) is: functors may agree with nominal arguments. Keenan's motivation for (17) is that the reference of a nominal argument a can, in general, be determined independently of the interpretation of any functor expression depending on a, while the converse is not true. This dependence, according to Keenan, is reflected syntactically in the fact that the morphological form of a functor may vary with the form of an argument, but not vice versa. While we do not follow Keenan on points of detail, we believe that his principle is highly significant in attempting to identify concordant constituents on the basis of their semantic relationship. If interpreted as prohibiting any instances of agreement that it does not sanction, (17) places an interesting constraint on the class of agreement systems made available within linguistic theory. Under our assumptions about semantic structure, it provides the basis for explaining why there is agreement between subjects and verb phrases in English, between verbs and their direct objects (as well as their subjects) in others, between adjectives and the nouns they modify, and so on for numerous known agreement phenomena.

Our theory of agreement involves an extension of Keenan's semantically driven principle. Instead of referring to function–argument application we follow Bach and Partee (1980) and introduce a notion of *control* that subsumes it. We do not pretend to be offering anything like a complete account of agreement phenomena, and numerous thorny problems will be left undiscussed.[9] We are concerned with the development of a universal theory of agreement and the inflectional poverty of English, our main language of exemplification, makes it a less than satisfactory source of data for our discussion. Consequently, we shall sometimes illustrate the theory with agreement patterns not found in English; agreement between nouns and nominal modifiers is a case in point. We shall also assume without argument that the distribution of reflexive pronouns in infinitival VPs is a manifestation of syntactic agreement, even though we do not treat the syntax and semantics of reflexives and reciprocals in the present work (but cf. Pollard and Sag 1983).

The relation of control holds between pairs of categories in a local tree that meet certain semantic criteria. There are two subcases to be considered. The first of these is essentially the same as that discussed by Keenan and arises when there are only two categories introduced by the rule. Such a pair of categories will nearly always[10] combine semantically as function and argument, and the argument-category will control the functor-category.

The functor category in the control relation will be called the (*agreement*) *target*. A target will contain a syntactic feature AGR or SLASH whose value is linked to some other category in the same local tree. AGR and SLASH are members of a set that we will call CONTROL features, and they are both category-valued.

There is a systematic correlation between the CONTROL feature specification on a nonlexical target and its semantic status in the kind of function–argument structure that is associated with the construction in which it occurs. We mentioned above that Keenan's principle requires an agreement target to denote a function of some kind. How do we know whether a constituent of a given category is interpreted as a function? This information is represented by the *semantic type* associated with the category. There are certain primitive types, the details of which do not concern us at the moment, and complex types defined in terms of them. Each semantic type determines a set of possible denotations for expressions of that type, and again the details of these sets are irrelevant at the moment. What is germane is first that a complex type is always of the form $\langle a, b \rangle$, where a and b are also types; and second, that expression of type $\langle a, b \rangle$ denote functions from objects of the sort denoted by expressions of type a to objects of the sort denoted by expressions of type b. Whenever C is a syntactic category, we use '$TYP(C)$' to mean the semantic type associated with C.

Let us return now to our discussion of CONTROL features. If $f \in$ CONTROL and C is a nonlexical category which contains the specification $[f\ C']$, then the type of C is $\langle TYP(C'), a \rangle$, for some type a. This is just another way of saying that a constituent of category $C[f\ C']$ will be interpreted as a function that combines with arguments of type $TYP(C')$. The following illustrates this for both AGR and SLASH:

(18)   a. $TYP(\text{VP[AGR NP]}) = \langle TYP(\text{NP}), TYP(\text{S}) \rangle$
= a function from NP-type objects to S-type objects
$TYP(\text{Det[AGR N}^1]) = \langle TYP(\text{N}^1), TYP(\text{NP}) \rangle$
= a function from N^1-type objects to NP-type objects
       b. $TYP(\text{S[SLASH AP]}) = \langle TYP(\text{AP}, TYP(\text{S}) \rangle$
= a function from AP-type objects to S-type objects
$TYP(\text{VP[SLASH NP]}) = \langle TYP(\text{NP}), TYP(\text{VP}) \rangle$
=a function from NP-type objects to VP-type objects

Thus, according to (18), the type of VP is $\langle TYP(\text{NP}), TYP(\text{S}) \rangle$. This means that an expression of category VP denotes a function from NP-type denotations to S-type denotations.[11] To sum up: given a binary branching local tree, the agreement target is always the category which has the type of a functor, while the controller is the category with the type of an argument.[12] In the following binary branching local trees, the agreement target is flanked by an indication of its type.

(19)   a.   S

    NP
    VP $\langle TYP(\text{NP}), TYP(\text{S}) \rangle$

    b.   S

    XP
    S/XP $\langle TYP(\text{XP}), TYP(\text{S}) \rangle$

    c.   NP

    Det $\langle TYP(\text{N}^1), TYP(\text{NP}) \rangle$
    N^1

    d. N^1

    AP $\langle TYP(\text{N}^1), TYP(\text{N}^1) \rangle$
    N^1

A second sort of control involves control predicates. A control predicate is a lexical head subcategorized for complements belonging to a predicative category, where a predicative category is one of type $\langle TYP(\text{NP}), a \rangle$. That is, an expression belonging to a predicative category denotes some kind of function on NP denotations.[13] Mostly we will be concerned with the predicative category VP, of type $\langle TYP(\text{NP}), TYP(\text{S}) \rangle$. Complements belonging to this category include infinitival VPs and instantiations of XP[+PRD] such as predicate nominals and adjective phrases. Control predicates correspond to a class of verbs and adjectives which includes auxiliary verbs, and the 'raising' and 'equi' predicates of classical transformational grammar. The only predicates subcategorized for complements of a predicative category whose type is not $TYP(\text{VP})$ are the adjectives of the *tough*-class. According to our analysis of missing-object constructions (chapter 7), such adjectives take complements of category VP[SLASH NP], and this, as we saw in (18) above, has the type $\langle TYP(\text{NP}), TYP(\text{VP}) \rangle$.[14]

The predicative complements of control verbs and adjectives are always potential agreement targets in local trees, even though there may be no controlling sister category. In some cases however the lexical head *mediates* control between an NP complement and the predicative. Control mediators are the 'object-controlled equi' and 'raising-to-object' verbs. Our semantic analysis of control mediators analyzes them as functions which combine consecutively with a VP complement and an NP object to make a VP expression. Their type is therefore $\langle TYP(\text{VP}), \langle TYP(\text{NP}),$ $TYP(\text{VP})\rangle\rangle$.[15] (20) displays the lexical ID rule that introduces 'raising-to-object' verbs:

(20)   VP → H[17], NP, VP[INF]

Summarizing the last few paragraphs, it turns out that a category C is controlled by another category C' in a constituent C_0 if one of the following situations obtains at a semantic level: either C is a functor that applies to C' to yield a C_0, or else there is a control mediator C'' which combines with C and C' in that order to yield a C_0. This gives rise to the following definition.

> *Definition 3*: Control (preliminary version)
> If ϕ is a projection of r, where $r - C_0 \rightarrow C_1, \ldots, C_n$, then a category $\phi(C_i)$ *controls* $\phi(C_j)$ in ϕ, $1 \le i, j \le n$, if and only if
> (i) $TYP(\phi(C_j)) = \langle TYP(\phi(C_i)), TYP(\phi(C_0))\rangle$, or
> (ii) $TYP(\phi(C_j)) = TYP(\text{VP})$ and one of the types associated with the head of r is $\langle TYP(\phi(C_j)), \langle TYP(\phi(C_i)), TYP(\text{VP})\rangle\rangle$.

The situation is complicated slightly by the possibility of instantiated **FOOT** feature specifications, as discussed in the previous section. In a local tree like (21a), for example, we still want the subject NP to be the controller of the VP even though the instantiation of [SLASH NP] has changed the VP's semantic type so as to make our current definition inapplicable.

(21)   a.   S/NP
                   NP
                   VP/NP

        b.   VP/NP
                   V[17]
                   NP/NP
                   VP[INF]

Similarly, in (21b) the NP/NP must control its VP sister, but does not under our present assumptions.

To rectify this situation, we must modify the definition of control in such a way that it ignores perturbations of semantic type occasioned by the presence of instantiated **FOOT** features. In fact, it is just **HEAD** feature specifications (other than those which are also **FOOT** feature specifications) and inherited **FOOT** feature specifications that determine the semantic types relevant to the definition of control. Hence let us adopt the notation $\chi(\phi(C_i))$ to designate $\phi(C_i)|((\textbf{HEAD} - \textbf{FOOT}) \cup (DOM(C_i |\textbf{FOOT})))$.[16] We may modify Definition 3 as follows:

> *Definition 4*: Control
> If ϕ is a projection of r, where $r = C_0 \rightarrow C_1, \ldots, C_n$, then a category $\phi(C_i)$ controls $\phi(C_j)$ in ϕ, $1 \le i, j \le n$, if and only if
> (i) $TYP(\chi(\phi(C_j))) = \langle TYP(\chi(\phi(C_i))), TYP(\chi(\phi(C_0)))\rangle$, or
> (ii) $TYP(\chi(\phi(C_j))) = TYP(\text{VP})$ and one of the types associated with the head of r is $\langle TYP(\text{VP}), \langle TYP(\chi(\phi(C_i))), TYP(\text{VP})\rangle\rangle$.

Our notion of control is like Keenan's principle in that it is intended as a language universal, and only determines which constituents can agree with each other, not which constituents do agree. It needs to be supplemented with language particular statements if we are to account for the pattern of agreement that is in fact manifested in a given language. In order to illustrate our approach, let us adopt the conservative position that the only constituents in English which show morphological agreement are Vs and VPs.[17] Prepositions do not agree with their NP objects in English,[18] and we do not wish our grammar to predict that agreement does take place. One solution is to say that the category of prepositions never takes a value for AGR in English. This could be accomplished with an FCR such as the following, according to which any category specified as a lexical P is undefined for the feature AGR:

(22)   FCR: $[-\text{N}, -\text{V}, \text{BAR } 0] \supset \sim[\text{AGR}]$

However, given our conservative stance on agreement in English, we can make a much stronger statement namely (23).

(23)   FCR 12: $[\text{AGR}] \supset [-\text{N}, +\text{V}]$

This embodies the claim that a category is only defined for the feature AGR if it is a 'projection' of the lexical category V, and thus entails (22) and many similar FCRs.[19]

At this point, let us briefly sketch how AGR feature specifications might determine the morphological form of verbs. The paradigm for a lexical item like *walk* will contain an entry, /walks/ with the specification [−PAST, AGR NP[PER 3, −PLU]]. The Head Feature Convention discussed in the next section will ensure that this form will only occur in a terminated tree when the same specification also occurs on the VP which immediately dominates the lexical V node (since AGR is a **HEAD** feature). In conjunction with [−PAST], any other specification of AGR will be morphologically realized as the form /walk/.[20]

Taking stock of our discussion up to this point, we have claimed that the VP in simple sentential structures is an agreement target controlled by the subject NP. We have also proposed that the AGR value on a VP will determine, via the Head Feature Convention, the morphological form of a lexical head dominated by that VP. What we still lack is a mechanism for ensuring that the VP does in fact agree with the subject NP. This task is accomplished by the Control Agreement Principle, which is one of the conditions placed on admissible local trees. The Control Agreement Principle says, roughly, that if a potential agreement target C in a local tree has a controller C', then the value of the CONTROL feature of C must be equal to C'; otherwise, if C is a predicative category with no controller, then the value of the CONTROL feature of C must be equal to the value of the CONTROL feature of its mother, C_0. More precisely, the required equality involves only those feature specifications that were relevant in defining the notion of *control* a moment ago, i.e. specifications for non-**FOOT HEAD** features and inherited **FOOT** feature specifications. Let us henceforth refer to this class of feature specifications as χ-*specifications*.

We saw above that there are two possible CONTROL features that a category might have, AGR and SLASH, but we still lack some way of choosing between them in any given case. Notice that, in general, AGR is not specified on categories in ID rules, but can be instantiated on the extending categories in a corresponding local tree. By contrast, SLASH is specified on categories in ID rules in certain crucial cases, and in fact only counts as a CONTROL feature on a category when it has been inherited from the licencing category. Thus, we have the following definition:

> *Definition 5*: CONTROL feature
> Suppose C_i is a category in a rule r, C_i (BAR) $\neq 0$, and ϕ is a projection of r. Then a feature f is *the CONTROL feature of* $\phi(C_i)$ if and only if
> (i) $f = $ SLASH and $f \in DOM(C_i)$, or
> (ii) SLASH $\notin DOM(C_i)$ and $f = $ AGR.

We can now give a formal statement of the Control Agreement Principle.

> *Definition 6*: Control Agreement Principle (CAP)
> Let Φ_r be the set of projections from r, where $r = C_0 \rightarrow C_1, \ldots, C_n$. Then $\phi \in \Phi_r$ *meets the CAP on* r if and only if
> (i) if $\phi(C_j)$ controls $\phi(C_i)$, then
> $\phi(C_i)(f_i) = \chi(\phi(C_j)) \bigsqcup \phi(C_j)|\{f_i\}$, where f_i is the CONTROL feature of $\phi(C_i)$.[21]
> (ii) if there is a $\phi(C_i)$ which is a predicative category with no controller, then $\phi(C_i)(f_i) = \phi(C_0)(f_0)$, where f_i and f_0 are the CONTROL features of $\phi(C_i)$ and $\phi(C_0)$, respectively.

According to clause (i) of this definition, the feature specifications associated with the control feature f of a target C_i are identical to the χ-specifications of the controller of C_i. As an example of what this would cover, consider the local trees below:

(24)   a.   S

NP[PER 3, −PLU]
VP[AGR NP[PER 3, −PLU]]

b.   S

NP[PER 3, −PLU]
VP[AGR NP[PER 2, +PLU]]

As we saw earlier, the NP controls the VP in trees such as these and the control feature of VP is AGR. (24a) meets the CAP, since VP(AGR) = NP[PER 3, −PLU], but (24b) does not, since VP(AGR) = NP[PER 2, +PLU] instead of NP[PER 3, −PLU].

Continuing with clause (i), next consider a case in which there is a **FOOT** feature in a rule. An example would be the rule S → X², H/X², which introduces topicalized constituents, relative clauses, *wh*-interrogatives, etc. (see chapter 7). In any projection ϕ of this rule, ϕ(H/X²) translates as a function that takes a ϕ(X²) argument into an S denotation, so it is controlled by ϕ(X²). The CONTROL feature of the target is SLASH, because SLASH is inherited from the licencing rule. Hence the feature specifications of the X² that SLASH takes as its value must match the χ-specifications of the controller. This determines that the fronted category will be the right one to be missing from the body of the sentence. The point is illustrated in the following three local trees compatible with the topicalization rule.

(25)   a.   S

AP
S[SLASH NP]

b.   S

NP[PER 3, −PLU]
S[SLASH NP[PER 3, +PLU]]

c.   S

NP[PER 3, −PLU]
S[SLASH NP[PER 3, −PLU]]

Only (25c) meets the CAP. (25a) violates it because an AP filler is associated with an NP gap. If not excluded, such a local tree would give rise to strings like *Proud to be considered, everyone says Sandy kicked.* And (25b) violates the CAP because it fails to ensure agreement between 'extracted' NPs and elements dependent on the positions they are

'extracted' from (cf. *This guy, everyone thinks* ＿＿＿ *is a drip* but not
*Those guys, everyone thinks ＿＿＿ *is a drip*).

To illustrate clause (i) of the CAP further, let us relax the restriction that
AGR is only defined for verbal categories. Then (26) contains schematic
local trees which are compatible with some of the ID rules in (18). The
CAP requires that in each structure, the two occurrences of * must be
assigned that same set of feature specifications.

(26)   a.   NP
                 Det[AGR N^1[*]]
                 N^1[*]
     b. N^1
                 AP[AGR N^1[*]]
                 N^1[*]

Similarly, any local tree of the form (27) must contain identical feature
instantiations of * in order to meet the CAP on rule (20) presented above.

(27)   VP
           V[17]
           NP[*]
           VP[INF, AGR NP[*]]

This is because V[17] mediates control between the predicative category
VP and the controller NP.

Clause (ii) deals with those rules in which there is a predicative category
C_i but no controller. In such a case, it says that the feature specifications of
$\phi(C_i)$, are identical to the specifications of the control feature of the
mother in the tree. Consider an ID rule like the following:

(28)   VP → H[13], VP[INF]

This introduces verbs such as *tend* together with VP complements like *to
burn themselves out*. According to clause (ii), in any local tree meeting the
CAP on this rule, the control feature value of the target has the same
specifications as the control feature value of the mother VP. Two cases are
illustrated below.

(29)   a.   VP[AGR NP[PER 3, +PLU]]
                V[13]
                VP[AGR NP[PER 3, +PLU]]
     b.   VP[AGR NP[PER 2, +PLU]]
                V[13]
                VP[AGR NP[PER 3, +PLU]]

The control feature on the daughter VP is AGR. Suppose the value of
AGR on this VP is instantiated as NP[PER 3, +PLU]]. Then by clause

(ii), the dominating VP node will have the same feature specification for its AGR value. (29a) meets this condition, while (29b) does not, giving rise to the contrast *They tend to burn themselves out* but not **You tend to burn themselves out.*[22]

Consider next the rule in (30); this introduces the verb *promise*, whose type is $\langle TYP(NP), \langle TYP(VP), TYP(VP) \rangle \rangle$.[23] Such verbs will not mediate control, and hence the predicative complement will not have a controller.

(30)   VP → H[19], (NP), VP[INF, AGR NP[NORM]]

If (31) is a local tree compatible with this rule, it will only meet the CAP if the two occurrences of * are instantiated identically with respect to feature specifications.

(31)   VP[AGR NP[*]]
           V[19]
           NP
           VP[AGR NP[*]]

This restriction plays a part in accounting for distinctions of the following sort:

(32)   a.   They promised him to wash themselves.
           b.   *They promised him to wash himself.

A parallel situation arises with the rule that analyzes missing object constructions.

(33) A^1 → H[42], V^2[INF, SLASH NP]

In any local tree admissible from (33), the specifications of the value of SLASH must be the same as those of the value of AGR on the A^1 mother. Since VP[SLASH NP] is a predicative (being of type $\langle TYP(NP), TYP(VP) \rangle$), and has no controlling sister (one of the types associated with A[42] being $\langle TYP(VP[SLASH NP]), TYP(A^1) \rangle$), the CAP will ensure agreement of the kind indicated in (34).

(34) A^1[AGR NP[*]]
           A[42]
           VP[SLASH NP[*]]

Finally, consider how our proposal deals with rules which terminate unbounded dependencies. Slash Termination Metarule 1 (see chapter 7) will map a rule like (35a) into (35b).

(35)   a.   VP → H[17], NP, VP[INF]
           b.   VP → H[17], NP[+NULL], VP[INF]

Since the VP complement is a predicative controlled by NP[+NULL], its

AGR value must agree with its controller on feature specifications. Hence, by itself, the CAP requires trees of the sort shown in (36a). However, FCR 19 (which we will present in chapter 7) and the FFP place further constraints on local trees projected from (35b), namely that [SLASH NP[*]] is instantiated on both the NP[+NULL] and the VP mother. These requirements combine to ensure that admissible projections from rule (35b) in fact all satisfy the agreement pattern illustrated in (36b).

(36)   a.   VP
               V[17]
               NP[+NULL, *]
               VP[AGR NP[*]]
        b.   VP[SLASH NP[*]]
               V[17]
               NP[+NULL, *, [SLASH NP[*]]]
               VP[AGR NP[*]]

This is relevant in providing a proper account of such dependencies as those illustrated in (37).

(37)   a.   Which man did you persuade to wash himself /*myself/
               *yourselves.
        b.   The culprits, we believe to have killed themselves/*your-
               self.

In addition, the CAP provides an account of agreement in UDCs terminated by outputs of Slash Termination Metarule 2 (see chapter 7). The latter will map from (38a) to (38b).

(38)   a.   VP → H[40], S[FIN]
        b.   VP/NP → H[40], VP[FIN]

Since the VP[FIN] complement in (38b) is a predicative without a controlling sister, the clause (ii) of the CAP will restrict local trees admissible from (38b) to those in which the specifications of the AGR value of the complement are the same as those of the SLASH value of the VP mother:

(39)   VP[SLASH C[*]]
        V[40]
        VP[FIN, [AGR C[*]]]

This provides an account of agreement phenomena of the sort illustrated in (40).

(40)   Which men did you say were/*was happy.

Taken together, the HFC, the FFP, and the CAP provide the basis for an effective theory of agreement within GPSG. As far as the phenomena considered here are concerned, the only parochial rule of agreement in English is FCR 12 in (23). The CAP also permits a fairly natural treatment of case government: the inclusion of the following FCR in the grammar of English will force nominative case onto the subjects of tensed sentences.[24]

(41)   FCR 13: [FIN, AGR NP] $\supset$ [AGR NP[NOM]]

Thus, a broad range of facts fall out as a consequence of universal principles of grammar, given the independently established details of English phrase structure and the associated semantic types.

4 The Head Feature Convention

Given the notion of head defined in chapter 3, we can define the feature convention that gives substance to that notion, namely the Head Feature Convention (HFC, hereafter). The HFC is part of the mapping from ID rules to structures. That is, it imposes certain conditions on how categories may be assigned to nodes in a local tree. Like the other feature instantiation principles in this book, the HFC narrows down the class of local trees which are compatible with a given ID rule. In order to give an informal account of what it means for a local tree t to meet the HFC relative to a headed ID rule r, we will first state an oversimplified version, and then progressively refine it.

To begin with, we will assume that every rule introduces exactly one head (C_h). Then the simplest conceivable version of the HFC will just require identity between the **HEAD** features on the mother and those on the head daughter. We can state this as follows:

(42) $\phi(C_0)|\textbf{HEAD} = \phi(C_h)|\textbf{HEAD}$

This can be expressed equivalently, though more longwindedly, in the following form:

(43)   i. $\phi(C_0)|\textbf{HEAD} \sqsubseteq \phi(C_h)|\textbf{HEAD}$
        ii. $\phi(C_h)|\textbf{HEAD} \sqsubseteq \phi(C_0)|\textbf{HEAD}$

The problem with this definition is that it enforces an absolute identity, and makes no allowance for the fact that the daughter may be independently required to carry (or not to carry) a **HEAD** feature specification which (or whose absence) is incompatible with those on the mother (i.e. no legal extension of the mother carries (fails to carry) such a specification) or the mother may be required to carry (or not to carry) a **HEAD** feature specification which (or whose absence) is incompatible with the daughter. These requirements can arise either because the 'problematic' feature specification is stipulated in the rule, or because its presence or absence is required by FCRs, or because its presence or absence is required by the FFP or CAP. If we leave the HFC as we have currently formulated it, then rules that give rise to 'problematic' feature specifications will simply not induce any local trees. To avoid this consequence we have to modify the HFC so that it only seeks to equate those **HEAD** feature specifications which can be freely equated. In looking at the head we must restrict attention to those feature specifications which *can* appear on the mother, and in looking at the mother we must restrict attention to those feature specifications that *can* appear on the head. In order to restrict our attention in this way, we need a notion of 'free' feature specifications, i.e. the set of feature specifications that *can* be instantiated on the category in the context of the rule in which it finds itself. We will define this notion of *free* by defining a function ψ which takes as arguments a category in a rule, and a set of projections from that rule, and returns the union of the instantiations of the category found in the set of projections.

> *Definition 7*: Free feature specification sets.
> Let C_i be a category in a rule r, and let Ψ_r be a set of projections of r. Then the set of *free feature specifications on C_i in Ψ_r* is $\psi(C_i, \Psi_r)$, where
> $\psi(C_i, \Psi_r) = \{\langle f, v \rangle : \exists \psi \in \Psi_r[\langle f, v \rangle \in \phi(C_i)]\}$

Intuitively, the *free* feature specifications on a category is the set of all feature specifications which can legitimately appear on extensions of that category: feature specifications which conflict with what is already part of the category, either directly, or in virtue of the FCRs, FFP, or CAP, are not *free* on that category. In the discussion that follows we will use Φ_r to stand for the set of projections from r that meet the FFP and CAP.

Then we revise (43) to read as follows:

(44) i. $(\phi(C_0) \cap \psi(C_h, \Phi_r))|\textbf{HEAD} \sqsubseteq \phi(C_h)|\textbf{HEAD}$
     ii. $(\phi(C_h) \cap \psi(C_0, \Phi_r))|\textbf{HEAD} \sqsubseteq \phi(C_0)|\textbf{HEAD}$

This says (i) that the **HEAD** feature specifications on the head are an extension of the **HEAD** features of the category created by taking the intersection of the mother with the free feature specifications on the head. And (ii), that the **HEAD** feature specifications on the mother are an extension of the **HEAD** features of the category created by taking the intersection of the head with the free feature specifications on the mother. This achieves exactly the result we want.[25]

Unfortunately, (44) only caters for the situation in which a rule has a single head. Catering for the possibility of multiple heads complicates matters considerably. To begin with, we will simplify things by ignoring the issue that 'problematic' feature specifications give rise to. In this case the HFC has a straightforward definition.

$$(45) \qquad \phi(C_0)|\textbf{HEAD} = \bigcap_{C_i \in W_H} \phi(C_i)|\textbf{HEAD}$$

This says that the **HEAD** features on the mother are identical to the **HEAD** features on the category that results from taking the intersection of all the head daughters. Notice that in the single-headed case, where $W_H = \{C_h\}_m$, (43) simply reduces to (42). But, as we have said, (45) makes no allowance for 'problematic' feature specifications. In order to take these into account we will begin by reformulating (45) into the more verbose, but equivalent (46):

$$(46) \qquad \text{i.} \quad \phi(C_0)|\textbf{HEAD} \sqsubseteq \bigcap_{C_i \in W_H} \phi(C_i)|\textbf{HEAD}$$

$$\qquad \text{ii.} \quad \bigcap_{C_i \in W_H} \phi(C_i)|\textbf{HEAD} \sqsubseteq \phi(C_0)|\textbf{HEAD}$$

And this, in turn, can be reformulated as (47):

$$(47) \qquad \text{i.} \quad \forall C_i \in W_H[\phi(C_0)|\textbf{HEAD} \sqsubseteq \phi(C_i)|\textbf{HEAD}]$$

$$\qquad \text{ii.} \quad \bigcap_{C_i \in W_H} \phi(C_i)|\textbf{HEAD} \sqsubseteq \phi(C_0)|\textbf{HEAD}$$

This ugly bit of formalism is exactly equivalent to (45) but, of course, it is much harder to make any intuitive sense of it. Its virtue, in the present context, is that it allows us to add the restrictions to free features that we have already seen to be necessary in our discussion of the single head case. We thus unify definitions (44) and (47) to arrive at (48):

$$(48) \qquad \text{i.} \quad \forall C_i \in W_H[(\phi C_0) \cap \psi(C_i, \Phi_r))|\textbf{HEAD} \sqsubseteq \phi(C_i)|\textbf{HEAD}]$$

$$\qquad \text{ii.} \quad (\bigcap_{C_i \in W_H} \phi(C_i) \cap \psi(C_0, \Phi_r))|\textbf{HEAD} \sqsubseteq \phi(C_0)|\textbf{HEAD}$$

This is essentially the final form of the HFC. It is less than entirely perspicuous and the best way to understand it is in terms of its reductions in various special cases: (a) if there is only a single head, then (48) reduces to (44); (b) if there are multiple heads but 'problematic' feature specifications do not arise, then (48) reduces to (45); and, finally, if there is only a single head and no 'problematic' feature specifications arise, then (48) reduces to (42) – which is where we started from.

One final matter needs attention: the notion 'head' is intimately tied up with the assumptions of the X-bar system. In particular, we do not want minor categories (instantiated categories that lack a bar specification) to either *be* heads, or to *have* heads. But nothing we have said so far will prevent this, since BAR is a feature like any other, and may or may not be instantiated. Accordingly, we augment our definition of the HFC with a clause requiring the presence of a specification for **BAR** (not necessarily the *same* specification) on the mother and all the head daughters.

> *Definition 8*: Head Feature Convention (HFC)
> Let Φ_r be the set of projections from r which meet the FFP and the CAP, and where $r = \langle\langle C_0, \{C_1, \ldots, C_n\}_m\rangle, W_H\rangle$. Then $\phi \in \Phi_r$ meets the HFC on r if and only if
> (i) $\forall C_i \in W_H[(\phi(C_0) \cap \psi(C_i, \Phi_r))|\textbf{HEAD} \sqsubseteq \phi C_i)|\textbf{HEAD}]$
> (ii) $(\bigcap_{C_i \in W_H} \phi(C_i) \cap \psi(C_0, \Phi_r))|\textbf{HEAD} \sqsubseteq \phi(C_0)|\textbf{HEAD}$
> (iii) $\forall C_i \in W_H[\textbf{BAR} \in DOM(\phi(C_0)) \cap DOM(\phi(C_i))]$

Notice that this definition entails that *any* projection of a rule that introduces no heads will satisfy the HFC.

In order to illustrate the HFC here, we will confine our attention to single-headed constructions. First we remind the reader of the membership of **HEAD**:

(49)   **HEAD** = {N, V, PLU, PER, VFORM, PFORM, AUX, ADV, SUBJ, INV, PAST, PRD, SLASH, AGR, SUBCAT, BAR, LOC}

Consider the pair of rules in (50) and (51):

(50)   VP → H[10], S[BSE]

(51)   S → X², H[−SUBJ]

Rule (50) is the lexical ID rule which introduces verbs like *insist* that take a complement clause whose head is in base form (cf. *I insist that you be here by nine o'clock*), while (51) is the familiar S expansion rule (in a somewhat unfamiliar guise). Two of the local trees compatible with (50) are the following:

(52)   VP[FIN]
          X⁰[10]
          S[BSE]

(53)   VP[FIN, −PLU]
          V⁰[10, FIN, +PLU]
          S[BSE]

Both of these trees fail to meet the HFC with respect to rule (50). The set of free **HEAD** features on the mother category in (52) is {⟨N, −⟩, ⟨V, +⟩, ⟨VFORM, FIN⟩}. Note that ⟨BAR, 2⟩, though a **HEAD** feature and present on the mother, is not a free **HEAD** feature in this example, since FCRs force the lexical head to contain ⟨BAR, 0⟩. Example (52) fails to meet the HFC on rule (50) because none of the free **HEAD** features from the mother have been instantiated on the head daughter. On the other hand, (53), fails because the set of free **HEAD** features on the mother category is $\{\langle N, - \rangle, \langle V, + \rangle, \langle VFORM, FIN \rangle, \langle PLU, - \rangle\}$ whereas the instantiated free **HEAD** features on the head daughter are $\{\langle N, - \rangle, \langle V, + \rangle, \langle VFORM, FIN \rangle, \langle PLU, + \rangle\}$. These two sets intersect, but neither is an extension of the other, and (53) fails to meet the HFC with respect to rule (50).

Next, examine the local trees in (54).

(54)   VP[FIN]
              V[10, FIN]
              S[BSE]

(55)   S[BSE]
              NP
              VP[BSE]

(54) does meet the HFC on rule (50), and (55) meets the HFC on rule (51). Consequently, the rules together will admit the tree (56), because each local subtree in (56) is compatible with the rules.

(56)

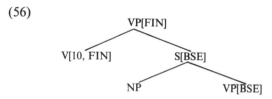

Imagine we were randomly generating all the local trees admitted by the two ID rules just discussed. There is nothing to guarantee that the mother in any given local tree compatible with the S expansion rule will match the complement daughter in a given local tree compatible with the VP expansion rule. And indeed none of the feature instantiation principles in our grammar is intended to ensure such a matching. But in order for the grammar to admit the nonlocal tree (56), it is quite sufficient if each of its local subtrees turns out to be one of the many local trees compatible with the relevant ID rules, and this we know to be true. What the HFC ensures is that we get a [VFORM FIN] specification on the mother VP category if and only if we get the same specification on the V[10] category, and that we get a [VFORM BSE] specification on the S category if and only if we get it on its daughter VP category. What happens when we combine the HFC with the definition for admitting nonlocal trees is that the subcategorization requirement for a bare infinitive demanded by verbs of class V[10] gets transmitted down to the VP head of the S complement in the way just described. Analogous reasoning shows that the requirement would also be transmitted down to the lexical head of any VP that sprouted from the appropriate node in (56).

5 Tree admissibility

In the foregoing section we have outlined the fundamental feature instantiation principles responsible for ensuring the proper distribution of features in trees. But we have said little about how these principles interact with each other, and we have not explained how they interact with the system of feature specification defaults discussed in chapter 2, section 4. It is to this question that we turn our attention now.

The heart of our theory of the mapping from ID rules to structural descriptions is a relation that we call local admissibility. Local admissibility invokes the three feature instantiation principles that we have discussed in preceding sections: the Head Feature Convention, the Control Agreement Principle, and the Foot Feature Principle. It also invokes the LP statements for the language, the feature co-occurrence restrictions and the feature specification defaults.

Before turning to the formulation of local admissibility, however, some further definitions are required. To begin with, we give a precise account of what it means for a local tree to observe LP statements.[26] This we do as follows:

> *Definition 9*: LP-Acceptable
> Let Φ_r be the set of projections induced by a rule r, where $r = C_0 \to C_1, \ldots, C_n$, and $\prec$ is the relation of linear precedence determined by the grammar, then $\phi \in \Phi_r$ is *LP-acceptable* if and only if whenever $\phi(C_i) \prec \phi(C_j)$ (i.e. precedes in the tree) there are no categories C_i', C_j' such that $\phi(C_i)$ extends C_i', $\phi(C_j)$ extends C_j', and '$C_j' \prec C_i'$' is an LP-rule.

For example, consider the rules in (57).

(57)　i.　　VP → H, NP, PP
　　　　ii.　　NP $\prec$ PP

By the preceding definition, the local tree in (58) is not LP-acceptable.

(58)
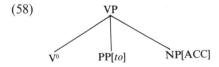

The reason is that PP[*to*] precedes NP[ACC] in the tree, PP[*to*] is an extension of PP, NP[ACC] is an extension of NP, and 'NP $\prec$ PP' is given as an LP-rule in (56ii).

The definition of local admissibility will be stated in two stages. First we characterize a notion of candidate projection which takes into account all the feature instantiation principles except those involving defaults. This is a straightforward application of the ideas developed earlier in the chapter.

> *Definition 10*: Candidate projection
> Let Φ_r be the set of projections induced by a headed ID rule r, where $r = \langle C_0 \to C_1, \ldots, C_n, W_H \rangle$. Then $\phi \in \Phi_r$ *is a candidate projection of r* if and only if
> (i) ϕ is LP-acceptable, and
> (ii) ϕ meets the HFC, CAP and FFP on r.

Before we complete our definition, we need to consider the role of feature specification defaults. In general a feature is exempt from assuming its default specification if it has been assigned a different value in virtue of some ID rule or some principle of feature instantiation. Oversimplifying somewhat, suppose that in every candidate projection of rule r, the instantiated categories $\phi(C_i)$, for some C_i in r, always agree on the feature f. Then we can conclude that the value of f is indeed the way it is as a result of some ID rule or principle of feature instantiation: such a feature specification is *privileged*. By contrast, if the categories $\phi(C_i)$ in the various trees resulting from candidate projections of r assign different values to f, values which vary independently of anything else in the projections, then we want to exclude those trees in which f fails to take its default value.

It will be helpful to illustrate this fundamental point with an example. First, we list the FSDs that we assume in this book:

(59) a. FSD 1: $[-\text{INV}]$
      b. FSD 2: $\sim[\text{CONJ}]$
      c. FSD 3: $\sim[\text{NULL}]$
      d. FSD 4: $\sim[\text{NOM}]$
      e. FSD 5: $[\text{PFORM}] \supset [\text{BAR } 0]$
      f. FSD 6: $[+\text{ADV}] \supset [\text{BAR } 0]$
      g. FSD 7: $[\text{BAR } 0] \supset \sim[\text{PAS}]$
      h. FSD 8: $[\text{NFORM}] \supset [\text{NFORM NORM}]$
      i. FSD 9: $[\text{INF}, +\text{SUBJ}] \supset [\text{COMP } for]$
      j. FSD 10: $[+\text{N}, -\text{V}, \text{BAR } 2] \equiv [\text{ACC}]$
      k. FSD 11: $[+\text{V}, \text{BAR } 0] \supset [\text{AGR NP[NORM]}]$

Consider (59b). Loosely speaking, this says that the default specification for CONJ is to have no specification at all. We interpret this to mean that if it is possible for a category in a candidate projection to lack a CONJ specification, then that category must lack a CONJ specification.

Or, in other words, a CONJ specification is only permissible if it is explicitly required by a rule. Defaults excluded, nothing prevents (28) from being instantiated as the local tree in (60).

(60)   VP
          V[13, CONJ *or*]
          VP[INF, CONJ *and*]

On the other hand, we have also seen that there are candidate projections of (28) which lack these CONJ specifications. Since CONJ is not required by the rule to have anything other than its default specification, our convention for defaults says that CONJ must have its default specification, i.e. must be absent altogether. Consequently, we will not generate strings like *Lee or was and kissed by Lou.*

So far, we have not said anything about defaults occurring on mother categories. Suppose that we allowed a CONJ specification to freely occur on the root of a projection of (28):

(61)   VP[CONJ *and*]
          V[13]
          VP[INF]

If this were permissible, it would allow us to generate strings such as *Lee both wants to try tends to succeed*, where there is a coordinating conjunction missing from the position between *try* and *tends*. Examples like these show that FSDs must apply to mother categories in a rule as well as to daughters. Once again, the principle of defaults that we have suggested will exclude the feature specification illustrated on the mother of (61), since nothing obliges [CONJ *and*] to be there. In fact, the only way in which a CONJ specification is ever present on an admissible tree is by virtue of a rule like (62) which explicitly requires there to be such a specification:

(62)   X → H[CONJ a_0], H[CONJ a_1]

Let us sum up. We have defined what it is for a local tree to be induced by a candidate projection of an ID rule. However, we wish to draw a distinction between being a *candidate projection*, and being an *admissible projection*, of an ID rule. A projection ϕ only has the second property if it both satisfies the conditions for being a candidate projection of the rule and meets the requirements of the default specifications. In order for a projection ϕ of rule r to meet default specifications, roughly the following is required: for every category $\phi(C)$ to which some default applies, either no candidate projection of r makes the default true of $\phi(C)$ (and hence the category is *privileged* in respect of that default), or else $\phi(C)$ *does* make the default true.

Although this treatment of defaults gives the right results in most cases, there is an important class of cases for which it is still inadequate, namely those in which a given feature is found in two distinct categories in the local tree, and the values of the two occurrences covary. The HFC, FFP, and CAP can all give rise to instances of such covariation. For example, the situation occurs whenever the grammar permits recursion via a head category: rules introducing adverbial modifiers typically have this form, as do coordination rules. This leads us to define a potentially more liberal notion of *privileged* than that presupposed in our discussion so far.

Before we get to that definition, it will simplify matters somewhat if we introduce an equivalence class relation holding between projections of the same rule. The intuitive idea here is the same as the idea familiar from the standard model theory for quantifiers: the idea of considering a set of assignments all of which yield the same value for some set of variables. In the present instance we are concerned to characterize sets of projections all of which instantiate some subset of the categories mentioned in the rule in the same way. Our equivalence class relation will thus be relativized to a set of categories, as follows:

> *Definition 11*: K-equivalence
> Let K be a subset of the categories in a rule. Then
> $\phi \approx_K \phi'$ if and only if $\forall C \in K[\phi(C) = \phi'(C)]$.

In the two definitions that follow, we adopt the following notational conventions: C is a category in a rule r, where $r = \langle\langle C_0, \{C_1, \ldots, C_n\}_m, W_H\rangle$, K is a subset of the categories mentioned in r, Φ_r is the set of candidate projections induced by r, and d is a default. Given these conventions, and the equivalence relation just defined, we can define the notion *privileged* as follows:

> *Definition 12*: Privilege
> A category C is *privileged with respect to r, d, ϕ, and K* (written
> 'PRIVILEGED(C, r, d, ϕ, K)' if and only if
> $\forall \phi' \in \Phi_r[\phi' \approx_{K-\{C\}} \phi \supset d(\phi'(C))=0]$

This says that a category C is privileged with respect to a default and a set of categories K just in case the default is false of the category in every projection which is equivalent modulo $K-\{C\}$. Rather than discuss this definition in the abstract any further, we will consider its implications once we have completed the task of incorporating feature defaults into the definition of admissible projections.

> *Definition 13*: Admissible Projections
> A candidate projection ϕ of r is *an admissible projection of r* if
> and only if, for all defaults d, and categories C in r:

(i) $d(\phi(C)) = 1$, or
(ii) PRIVILEGED$(C, r, d, \phi, \{\})$, or
(iii) if $\bigcap_{\phi' \in \Phi_r} \phi'(C)(\text{BAR}) = 0$, then

   PRIVILEGED $(C, r, d, \phi, \{C_k: 1 \leq k \leq n\})$,
   otherwise PRIVILEGED$(C, r, d, \phi, \{C_k: 0 \leq k \leq n\})$.

Given this definition, we can say that a local tree $\phi(r)$ is *(locally) admissible* from a rule r just in case ϕ is an admissible projection of r.

We will attempt to provide a gloss on definition 13 in order to convey its intuitive sense. What it says is this: a candidate projection meets the defaults if and only if for every category and default, (i) the default is true of the category, or (ii) no candidate projections exist in which the default is true of that category, or (iii) the default is false of the category but making it true would necessitate changing some other category in the local tree (in particular, changing a sister if the category is a lexical daughter). The final clause would be simpler if one just said, in effect, that a category was exempt from a default (i.e. privileged) whenever it covaried, in relevant respects, with some other category in the local tree. However, this simpler formulation is inadequate since it entails that lexical heads will always be exempt from defaults that relate to their **HEAD** features: these are either fixed by the rule, or else they covary with the head features in the mother. Accordingly, the final clause needs to distinguish lexical categories, which become exempt from a default only if they covary with a sister,[27] and nonlexical categories, which become exempt from a default if they covary (in relevant respects) with *any* other category in the local tree.

To illustrate the way the definition works out, we will consider here a couple of rules and an FSD.

(63)   a.   A → B
       b.   A → B[F]
       c.   FSD: ∼[F]

Suppose that the candidate projections that (63a) gives rise to are (64a)–(64d), and that those that (63b) gives rise to are (64c) and (64d).

(64)   a.   A
            B
       b.   A[F]
            B
       c.   A
            B[F]
       d.   A[F]
            B[F]

Assume to start with that the feature specification F is unrelated to any other, whether by FCR, or by the HFC, FFP, or CAP. Then the only admissible projection of (63a) is (64a) – thanks to clause (i) of definition 13, above. Violation of the default blocks admissibility of the other three candidates. The only admissible projection of (63b) is (64c) – thanks to clause (ii) which is satisfied by the fact that *every* candidate projection of (63b) violates the default on the daughter category (though this is not true of the mothers). Now suppose that F is a **HEAD** feature, and that B is the nonlexical head of A in the two rules. In this case, (64a) and (64d) are the only candidate projections of (63a), and *both* are now admissible – thanks to the second part of clause (iii). Likewise, (63b) has (64d) as its only candidate projection and this is also admissible (by clause (ii)). Finally, consider the case where F is a **HEAD** feature and B is the lexical head of A. Now the first part of clause (iii) applies, and only (64a) qualifies as an admissible projection of (63a). However, (64d) remains an admissible projection of (63b) (by clause (ii), again).

The reader may have noticed that we have made no provision for introducing lexical items into trees. That is, we have the resources to define local trees like (65), but not ones like (66).

(65)   V[BAR 2, BSE, $-$SUBJ]
         |
         V[1, BAR 0, BSE]

(66)   V[1, BAR 0, BSE]
         |
         die

Lexical items like *die* will not be further analyzed, and they constitute the terminal symbols of our grammar. A tree will be said to be *terminated* if and only if every leaf node is labeled by a terminal symbol. We shall assume that terminated local trees like (66) are generated by the lexicon, and that the principles by which this happens are outside the scope of this book. However, we shall also suppose that any terminated local subtree which is provided by the lexicon is accessible to the syntax. Having augmented the set of admissible local trees in this way, we now give a definition of admissibility for nonlocal trees.

> *Definition 14*: Admissibility
> Let R be a set of ID rules. Then a tree t is *admissible from R* if and only if
> (i) t is terminated, and
> (ii) every local subtree in t is either terminated or locally admissible from some $r \in R$.

The theory of grammar outlined in this chapter claims that the grammar of a natural language contains five components, as summarized in (67).

(67)   i.   Immediate dominance rules
        ii.   Metarules
        iii. Linear precedence statements
        iv.   Feature co-occurrence restrictions
        v.   Feature specification defaults

In the content of these components, there is at least some freedom for human languages to differ from one another in their grammars. We claim that there are no other parochial syntactic components. Such other principles as there are – for feature instantiation and for semantic interpretation, in particular – are claimed to be universal.

Organizing the grammar in the way that we have makes a number of nontrivial empirical claims.

(i)   Metarules apply to ID rules, not to local trees, and so they cannot make reference to features assigned by default, or in virtue of the HFC, CAP, or FFP.

(ii)   Metarules cannot make reference to ordering relations holding between sisters (or any other ordering relation, for the matter). So, for example, we would not expect to find a language in which the availability of passive VPs was somehow conditioned by the order of daughters in the corresponding active VPs.

(iii) By determining linear precedence simultaneously with feature instantiation, the grammar leads us to expect that there will be languages which, for example, order lexical heads differently according to category,[28] or which have linearization principles that make reference to features assigned by convention, default, or free instantiation (as opposed to being assigned by explicit mention in some rule).[29]

(iv)   By requiring that linear precedence statements be satisfied in the same way as other principles of local admissibility, i.e. locally for each mother-and-daughters substructure rather than globally over whole trees at once, we predict that ordering constraints in natural languages are limited to sisters – for example, that order of verb and object cannot depend on whether there is an adverb in a nearby AP – without having to stipulate this as an extra condition on linearization rules.

(v)   In addition, interesting consequences follow from the fact that only lexical ID rules can be input to metarules. Some of these will be discussed in chapter 7.

Notes

1 To simplify things, we will ignore heads and the 'H' notation in our discussion of this example.

2 In the future, we will try to reserve the term 'admits' for talking about the relation between the grammar as whole (i.e. ID rules, LP statements, FCRs, FSDs, and feature instantiation principles) and a given tree. That is, by itself, an ID rule will be compatible with a given local tree, rather than admitting it.

3 For the reader familiar with sets, but not multisets, an apparent problem may arise in applying a function such as ϕ to a multiset such as $\{X, X\}_m$. On the one hand, we do not necessarily want ϕ to assign the same value to each repetition of X. On the other hand, it seems that these are two repetitions of the same element, and therefore ϕ cannot assign different values to each repetition. But the problem here is only apparent, not real. By virtue of what a multiset is, multiple occurrences of 'the same object' are different from the perspective of some function on that multiset. If this were not the case, then it would make no sense to say that the multiset $\{X, X\}_m$ had a different cardinality than the multiset $\{X\}_m$.

4 The term, due originally to Carl Pollard, alludes to the fact that these features contrast with familiar varieties of **HEAD** features as regards their distribution in phrases and subphrases: they generally have their morphological effects in non-head subconstituents of the constituents on which they appear.

5 Gazdar and Sag say glibly that they 'assume that independently needed feature conventions allow' the relevant things to happen, but they do not provide those conventions.

6 We shall only refer to the three members named, but in principle it is possible that there could be additional members. For example, in unpublished work, Dan Flickinger has suggested that the distribution of the English possessive clitic should be handled with a **FOOT** feature, and Paul Schachter has proposed that the distribution of resumptive pronouns should be dealt with by means of a **FOOT** feature RESUM (though see Sells 1984 for arguments that resumptive pronouns do not behave in the manner this would predict).

7 As we shall see in chapter 7, rule (11b) arises as a result of a metarule. But the distinction between listed rules and those produced by metarule is not relevant to feature instantiation.

8 Interesting exceptions are Bach 1981, 1983 and Lapointe 1981.

9 A wide variety of these are discussed in Borsley 1984b, Cann 1984, Corbett 1983a, b, Morgan 1972, and Sag et al. forthcoming.

10 The exception is the case of coordination rules.

11 For further discussion of semantic types, see chapter 9 and references therein. It should be pointed out that a CONTROL feature specification does not determine the type associated with a particular category. This is a consequence of our use of X-bar notation as opposed to some kind of categorial analysis of syntactic categories.

12 The treatment of the CAP in Sag and Klein 1982 makes reference to the

semantic translations that are associated with constituents in a structure. However, this is avoided in the present context given our claim that semantic type determines translation (see chapters 9 and 10 for details).

13 This definition of a predicative category is due to Keenan (1983), except that we ignore Keenan's generalization from NPs to a broader class of 'argument categories'.

14 Adjectives of the *tough*-class, according to our analysis, also allow S/NP complements, whose semantic type is $\langle TYP(\text{NP}), TYP(\text{S}) \rangle$. This apparent difficulty is resolved by assigning two distinct lexical translations to such adjectives. For further discussion, see section 4 of chapter 10.

15 The precise details of how this type assignment interacts with other semantic properties of control verbs can safely be ignored for the time being; a fuller discussion is given in chapter 9.

16 There are a number of alternatives to the 'contextual' definition of the function χ just given, each with subtly different empirical consequences. The present formulation is motivated primarily by expository convenience in subsequent discussion.

17 A more liberal stance, such as that taken by Barlow (1983), might regard examples like those below as showing that determiners and adjectives agree in English:

> (i)   all/*each boys
> (ii) the many/*much boys
> (iii) the problems were many/*much

18 We predict that it is possible for prepositions to agree with their objects in a natural language, however, and this appears to be correct: Arnold Zwicky has reminded us of the case of inflected prepositions in Welsh, which can be regarded as agreement with pronominal NP objects, and Ed Keenan suggests that the Melanesian language Arosi is another case (see Capell 1971, pp 74 ff.).

19 For an interesting discussion of language-particular agreement parameters, and an alternative solution, see Cann 1984.

20 We leave open the question of how the lexicon determines verb paradigms, and how to minimize the redundancy that would occur if we distinguished between, say, /walk/ as AGR NP[PER 2, +PLU] and /walk/ as AGR NP[PER 3, +PLU]. One strategy would be to allow lexical specifications of the form [−PAST, ~[AGR NP[PER 3, −PLU]]].

The reader may have noticed that our treatment of verb agreement does not allow, as it stands, for the possibility of object agreement, as manifested in languages like Basque or Makua (cf. Stucky 1983 for a discussion of the latter with GPSG). The obvious way of extending our apparatus would be to allow AGR to take a sequence of categories as value. Since a generalization along these lines would duplicate information encoded in the SUBCAT feature, one might collapse the two along the lines suggested by Pollard (1984) and Shieber et al. (1983).

21 In the context of the grammar of English, the equation '$\phi(C_i)(f_i) = \chi(\phi(C_j))$' could be replaced by '$\phi(C_i)(f_i) = \phi(C_j)|\textbf{HEAD} - \textbf{FOOT}$'. In principle there could be empirical ways to distinguish the two.

22 We presuppose here an analysis of reflexives in which a VP like *burn themselves out* must be specified as [AGR NP[PER 3, +PLU]]. See Gazdar and Sag 1981, and Pollard and Sag 1983 for two such analyses.

23 For discussion of this point see chapter 10.

24. A rather more general formulation of this FCR is necessary if the presence of nominative case in the constructions discussed by Weeda (1981) is to be accounted for.

25 The fact that this definition of the HFC allows for head features on a head daughter to differ from those on the mother under certain circumstances ought to provide a solution to the problem discussed in Cooper 1981, 1982. However, we have yet to investigate whether it does so.

26 We note at this point an error in the original exposition of ID/LP format, in Gazdar and Pullum 1981. They propose (see e.g. p. 120) to formulate some LP statements in terms that mention the symbol 'H'. Shieber (1984) points out that this allows for non-ECPO grammars to be expressed in ID/LP format. However, such malign LP rules cannot be meaningfully formulated under the definitions adopted in the present work.

27 Cf. the discussion of dummy pronouns in Raising constructions in chapter 6.

28 For example, Farsi, Classical Latin, and modern Nahuatl are verb-final but have postpositions; German has head-final nonfinite verb phrases but head-initial N^1 constituents; Guajajara and Yagua (both spoken in Amazonia, though unrelated to each other) are verb-initial but have postpositions (see Derbyshire and Pullum forthcoming) and so on.

29 German linearizes verbs differently according to whether they are finite; Dyirbal normally has absolutive case-marked NPs earlier than other NPs; Navajo linearizes animate NPs to the left of inanimate ones; Haida places nonpronominal NPs before pronominal ones regardless of grammatical relations status; Spanish orders its clitic pronouns according to person specifications; and so on.

6

The constituent structure
of English

1 Introduction

This chapter serves a dual purpose. On the one hand, the sketch of phrasal constituent structure and subcategorization that we present will allow us to illustrate a variety of the theoretical devices that have been introduced in the preceding chapters. On the other hand, the analyses we present here will also provide a foundation for the discussion of unbounded dependency constructions that follows in chapter 7. The next four sections will be devoted to the basic structure of VPs, APs, NPs and PPs in English. We will adopt the view that the maximal projection of each category is bar-level 2, and will give a very brief account of our assumptions about the syntactic role of specifiers and modifiers within this system. We will then examine some issues in the subcategorization of the lexical categories, V, A, N and P. Subcategorized complements to major lexical categories will always be introduced by rules of the form

$$C \rightarrow H, \ldots$$

where C is a bar-level 1 or 2 projection of the lexical head. Semantically, the complements of a lexical head will denote arguments of the function denoted by the head.

In our remarks above, we used the word 'sketch' advisedly. It is not our intention here to provide a detailed grammar of English constituent structure. We believe that the analyses formulated in this chapter are plausible as far as they go, but we are also well aware of their limited scope. There are many details of phrasal constituent structure which still lack an elegant account, and about which we simply remain silent.

2   Verb phrases

The basic facts of verb subcategorization are analyzed in terms of rules
like the ones in the following list.

(1) a.   VP → H[1]
     b.   die, eat, sing, run, . . .
     c.   runs

(2) a.   VP → H[2], NP
     b.   sing, love, close, prove, . . .
     c.   prove the theorem

(3) a.   VP → H[3], NP, PP[*to*]
     b.   give, sing, throw, . . .
     c.   give the scissors to Sandy

(4) a.   VP → H[4], NP, PP[*for*]
     b.   buy, cook, reserve, . . .
     c.   bought a record for Lee

(5) a.   VP → H[5], NP, NP
     b.   spare, hand, give, buy, . . .
     c.   hand Kim the onions

(6) a.   VP → H[6], NP, PP[+LOC][1]
     b.   put, place, stand, . . .
     c.   put the magazines in the rack

(7) a.   VP[+AUX] → H[7], XP[+PRD]
     b.   be
     c.   is standing in the garden

These ID rules give rise to local trees in accordance with the definition
of admissible projection presented in the previous chapter. In particular,
various specifications of VFORM will be instantiated on the [+V, −N]
categories licenced by the rules. We shall assume that VFORM can take at
least FIN (finite), INF (*to*-infinitive), BSE (bare infinitive), PRP (present
participle), PSP (past participle), and PAS (passive participle), as values.[2]
Among the LP statements we crucially assume are those in (8).

(8) a.   [SUBCAT] ≺ ∼[SUBCAT]
     b. N^2 ≺ P^2 ≺ V^2

Given these, we generate structures like (9) and (10).

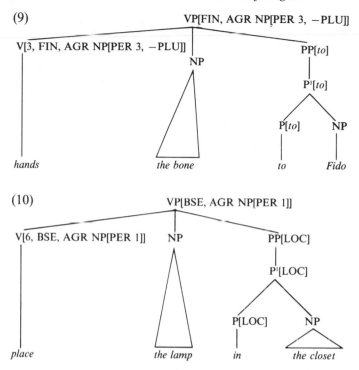

(9) / (10) tree diagrams

The XP[+PRD] in rule (7) licences complements that are NP[+PRD], AP[+PRD], PP[+PRD] or, because of the FCR in (11), VP[+PRD, PAS] or VP[+PRD, PRP].

(11)   FCR 14: ([+PRD] & [VFORM]) ⊃ ([PAS] ∨ [PRP])

Hence the rule in (7) licences the VPs in all the following examples.

(12)   a.   Dana is a Democrat.
        b.   Gerry was extremely happy about the decision.
        c.   Leslie is in trouble.
        d.   They were given ample warning by the authorities.
        e.   We are beginning to understand the problem.

Note that several verbs appear in more than one list in (1) through (7). This reflects the fact that many verbs allow multiple subcategorization frames. The regularities of multiple subcategorization are expressed within the semantics. Following Dowty 1978a, 1979a and Thomason 1976a, b, we assume the existence of meaning postulates that impose systematic relations between the meanings of homophonous verbs that are multiply listed. For example, a verb like *give* is listed in the lexicon as belonging to two distinct (though closely related) categories: V[3] and

V[5]. Since the preposition *to* functions semantically as an identity function on NP-meanings and a PP[*to*] therefore has the same semantic type as an NP, we may state a single meaning postulate relating the interpretations of V[3]s and V[5]s in the desired way.[3] This meaning postulate guarantees that pairs of sentences like those in (13) will be truth-conditionally equivalent.

> (13)   a.   Terry gave Lou the book.
>   b.   Terry gave the book to Lou.

Before presenting an analysis of these verbs, however, we must digress briefly into the matter of how embedded clauses are distinguished syntactically, and more generally, how projections of V are realized as complements.

We assume a feature COMP whose values include the names of the complementizers *for* and *that*. The distribution of these complementizers is governed by the following feature co-occurrence restrictions.

> (14)   a.   FCR 15: [COMP] ≡ [+SUBJ]
>   b.   FCR 16: [WH, +SUBJ] ⊃ [COMP NIL]
>   c.   FCR 17: [COMP *that*] ⊃ [FIN] ∨ [BSE]
>   d.   FCR 18: [COMP *for*] ⊃ [INF]

It is important to recall how the presence of a bare feature name (as opposed to a bare value name) on the left-hand side of an FCR, such as [COMP] in (14a) above, is interpreted. What it means is that the feature is in the domain of the relevant category, and thus receives some value (cf. chapter 2, section 3). So (14a) says that any category in which COMP is assigned a value is one in which the feature SUBJ is assigned the value +. In other words, the only category which can contain a feature specification [COMP *that*], [COMP *for*], or [COMP NIL] is V^2[+SUBJ].[4] If the feature WH appears on a sentence, as happens in relative clauses and constituent questions, for example, then (14b) requires the sentence to have NIL as its COMP value. If a category has *that* as its value for COMP, (14c) requires that it have FIN or BSE as its VFORM value, which allows for tensed *that*-clauses and the tenseless 'subjunctive' *that*-clauses studied in somewhat more detail by Weeda (1981). Some speakers find sentences like *We require it be tensed* grammatical; for them, (14b) should also allow BSE. Finally, FCR (14d) ensures that whenever [COMP *for*] is specified on a category, the VFORM value of that category is INF.

In addition to these FCRs, we state the following FSD for COMP:

> (15)   FSD 9: [INF, +SUBJ] ⊃ [COMP *for*]

Together with the rule in (16) which expands clauses positively specified for complementizer features, the default assignment just stated and the

FCRs governing the complementizers ensure that any clausal category appearing on the right-hand side of a rule will expand in the appropriate fashion.

(16)   S[COMP *α*] → {[SUBCAT *α*]}, H[COMP NIL]
        where *α* ∈ {*that, for, whether, if*}

The category {[SUBCAT *α*]} will, unsurprisingly, be lexically realized as *α*. That is, where the name of some terminal symbol (word or morpheme in the language) appears as the value of SUBCAT, rather than an integer, that item belongs (usually uniquely) to the grammatical category in question: the category of the complementizer *that* is {[SUBCAT *that*]}, and so on.

The structure that we assign to *for–to* clauses is illustrated in (17):

(17)

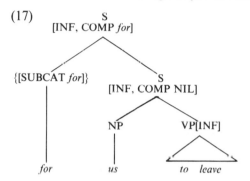

There are a number of constructions in which both *for–to* clauses and infinitival VPs (i.e. V²[INF, −SUBJ]) can occur:

(18)   Sentential Subjects:
        (*For us*) *to leave* is annoying.
        (*For us*) *to be late* would bother Lee.

        Infinitival Relatives:
        The man (*for us*) *to talk to* is here.

        too Complements:
        They are too crazy (*for us*) *to talk to*.
        It is too hot (*for us*) *to wear these clothes*.

        Purpose Clauses:
        I bought a book (*for you*) *to read to the children*.

We will not present analyses of all these constructions in this book. However, they illustrate that the alternation between infinitivals with and without NP subjects occurs in a wide variety of contexts. On our approach, the rules responsible will all introduce the category V²[INF], which is unspecified for the feature [SUBJ]. Since the latter is default-free, there will be two instantiations of this category: one where [+SUBJ] is instantiated, and one where [−SUBJ] is instantiated. The former gives rise to clauses; the latter to verb phrases. Some of the instantiation possibilities for V²s are illustrated in (19)–(21). In each case, the category in (a) is one that occurs as complement in some lexical ID rule, while (b) contains the relevant instantiated categories that would be licenced by (a) in admissible projections.

(19)   a.   V²[INF]
       b.   S[INF, COMP *for*]
            VP[INF]

(20)   a.   V²[+SUBJ, FIN]
       b.   S[FIN, COMP *that*]
            S[FIN, COMP NIL]

(21)   a.   V²[+SUBJ, BSE]
       b.   S[BSE, COMP *that*]
            S[BSE, COMP NIL]

Further rules expanding VP are illustrated in (22) and (23).

(22)   a.   VP → H[8], NP, S[FIN]
       b.   persuade, convince, tell, . . .
       c.   persuaded Lee (that) it was a good idea

(23)   a.   VP → H[9], (PP[*to*]), S[FIN]
       b.   concede, admit, . . .
       c.   conceded to the scientists that Jupiter has rings

As mentioned above, we follow Weeda (1981) in analyzing verbs that introduce 'subjunctive' clauses by rules like the following:

(24)   a.   VP → H[10], S[BSE]
       b.   prefer, desire, insist, . . .
       c.   insisted (that) the job be given to Lee

(25)   a.   VP → H[11], (PP[*of*]), S[BSE]
       b.   require, . . .
       c.   require of them that they write a paper.

Infinitival verb phrases in English are always introduced by the highly idiosyncratic item *to*. Our assumption about this item is that it is a peculiar nonfinite auxiliary verb. Comparatively theory-neutral arguments for this view are given in Pullum (1982), and various alternative analyses (that it is a preposition, a complementizer, a verbal 'particle' of some sort, a verb prefix, or whatever) are examined and shown to be unsatisfactory. The following VP rule is the special rule definitive of infinitival complements that any account of English structure must have, corresponding to the '$\overline{\text{VP}}$ → *to* VP' rule of some other analyses.

(26) a. VP[INF, +AUX] → H[12], VP[BSE]
      b. to
      c. to go home

There is a syntactically significant distinction to be drawn among three kinds of noun phrases: 'dummy' NPs whose realization is *it*, dummies whose realization is *there*, and the 'normal' NPs that have appeared in our examples thus far (proper names, quantified and determined NPs, referential pronouns and so forth). A given verbal element may require a particular kind of NP as its subject. Hence it is essential that our theory of categories distinguish one kind from another. To distinguish among the various kinds of NP, we employ the feature NFORM whose values are those shown in (27).

(27) {*it, there,* NORM}

The two expletive pronouns of English are assigned to the categories indicated by the lexical entries in (28).

(28) a. ⟨*it*, NP[PRO, −PLU, NFORM *it*], {}, *Δ*⟩
      b. ⟨*there*, NP[PRO, NFORM *there*], {}, *Δ*⟩

And the 'ordinary' NPs referred to above all are specified as [NFORM NORM].

The FSD in (29) ensures that the default value for NFORM is NORM.

(29) FSD 8: [NFORM] ⊃ [NFORM NORM]

In what follows we refer several times to V² categories bearing the feature specification [AGR NP[NFORM NORM]], which indicates compatibility with normal NPs and incompatibility with dummy subjects. We introduce the abbreviation ' +NORM' for this feature specification. Since NORM is not a binary feature (or even a feature), this cannot lead to ambiguity.

Let us now give some ID rules for several different classes of complement-taking verbs.

(30) a. VP → H[13], VP[INF]
      b. continue, tend, . . .
      c. continue to be unhappy

(31) a. VP → H[14], V²[INF, +NORM]
      b. prefer, intend, . . .
      c. prefers (for us) to stand alone

(32)   a.   VP → H[15], VP[INF, +NORM]
     b.   try, attempt, . . .
     c.   tried to leave

(33)   a.   VP → H[16], (PP[*to*]), VP[INF]
     b.   seem, appear, . . .
     c.   seems (to us) to be unhappy

(34)   a.   VP → H[17], NP, VP[INF]
     b.   believe, expect, . . .
     c.   believes Bobbie to be unhappy

(35)   a.   VP → H[18], NP, VP[INF, +NORM]
     b.   persuade, force, . . .
     c.   persuade them to give themselves up

(36)   a.   VP → H[19], (NP), VP[INF, +NORM]
     b.   promise
     c.   promise Leslie to behave

The various principles of feature instantiation presented in the previous chapter place a number of interesting constraints on the set of trees that are admissible from these rules. As we shall now illustrate, those principles form the basis of a general account of the distribution of expletive pronouns ('dummy' *it* and *there*) in infinitival constructions. Hence it is guaranteed that in general if a rule introduces an NP daughter that contains no specification for NFORM, that daughter will licence only 'ordinary' NPs.

The expletive pronouns, which occur in the following examples, have an extremely restricted distribution.

(37)   a.   It appears that Kim is happy.
     b.   It bothers us that Sandy can't come.
     c.   It would be unlikely for Pat to be called upon.

(38)   a.   There is nothing in the box.
     b.   There was a pig roasted.
     c.   There were two women teaching the class.
     d.   There were a number of students sick that day.

For example, no expletive may be the subject of any of the VPs we have analyzed so far.[5]

(39)   a.   *It put the book on the table.
     b.   *It said that Kim was happy.

(40)   a.   *There put the book on the table.
     b.   *There preferred for Sandy to get the job.

Conversely, the 'ordinary' NPs that have appeared in all our examples so far can never appear as subjects of those VPs which take expletive subjects. Compare (37)–(38) with the following.

(41) a. *Sandy appears that Kim is happy.
      b. *Dana would be unlikely for Pat to be called upon.

(42) a. *Robin is nothing in the box.[6]
      b. *He was a pig roasted.

A fundamental concern in the syntax of expletive pronouns is to systematize their restricted distribution and to predict the incompatibility of non-expletive NPs with VPs that allow expletive subjects.

We deal first with dummy *it*. Many verbs in English occur with the expletive pronoun *it* as their subject and a sentential constituent in 'extraposed' position.

(43) a. It bothered Lou that Robin was chosen.
      b. It would bother Lou (for Chris) to do that.
      c. It should be obvious that they will resign.
      d. It seems that Pat was unhappy.
      e. It appears that Leslie will be late.

Some, but not all, of these also allow a sentential subject.

(44) a. That Robin was chosen bothered Lou.
      b. (For Chris) to do that would bother Lou.
      c. That they will resign should be obvious.
      d. *That Pat was unhappy seems.
      e. *That Leslie will be late appears.

The essential regularity is that any verb which takes a sentential subject also allows an extraposed clause, but not conversely.

In order to accommodate examples like (44a–c), we posit rules like (45)

(45) a. VP[AGR S] → H[20], NP
      b. bother, amuse, . . .
      c. bothered Lou

The specification [AGR S] in (45) allows VPs of this class to take sentential sentential subjects[7] because the CAP ensures the agreement illustrated in trees like (46) in virtue of the fact that the sentential subject is the controller of the VP:

(46)

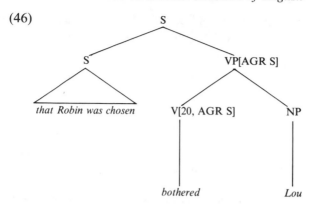

The key properties of the sentential extraposition construction are captured by the following metarule.

(47)   Extraposition Metarule

$$X^2[\text{AGR S}] \rightarrow W$$
$$\Downarrow$$
$$X^2[\text{AGR NP}[it]] \rightarrow W, S$$

This maps (45) into (48) (and similarly for other rules which we will not discuss in detail here).

(48)   a.   VP[AGR NP[it]] → H[20], NP, S
         b.   bother, amuse, . . .

The feature specification [AGR NP[it]], which will abbreviate as '+it' from now on, is distributed in accordance with the same general principles we have been discussing. Hence, given the categorization of it in (36a), we have trees like (49).

(49)

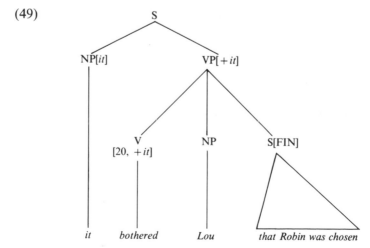

Note that the treatment of defaults defined in chapter 5 exempts subjects from being required to assume the default value NORM for the feature NFORM. However, because the default value of AGR on verbs is NP[NFORM NORM] (see FSD 11, in section 5 of chapter 5), such feature specifications as [AGR NP[NFORM *it*]] or [AGR NP[NFORM *there*]] cannot be instantiated on the lexical heads of the structures licenced by the ID-rules presented earlier. But the rules just presented contain VP mothers whose AGR value is distinct from the default, and the effect of this is that the relevant defaults are 'overridden' because the HFC forces the nondefault value onto the lexical head (see the discussion of FSDs in chapter 5).

The exceptional nature of *seem* and *appear* is accommodated by positing the following rule.

(50) a. VP[+*it*] → H[21], (PP[*to*]), S[FIN]
      b. seem, appear, . . .
      c. seems (to us) that Pat was unhappy

Although this looks like output from the extraposition metarule, it is not. The rule simply lists the fact that these verbs allow a dummy *it* subject.

Our analysis of the expletive pronoun *there* is similar to our account of dummy *it*. We follow Jenkins (1975) and Williams (1984) in assuming that the elements after *be* in *there*-sentences like those in (51) constitute a single NP constituent.

(51) a. There was a lion in the zoo.
      b. There were three wolves sick that day.
      c. There was a dog chewing a bone.

We implement this position by adopting the following rule:

(52) a. VP[AGR NP[*there*, αPLU]] → H[22], NP[αPLU]
      b. be, . . .
      c. was a lion in the park.

This rule also allows for sentences of the following sort:

(53) a. There is a Santa Claus.
      b. There are unicorns.

The rule just given interacts with previously discussed principles to generate structures like the following.

(54)

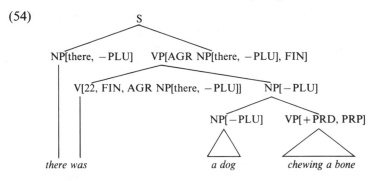

Our analysis of this construction allows any NP to appear as a complement within a VP[AGR NP[*there*]].[8] Note again that because the rule in (52) specifically mentions an AGR value distinct from the default value, verbs admitted from this rule 'override' the FSD governing AGR on verbs.

We are now in a position to illustrate our analysis of expletive pronouns in infinitival constructions, which introduce problems of long-distance agreement, as illustrated by the following examples.

(55)   { *There / *It / Kim }   continued to read books.

(56)   { There / *It / *Kim }   appeared to be nothing in the park.

(57)   { It / *There / *Kim }   seems to bother them that Kerry resigned.

(58)   Leslie believed { *there / it / *Kim }   to have bothered us that Lee lied.

(59)   We believed { there / *it / *Kim }   to be no flaws in the argument.

These examples all point to the conclusion that in the following structures, there must be identity of features, as indicated.

(60)

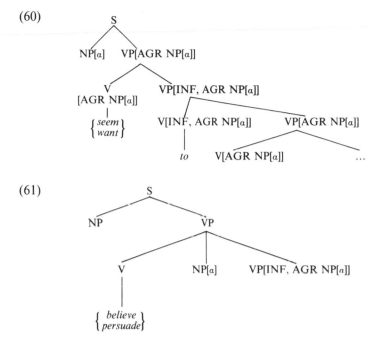

(61)

The agreement principles outlined in chapter 5 ensure exactly this agreement. In structures like (61) the NP complement is the controller of its VP sister. Hence the latter's AGR value must agree with the NP controller by the first clause of the CAP. In the case of structures like (60), however, the VP complement has no controller. Hence its AGR value must match that of its VP mother (by the second clause of the CAP) which in turn must match the subject NP of the sentence (by the first clause of the CAP). This correctly systematizes the contrasts illustrated in (55) through (59) above. Finally, note that the theory of defaults presented in chapter 5 has the effect of not requiring that the subject and object NPs in these examples bear the default specification NORM for the feature NFORM. Such controller NPs turn out to be *privileged* in respect of agreement features, and thus exempt from the relevant defaults. Thus dummy pronouns are systematically allowed to be controllers. However, because the rules introducing 'equi' verbs like *try*, *persuade* and *promise* introduce complements specified as [+ NORM] (see the rules in (32), (35) and (36)), it follows that none of the examples in (62) are generated:

(62) a. *There/it tried to be a riot in the park.
     b. *Dana persuaded there/it to be a riot in the park.
     c. *There/it promised Leslie to be nothing in the bag.

This is just the desired result.

Finally, we note that the agreement pattern of reflexive and reciprocal pronouns in infinitival constructions is identical to that just explicated for expletive pronouns. GPSG analyses of reflexives and reciprocals, e.g. that of Pollard and Sag (1983), have the property that they introduce a FOOT feature (RE in the case of the present feature system) on complements that contain reflexive or reciprocal elements. Agreement principles guarantee that these reflexive or reciprocal elements agree with the AGR value of the VPs that contain them (in a significant class of cases). This being the case, the contrasts in (63) through (65) are explained in exactly the same way as the analogous expletive pronoun examples just discussed.

(63)   *They* seem to like themselves/*myself/*herself.

(64)   I persuaded *them/*him* to talk to each other.

(65)   We believed *her* to have hurt herself/*themselves/*yourself.

3   Adjective phrases

Degree modifiers like *how, so, too, more, less,* and *as,* which we assign to the minor category Deg, play a role within AP which is somewhat similar to that of determiners within NP, i.e. members of the minor category Det. Consider now the rule in (66).

(66) $A^2 \rightarrow (\{\langle SUBCAT, 23\rangle\}), H^1$

It will be recalled that in chapter 2, we suggested that minor lexical categories are categories which contain a SUBCAT feature, but do not contain a BAR feature. Thus we will use 'Deg' as an abbreviation for the non-head category shown in (66).

(67) $Deg = \{\langle SUBCAT, 23\rangle\}$

Combined with rules for expanding A^1, the grammar will admit trees like (68).

(68)

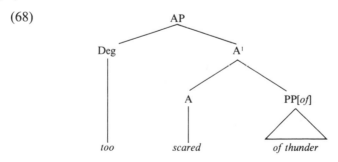

We assume an additional Boolean feature ADV, which is instantiated on [+N, +V] categories. Because of the FSD shown in (69), an AP daughter in a tree will in general be unspecified for ADV if its licencing category in an ID-rule is itself unspecified for ADV.

(69)   FSD 6: [+ADV] ⊃ [BAR 0]

Rule (66) will now give rise to structures like (70).

(70)

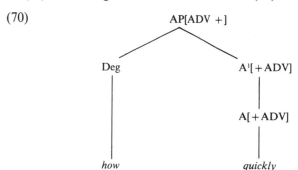

A further rule for expanding AP is (71a), and (71b) illustrates the kind of structure admitted by this rule:

(71)   a.   AP → (AP[+ADV]), H¹

         b.

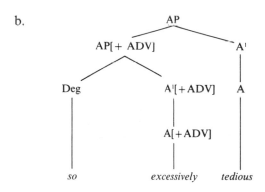

The following lexical ID rules indicate the kind of subcategorization that is required for adjectives.

(72)   a.   A¹ → H[24], PP[*about*]
         b.   angry, glad, curious, ...
         c.   angry about the decision

(73)   a.   A¹[AGR S] → H[25], PP[*to*]
         b.   apparent, obvious, certain, ...
         c.   apparent to us

(74)   a.   A¹ → H[26], S[FIN]
        b.   afraid, aware, amazed, ...
        c.   afraid that it was too late

(75)   a.   A¹ → H[27], S[BSE]
        b.   insistent, adamant, determined, ...
        c.   insistent that you be on time

An interesting fact about adjectives, and indeed nouns, is that they never seem to be subcategorized for obligatory complements. That is, there seems to be no adjective or noun which is like *destroy* in that it must co-occur with an argument phrase.[9] If this is a true generalization about the syntax of English, we can capture it by the following metarule.

(76)   Complement Omission Metarule
        [+N, BAR 1] → H, *W*
                  ⇓
        [+N, BAR 1] → H

This metarule provides a general account of optionality and means that complements in lexical ID rules expanding A¹ and N¹ do not have to be parenthesized.

Adjectives taking infinitival complements are distinguished in much the same way as the raising and equi verbs discussed in the previous section.

(77)   a.   A¹ → H[28], VP[INF]
        b.   likely, certain, sure, ...
        c.   likely to leave

(78)   a.   A¹ → H[29], V²[INF, +NORM]
        b.   anxious, eager, ...
        c.   eager (for us) to leave

These rules give rise to structures like (79) and (80).

(79)

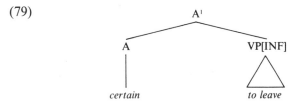

(80)

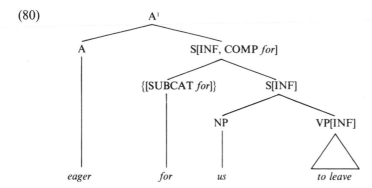

Given these analyses, we would expect A and its complement to appear sentence-initially in root interrogatives, as in fact they do.

(81)   a.   How ready (for us) to leave are they?
        b.   How eager (for the students) to take the exam did you say they were?

As Hendrick (1978) has pointed out, the complements of sentence-initial adjectives can be readily separated from their heads. We observe that a treatment of rightwards dependencies along the lines suggested by Gazdar (1981b) will interact with the rules responsible for (81) to produce the relevant examples.

(82)   a.   How ready are they (for us) to leave?
        b.   How eager did you say they were (for the students) to take the exam?

The constituency assigned by the rule in (78) also predicts that 'Right Node Raising' structures like (83) will be well-formed.

(83)   a.   They are willing, and we are eager, for the children to leave as soon as possible.
        b.   Kim is prepared, and indeed eager, for the children to leave as soon as possible.

Finally, note that the feature agreement principles and the theory of defaults outlined in chapter 5 interact with the rules in (77) and (78) to provide an account of the following contrasts, which are exactly analogous to the examples involving raising and equi verbs discussed in the previous section.

(84)   a.   There was likely to be a thug lurking in the park.
        b.   *There was eager to be a thug lurking in the park.
        c.   It is certain to bother them that you are quitting.
        d.   *It is silly to bother them that you are quitting.

4 Noun phrases

The overall picture of the structural analysis of NP that we assume is a fairly conservative one, very much as proposed by Chomsky (1970). It is shown schematically in (85).

(85)

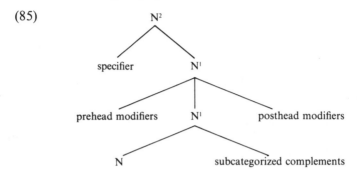

The phrasal level of N^2 expands as a specifier followed by the N^1 head. Specifiers comprise determiners, possessive phrases and a limited set of 'quantifying' APs (e.g. *many* and *few*). Optional modifiers are allowed to occur as sisters of N^1. These modifiers consist largely of APs, relative clauses, PPs and nonfinite VPs. Finally, beneath N^1 is the lexical head of the NP, together with any complements for which it is subcategorized. The tree below illustrates (85) more concretely.

(86)

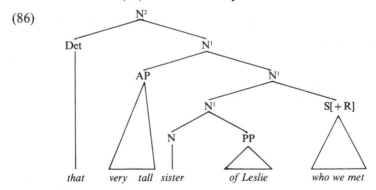

We will not discuss all aspects of this structure in detail (cf. Andrews 1983), but will turn instead to the rules which expand N^1.

There are strong parallels between the range of complements allowed by nouns and verbs. This is particularly noticeable in the case of deverbal nominalizations. Thus the N^1 phrases in (87) correspond to the VPs in (88).

(87) a.   disappearance
      b.   argument with Beverley about the meal
      c.   proof that the set is infinite
      d.   insistence that you be quiet
      e.   plan to leave

(88) a.   disappear
      b.   argue with Beverly about the meal
      c.   prove that the set is infinite
      d.   insist that you be quiet
      e.   plan to leave

We will assume that the lexical relatedness of nouns and their verbal sources will be characterized by redundancy rules in the lexicon, an issue which we will not attempt to address in this volume. The syntactic analysis of phrases like (87) will be accomplished by the following rules:

(89) a. $N^1 \rightarrow H[30]$
           death, disappearance, laughter
      b. $N^1 \rightarrow H[31]$, PP[*with*], PP[*about*]
           argument, consultation, conversation
      c. $N^1 \rightarrow H[32]$, S[COMP *that*]
           belief, implication, proof, notion, idea
      d. $N^1 \rightarrow H[33]$, S[BSE, COMP *that*]
           request, insistence, proposal
      e. $N^1 \rightarrow H[34]$, V^2[INF]
           plan, wish, desire

In the case of an ID rule like (89b), LP rules will not specify any precedence between the two PPs. Consequently, the local trees admitted by this rule will allow for the alternation exhibited in (90):

(90   the arguments with Lee about malathion
      the arguments about malathion with Lee

There is a further class of N^1s which correspond to VPs except that NP is replaced by a PP[*of*]. Compare (91) and (92):

(91) a.   seduction of Kim
      b.   gift of a book to the children
      c.   dislike of bathing

(92) a.   seduce Kim
      b.   give a book to the children
      c.   dislike bathing

The rules which analyze (91) are the following:

(93)   a. $N^1 \to H[35], PP[of]$
            love, seduction, criticism
       b. $N^1 \to H[36], PP[of], PP[to]$
            gift, announcement, surrender
       c. $N^1 \to H[37], PP[of, GER]$
            dislike, admission, memory, habit, prospect, idea

The structural parallelism between nouns and verbs is echoed in a
semantic parallelism. That is to say, many nouns are relational in the way
that verbs are. For example, *the seduction of Kim by Lee* denotes an event
in which Kim and Lee stand in the relation which holds when *Lee seduces
Kim* is true. However, not all relational nouns are nominalizations. So for
example, rule (93a), which accounts for nominals corresponding to
transitive verbs, will also introduce nouns such as those in (94).

(94)   a.   king, sister, inside . . .
       b.   king of France
            sister of Leslie
            inside of the box

A number of tests for identifying relational predicates have been suggested
in the literature.[10] First, even though relational terms can occur without
argument PPs, there is typically an entailment associated with them that
some entity stands in the appropriate relation. Thus inferences like (95)
are judged to be valid.

(95)   Lee is a sister.
       Therefore, Lee is a sister of someone.

A second criterion is that the preposition of an argument PP makes no
systematic semantic contribution to the interpretation of the phrase in
which it occurs. That is, the semantic role of the PPs in (94) vary according
to the interpretation of the head, and this is what one would expect if they
denoted arguments to the function denoted by the head. By contrast, a PP
like *from Spain* makes a constant semantic contribution to a noun phrase
in which it occurs. Similarly, within the verb phrase, optional modifying
PPs are distinct from argument PPs in that they freely co-occur with
arbitrary verbs (subject to semantic/pragmatic plausibility), and that they
have a constant semantic interpretation. A further criterion, suggested by
Bresnan (1982b), is the inability of argument PPs to undergo repetition.
Thus, there is a contrast between (96a) and (96b), which contain optional
modifier PPs.

(96)   a.   *I met the sister of Leslie of Gerry.
            *Louis was king of France of Spain.

b.   I met the student with long hair with freckles.
      The house by the stream by the woods is for sale.

However, as Dowty (1982b, pp. 116 ff.) observes, it is not always clearcut whether a given PP is to be interpreted as an argument or as a modifier. Consider, for instance, the PP[*of*] in (97).

(97)   This is a photograph of Leslie.

While it is tempting to suppose that *photograph* is subcategorized for PP[*of*] complements, it should be noted that the inference in (98) is much weaker than the one in (95). (One can imagine situations in which a photographic image has been produced by, say, faulty loading of the camera.)

(8)   This is a photograph.
       Therefore, this is a photograph of something.

While PPs that occur as daughters of N[1] will be interpreted as arguments of the nominal head, there will also be PPs introduced as sisters of N[1] by the rule in (99), and these will play the semantic role of modifiers.

(99)   N[1] → H, PP

Generalizing part of the preliminary LP statement given in (8b) above, we can give an LP statement that correctly linearizes the daughter constituents as follows:

(100) $[+N] < PP$

This says that a PP will follow any NP, N[1], N, AP, A[1], or A that stands in a sister relation to it. We will now obtain two analyses of *photograph of Leslie*, as illustrated in (101).

(101)a.

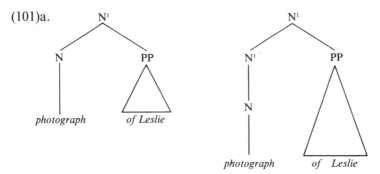

If the PP in (101b) is a modifier, then we would expect it to make an independent semantic interpretation. Evidence that it does in fact do so comes from the fact that it can occur in predicative position. Thus, observe the contrast in (102).

(102)   a.   This photograph is of Leslie.
         b.   *This sister is of Leslie.

Of course, given the rule introducing the verb *be* presented in the previous section, our grammar will generate both strings in (102). This is not a failing, however, since the deviance of (102b) is clearly semantic in nature. The meaning of *of* in (102a) – presumably a relation of depiction – is defined for things like photographs, but sisters will be outside its sortal range. It is this that gives rise to the anomaly in (102b).

It was pointed out by Lakoff (1970) that certain PPs cannot co-occur with the proform *one* as head. This is illustrated by pairs of examples like (103).

(103)   a.   Lou met the sister with long hair and I met the one with
               freckles.
         b.   *Lou met the sister of Leslie and I met the one of Gerry.

Jackendoff (1977, p. 58) attempted to explain this phenomenon by suggesting first, that *with long hair* is a sister of N^1 while *of Gerry* is a sister of N, and second, that *one* is a pro-N^1. For Jackendoff, as for us, sisters of N are interpreted as arguments of the head, while sisters of N^1 are interpreted as modifiers. According to this account, a noun cannot undergo *one(s)* anaphora when it co-occurs with a PP for which it is subcategorized, since that would involve the *one* replacing not the whole N^1 but a proper subpart of it, i.e. the lexical head.

An apparent difficulty arises when we consider a noun like *photograph*. It is subcategorized for a following PP[*of*], but it can undergo *one(s)* anaphora, as (104) shows.

(104)   Lou saw the photographs of Leslie and I saw the ones of Gerry.

Despite this difference, Jackendoff is unable to give any independent motivation for treating *photograph* differently from *sister*. However, as we have seen, there are good grounds for saying that *photograph* admits of a non-relational interpretation in a way that *sister* does not. Hence, (104) is acceptable because the phrase *of Gerry* can be interpreted as a modifying PP, rather than an argument. In the light of this consideration, we shall adopt Jackendoff's analysis of *one(s)* as a pro-N^1.

Let us consider now what predictions are made about the nouns discussed at the beginning of this section. We cannot *a priori* rule out the possibility that the post-head PPs analyzable by the rules in (93) will also be analyzable by rule (99). Consequently, we should not expect that the nouns which occur with such PPs will always resist *one(s)* anaphora. What we do predict, however, is that there will be a correlation between the acceptability of that complement occurring in predicate position and the acceptability of that complement also occurring with *one(s)*. The following data suggest that this prediction is correct.

(105) a. *The seduction was of Kim.
     b. *Their objection was to getting up at dawn.
     c. ?The gift was to the children.
     d. The argument was about malathion.
       The argument was with Lee.

(106) a. *The seduction of Kim was easier than the one of Gerry.
     b. *Their objection to getting up at dawn was matched only by their one to eating brown rice at every meal
     c. ?The gift to the children will be more expensive than the one to the teacher.
     d. The argument about malathion was as difficult as the one about disarmament.
       Those arguments with Lee were as pointless as the ones with Sam.

5 Prepositional phrases

Terms like 'lexical category' or 'major lexical category' are often used by grammarians, but have been given little in the way of explicit content. In particular, there has been no clear consensus as to whether prepositions are more on a par with minor, closed-class elements such as conjunctions, complementizers, and negation particles, or like the undisputed lexical vocabulary of a language – the nouns, verbs, and adjectives.

The position we take here is that prepositions are a major lexical category like nouns, verbs, and adjectives. This position is well established within recent work on English grammar, notably because of Jackendoff 1973, a work we shall rely on throughout this section, and subsequent work influenced by it (e.g. van Riemsdijk 1978). Jackendoff observes that linguists 'never seem to have taken prepositions seriously', being apparently inclined to 'deny that the category "preposition" has any real intrinsic syntactic interest other than as an annoying little surface peculiarity of English' (1973, p. 345). We accept Jackendoff's view that the structure of prepositional phrases has to be taken as seriously as the structure of any other kinds of phrase.

The view that prepositions are insignificant morsels of surface detail is clearly related to the fact that it is very common for prepositions to play the same role as do case-markers in languages like Latin that have case-inflected nouns. We recognize a distinction between case-marking (or similar) uses of prepositions and uses of prepositions to convey semantic content. The examples in (107) exemplify case-marking prepositions (italicized), which can be regarded as denoting identity functions on NP meanings. This means that they are semantically vacuous in a definable sense. The phrase that they head has a meaning identical with that of the noun phrase it contains; the preposition adds nothing.

(107)   I lent the lawnmower *to* Sandy.
         They don't approve *of* us.
         We were attacked *by* the dog.
         You can rely *on* that.
         We saw the interior *of* the box.
         We should have credited him *with* a little more intelligence.

Consider English indirect objects. We need to be able to guarantee that where a verb like *hand* occurs with a single prepositional phrase sister, then the latter will have *to* as its preposition (because while *She handed it to me* is grammatical, we want to block **She handed it for me*, **She handed it near me*, and so on). Thus we need to be able to mention in a rule of grammar that a given constituent is a prepositional phrase with *to* as its preposition. As noted in chapter 2, we allow the feature PFORM to take particular prepositions as its values, one of them being *to*. We enter *to* as being a lexical item of category P[PFORM *to*]. However, the homonymic directional preposition *to* as in *Sandy walked to the station* will be listed in the lexicon separately, and not treated as an instance of P[PFORM *to*]. Separate listing of these two prepositions is independently necessitated by the semantic difference between them. Now any rule that has to guarantee the presence of the preposition *to* in a prepositional phrase can simply introduce PP[FORM *to*]. PFORM is listed as a **HEAD** feature, so the Head Feature Convention (see chapter 5, section 2) will ensure that the P^0 in this PP is *to*, in the manner illustrated by the tree in (108).

(108)

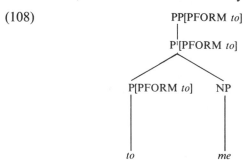

PFORM is freely instantiated onto $[-N, -V]$ categories, but because of the FSD in (109), a prepositional phrase will in general be unspecified for PFORM if it is licenced by a PP in an ID-rule that is itself unspecified for PFORM.

(109)   FSD 5: [PFORM] $\supset$ [BAR 0]

This places what appears to be the proper constraint on the distribution of subcategorized-for prepositions.

The examples in (110) contain prepositions (italicized) that have lexical meanings – meanings of a sort that, very roughly, map NP meanings into either adverbial modifiers or expressions denoting places or times.[11]

(110)   They placed the picnic table *between* the two trees.
         The car was found *under* the bridge.
         I'll see that something is done *before* dinner.
         We succeeded *despite* the efforts of our enemies to stop us.

Jackendoff (1973) shows clearly that there is enough parallelism between PPs, NPs, APs and VPs to justify a claim that the rules for introducing X^0 are virtually invariant across different values for X. He comments (p. 354):

> Is it coincidence that the correct generalization of the base rules for PPs is P $-$ (NP) $-$ (PP) and not P $-$ ($\left\{ \begin{matrix} \text{NP} \\ \text{PP} \end{matrix} \right\}$) or P $-$ (PP) $-$ (NP)...?
> There is one other syntactic category which allows NPs rather than just PPs in its complement, namely, the verb. And in verb phrases the NPs in the complement precede the PPs. This suggests that the structure of PPs is in fact not accidental.

The generalization Jackendoff is suggesting is captured in our terms by the constraints inherent in ID/LP format: if NP and PP are both introduced as non-head complements, whether to P or to anything else, they must either be freely ordered with respect to one another or (as happens in English) ordered in a fixed way regardless of the dominating category or the category of the head of their phrase. Thus, since 'V NP PP' is one possibility found in VP, but 'V PP NP' is not, we predict that either we will find 'P NP PP' but not 'P PP NP' in PPs, or PPs will not dominate strings containing both NP and PP.

Jackendoff also suggests that there is evidence from the internal syntax of PPs that they have at least two levels of bar structure. He points out parallels similar to those seen in (111a, b), where PPs and APs are compared.

(111)	a.	[Right [at the bottom of the wall]] they found a gold ring.
			My neighbor is [totally [without shame]].
			[Three feet [above the water]] the helicopter stopped descending.

	b.	[Immediately [adjacent to the house]] is a small shed.
			My neighbor is [totally [supportive of the local community]].
			[Three feet [closer to the wall]], the helicopter would have crashed.

The point is that adverbial or measure phrase modification in PPs parallels that found in APs. Jackendoff does not attempt to show that the structure of phrases like the ones bracketed in (111) has the label P^2 on the outer constituent and P^1 on the inner one. Both could be labeled P^2 if there were a rule of the form '$P^2 \rightarrow$ Modifier P^2'. One different prediction made by the two possible analyses is that '$P^2 \rightarrow$ Modifier P^2' predicts indefinitely iterated modifiers, while '$P^2 \rightarrow$ Modifier P^1' does not. The evidence from English on this point is somewhat equivocal. The modifier *right*, which is specific to PPs in the standard dialects of English, seems not to co-occur with other modifiers:

(112)	*Almost right out of the window bounced the shiny red ball.
	*That is right completely out of the question.
	*Nearly right over the moon flew the soaring frisbee.

Attempts to get other adverbial modifiers of different sorts to iterate on a PP meet with varying degrees of success, as the reader may verify, but the ones that sound best are often susceptible to an analysis in which the first adverb modifies the second (e.g. *almost totally out of control* can be analyzed as [[*almost totally*][*out of control*]] rather than as [*almost [totally [out of control]]]*). Thus the evidence of internal syntax favors the bar-level hypothesis proposed by Jackendoff, though only weakly.

We therefore adopt Jackendoff's (1973) position, and thus we assume that complements to P are in P^1, not P^2.

(113)	$P^1 \rightarrow$ H[38], NP

This one rule can take care of the syntax of both the full lexical prepositions like *underneath*, and the case-marking type uses of a preposition like *to*. The preposition *to* will be lexically listed both as P[SUBCAT 38] and as P[SUBCAT 38, PFORM *to*], whereas *underneath* will only be listed as belonging to category P[SUBCAT 38].

Note that *out* is not a member of P[38] for the many dialects in which **out the box* is ungrammatical as a PP (*out of the box* being the grammatical version), so it is not true that every preposition that takes a complement can take an NP complement. *Out* needs a rule like (114) in the dialects in question.

(114) a. $P^1 \rightarrow H[39], PP[of]$
       b.   out

[*of*] is the value of PFORM, and feature instantiation will have the effect of passing it from P^2 to P^1 to P by the HFC in the familiar way. P[39] contains *out*, and there may be other members; for example, for speakers who accept phrases like *forward of the railings* but not **forward the railings*, the preposition *forward* is a member of P[39], as may also be the idiomatic compound prepositions *in front* and (for American speakers) *in back* which appear to subcategorize for an obligatory PP[*of*].

Notes

1 LOC is a feature identifying locative phrases; cf. Bresnan and Grimshaw 1978.
2 See Gazdar et al. 1982 for some detailed discussion of the role of these and other features in the context of an analysis of the English auxiliary system. And see Warner forthcoming for a very promising alternative feature system.
3 See chapter 10, note 5.
4 In virtue of FCR 11, stated in chapter 4, section 3, any category which is [+SUBJ] is also a V².
5 We ignore irrelevant readings occasioned by the presence of the homophonous referential pronoun *it*.
6 Again there are irrelevant, though highly implausible, readings on which examples of this form are grammatical.
7 The fact that these verbs also belong to the category V[2] means that the subject may also be an NP, as in *Sandy bothered Pat.*
8 The examples in (i)–(iii) we take to be syntactically well formed, but deviant on semantic grounds.

     (i)   There was a student tall.
     (ii)   There were five students victims of his tyranny.
     (iii) There was every student in the hall.

For some suggestions about the semantic principles responsible for this deviance, we refer the reader to Milsark 1974, 1977, and Barwise and Cooper 1981.
9 The adjective *fond* is the only item we can find that looks like an exception to this statement; and even there, phrases like *fond memories* make the evidence less than conclusive. Maling (1983) shows that *like* and *worth*, which might appear to be counterexamples, are in fact prepositions.
10 In particular, see Dowty 1982b and Bresnan 1982b. These tests (like any tests in syntax) are not completely reliable, but they have considerable heuristic value.

11 To put our semantic proposals a little more precisely, a preposition of the case-marking sort will denote a function that takes the meanings of the prepositional object NP as argument and returns the same NP meaning as value. Some prepositions of the lexically meaningful sort will denote a function from NP meanings into functions from VP meanings into (distinct) VP meanings, while others will denote a function from NP meanings into expressions denoting regions of space or intervals of time, often in quite complex and context-dependent ways.

7

The analysis of
unbounded dependencies

1 Introduction

An *unbounded dependency construction* (UDC, hereafter) is one in which

(i)   a syntactic relation of some kind holds between the substructures in the construction, and

(ii) the structural distance between these two substructures is not restricted to some finite domain (e.g. by a requirement that both be substructures of the same simple clause).

Topicalization, relative clauses, constituent questions, free relatives, clefts, and various other constructions in English have been taken to involve a dependency of this kind. It is analytically useful to think of such constructions, conceptualized in terms of tree geometry (in the usual way, root up and leaves down), as having three parts: the top, the middle, and the bottom. The top is the substructure which introduces the dependency, the middle is the domain of structure that the dependency spans, and the bottom is the substructure in which the dependency ends, or is eliminated; (1) shows this schematically

(1)

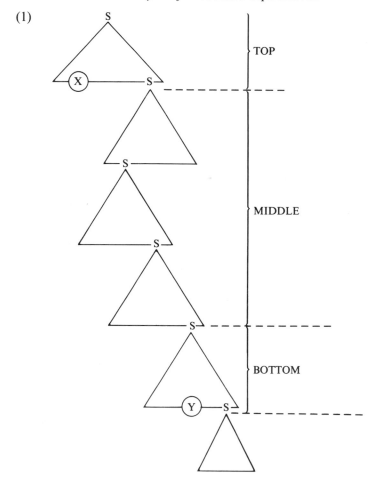

We shall present a theory of UDCs which claims that the principles which govern the bottom and the middle are completely general in character, and do not differ in syntactic characteristics from one UDC to another.

The account of **FOOT** features elaborated in chapter 5 is crucial to our analysis of UDCs. Indeed, our analysis of the middle of UDCs involves no more than the feature SLASH taken together with feature instantiation principles, in particular the Foot Feature Principle (FFP). Since this is at once the simplest and the most important part of our treatment of UDCs, we will begin with it. That is to say, we will begin in the middle. As will become evident as we proceed, the key feature of the GPSG analysis of UDCs is the claim that such dependencies are simply a global consequence of a linked series of local mother–daughter feature correspondences. No 'long-distance' statement is involved at all.

2 The percolation of SLASH features

In chapter 2, we introduced the category-valued feature SLASH, whose intuitive significance is that a constituent assigned to a category C[SLASH C'] (often written C/C') is an C-type constituent from which a C'-type subconstituent is missing.[1] There are two ways in which this rough intuitive characterization is misleading. First, 'missing' subconstituents are not exactly missing. Following Wasow (1972) and much subsequent work, we assume that the notion 'missing element' is in general to be explicated in terms of the presence of phonologically null constituents, often known as 'traces'.[2] Thus a constituent assigned to the category C/C' is in fact to be analyzed as a C-type constituent which contains a null constituent of category C'. We treat the latter in terms of the feature NULL. Second, it need not be just one subconstituent that is 'missing'. In the case of coordinate structures and certain other examples that have been discussed under the rubric of 'parasitic gaps', a constituent specified as [SLASH C'] contains more than one C'[+NULL] element. Thus an S/NP is a sentential constituent which may contain one or more NP[+NULL]s. We will return to both these points in the discussion that follows.[3]

In earlier GPSG work (e.g. Gazdar 1981b), the rules responsible for passing slash category information through a tree were arrived at by a metarule known variously as the 'derived rule schema', or the 'slash introduction metarule'. This metarule has no place in the present analysis. All of its effects, and certain other consequences as well, now follow as special cases of the effects of the FFP in feature instantiation. Indeed, the metarule account is now excluded in principle by our theory. Given the restriction on metarule application to lexical ID rules, it would no longer be possible to formulate a slash introduction metarule with the necessary properties.

The best way to grasp the effects of the FFP with respect to slash categories is to inspect an example of its application. Consider the set of ID rules shown in (2):[4]

(2) a. S → XP, H[−SUBJ]
     b. V² → H, X²[+ADV]
     c. VP → H[1]
     d. VP → H[2], NP
     e. VP → H[45], PP[*of*]
     f. VP → H[40], S[FIN]
     g. VP → H[13], VP[INF]
     h. VP → H[3], NP, PP[*to*]
     i. VP → H[17], NP, VP[INF]

j.   VP → H[9], (PP[*to*]), S[FIN]
k.   VP[+AUX] → H[7], X²[+PRD]
l.   VP[INF, +AUX] → H[12], VP[BSE]
m.   A¹ → H[24], PP[*about*]
n.   A¹ → H[42], VP[INF]/NP
o.   P¹ → H[38], NP

Let us consider now the local subtrees admitted by these rules, on the assumption that the specification [SLASH NP] is instantiated on one or more of the nonlexical daughters in the trees. In this case the feature instantiation principles outlined in chapter 5 predict that the resulting structures will be as shown in (3):

(3)   a.   S/NP
               NP
               VP/NP
           S/NP
               NP/NP
               VP/NP

      b.   VP/NP
               VP/NP
               PP[+ADV]
           VP/NP
               VP/NP
               PP[+ADV]/NP

      d.   VP/NP
               V[2]
               NP/NP

      e.   VP/NP
               V[45]
               PP/NP

      f.   VP/NP
               V[40]
               S[FIN]/NP

      g.   VP/NP
               V[13]
               VP[INF]/NP

      h.   VP/NP
               V[3]
               NP/NP
               PP[*to*]
           VP/NP
               V[3]
               NP
               PP[*to*]/NP
           VP/NP
               V[3]
               NP/NP
               PP[*to*]/NP

      i.   VP/NP
               V[17]
               NP/NP
               VP[INF]
           VP/NP
               V[17]
               NP
               VP[INF]/NP
           VP/NP
               V[17]
               NP/NP
               VP[INF]/NP

j. VP/NP
        V[9]
        PP[*to*]/NP
        S[FIN]
    VP/NP
        V[9]
        PP[*to*]
        S[FIN]/NP
    VP/NP
        V[9]
        PP[*to*]/NP
        S[FIN]/NP

k. VP[+AUX]/NP
        V[7]
        AP[+PRD]/NP

l. VP[+AUX, INF]/NP
        V[12]
        VP[BSE]/NP

m. A¹/NP
        A[24]
        PP[*about*]/NP

o. P¹/NP
        P[38]
        NP/NP

SLASH is a **FOOT** feature and the FFP requires that all **FOOT** feature specifications *instantiated* (as opposed to stipulated by a rule) on a daughter are also instantiated on the mother in any given local tree. This condition is met by all the structures in (3), but not, for example, by the local trees in (4):

(4)   S
            NP/NP
            VP
        S
            NP
            VP/NP

The FFP also ensures that no **FOOT** feature specification is instantiated on a mother unless the same specification has been instantiated on a daughter. Hence there are no local trees like those in (5):

(5)   S/NP
            NP
            VP
        N¹/NP
            N
        VP/PP
            V
            PP

And since the instantiated **FOOT** feature specifications of the mother must be the unification of the **FOOT** feature specifications instantiated on the daughters, there can be no discrepancies of the sort shown in (6):

(6)   S/NP
                   NP/PP
                   VP

           S/PP
                   NP
                   VP/NP

Finally, note that because SLASH is a **HEAD** feature as well as a
FOOT feature, it follows that whenever a SLASH specification is instantiated on a daughter, and hence on the mother in accordance with the FFP,
the same specification must be instantiated on the mother's head, if the
latter is nonlexical. This follows from the HFC, which requires that a
mother's **HEAD** feature specifications are also part of the head's **HEAD**
feature specifications (modulo FCRs). But the HFC does not force
SLASH onto lexical heads as this would lead to illegal extensions of those
heads in view of the following FCR (introduced above in chapter 2,
section 3):

(7)   FCR 6: [SUBCAT] $\supset$ $\sim$[SLASH]

Thus none of the following local trees is admissible, since they all violate
the HFC.

(8)   S/PP
                   NP/PP
                   VP

           NP/NP
                   N^1
                   PP/NP

           VP/NP
                   V/NP

We will consider the effects of these constraints in greater detail below, as
well as the further consequences of our feature instantiation principles
with respect to the rules governing coordinate structures and rules which
already include a slash category.

3   Slash termination, Metarule 1

We will turn our attention now to the bottom of UDCs, the part of the
structure in which the chain of slash categories (i.e. the 'projection path' in
the sense of Fodor (1980)) comes to an end and we reach an incomplete
constituent or gap.

(9)   Slash Termination Metarule 1 (STM1):

$$X \rightarrow W, X^2$$
$$\Downarrow$$
$$X \rightarrow W, X^2[+\text{NULL}]$$

This says that any rule which introduces an X^2 daughter has a counterpart in which that daughter bears the specification [+NULL]. Notice that, given the way our grammar is organized, STM1, being a metarule, can only apply prior to feature instantiation and can only apply to rules that specifically introduce a lexical category, i.e. the lexical ID rules. To show the effect it has, we exhibit in (10) all the rules that result from the application of STM1 to the rules in (2) when the pattern category X^2 is matched by AP, NP, or PP.

(10)   d.   VP → H[2], NP[+NULL]
        e.   VP → H[45], PP[*of*, +NULL]
        h.   VP → H[3], NP[+NULL], PP[*to*]
              VP → H[3], NP, PP[*to*, +NULL]
        i.   VP → H[17], NP[+NULL], VP[INF]
        j.   VP → H[9], PP[*to*, +NULL], S[FIN]
        k.   VP[+AUX] → H[7], X^2[+PRD, +NULL]
        m.   A¹ → H[24], PP[*about*, +NULL]
        o.   P¹ → H[38], NP[+NULL]

Feature instantiation in the local trees admitted by these rules is constrained by four considerations which interact to ensure that these rules are used only to terminate a UDC. Firstly, the following FSD prevents [+NULL] from showing up on the instantiations of any other rules:

(11)   FSD 3: ~[NULL]

Secondly, the following FCR forces [+NULL] categories to get instantiated with a SLASH feature of some kind:

(12)   FCR 19: [+NULL] ⊃ [SLASH]

Thirdly, we assume that among the lexical entries for the empty string is a schematic one which permits it to appear as a daughter of categories of the form $a[+\text{NULL}]/a$. Finally, the FFP guarantees that whatever specification is instantiated on a [+NULL] daughter is also instantiated on its mother. The resulting effect is that the (usable) instantiated extensions associated with these rules have the form shown in (13):

(13)   d.   VP/NP
              V[2]
              NP[+NULL]/NP

        e.   VP/PP
              V[45]
              PP[*of*, +NULL]/PP

        h.   VP/NP
              V[3]
              NP[+NULL]/NP
              PP[*to*]
              VP/PP[*to*]
              V[3]
              NP
              PP[*to*, +NULL]/PP[*to*]

        i.   VP/NP
              V[17]
              NP[+NULL]/NP
              VP[INF

        j.   VP/PP[*to*]
              V[9]
              PP[*to*, +NULL]/PP[*to*]
              S[FIN]

        k.   VP[+AUX]/NP[+PRD]
              V[7]
              NP[+PRD, +NULL]/NP[+PRD]
              VP[+AUX]/PP[+PRD]
              V[7]
              PP[+PRD, +NULL]/PP[+PRD]
              VP[+AUX]/AP[+PRD]
              V[7]
              AP[+PRD, +NULL]/AP[+PRD]

        m.   A^1/PP[*about*]
              A[24]
              PP[*about*, +NULL]/PP[*about*]

        o.   P^1/NP
              P[38]
              NP[+NULL]/NP

4   Topicalization

We are now in a position to discuss the top of UDCs and, in the light of our discussion so far, provide some concrete illustrative examples. The most basic and general rule responsible for introducing UDCs in English is that shown in (14), which says simply that a sentence can consist of an X^2 followed by a sentence which contains a null X^2 constituent.

(14) $S \rightarrow X^2, H/X^2$

This rule is responsible for, among other things, the topicalization

(15)

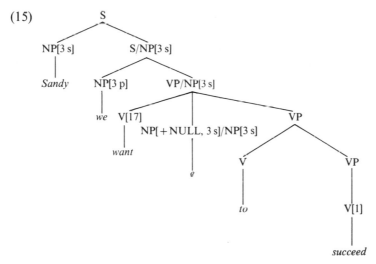

(16)

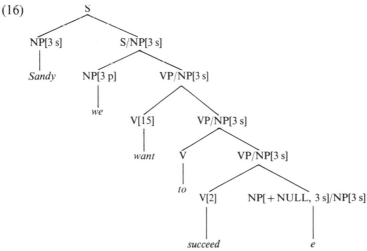

construction, as is illustrated by the trees in (15) and (16). In (15), we have the structure associated with the 'We want Sandy to succeed' reading of *Sandy we want to succeed*, whereas in (16) we have the structure associated with the 'We want to succeed Sandy' reading. Note that the agreement features of the topicalized constituent in these examples (where we use [3 s] and [3 p] to abbreviate [PER 3, − PLU] and [PER 3, + PLU] respectively) are 'passed down' into the SLASH values of all constituents on the projection path of the UDC. This is the combined effect of the CAP and the FFP. The former ensures that the X^2 and the SLASH value of the sentential daughter in (15) and (16) above are instantiated with identical values for agreement features (the sentential daughter is a controllee whose control feature is SLASH, and the X^2 corresponds to its phrasal controller). The FFP in turn ensures that whatever SLASH specifications are instantiated on the nonlexical daughters in the substructures in (15) and (16) are inherited by their mothers. Hence the agreement dependency between a trace and the dislocated constituent is properly transmitted. Our analysis of the topicalization construction is further illustrated by the examples in (17)–(19).

(17)

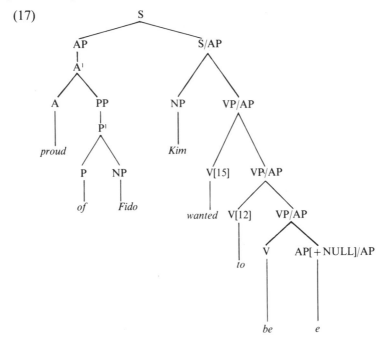

(18)

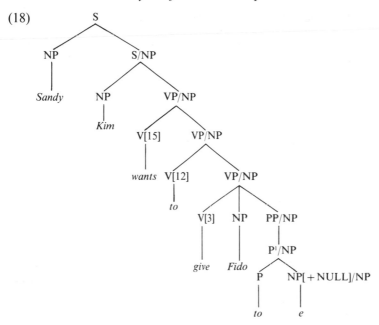

(19)

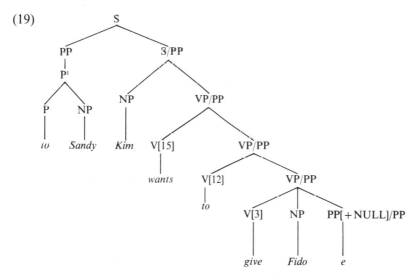

Examples (18) and (19) illustrate that the rules given allow both for NPs to be topicalized so as to strand prepositions, and for the whole PP to be topicalized. Thus the analysis gets the pied-piping facts exactly right, and will not permit examples such as (20) (from Iwakura's (1980) critique of Chomsky (1977)):

(20)   *To John, Julie gave a copy of her book to [*e*].

It is important to point out that in a local tree compatible with the topicalization rule we introduced in (14) above, the S mother cannot gain the SLASH specifications of its daughter S by feature instantiation. The local tree in (21b) is a projection of the topicalization ID rule, which we repeat here for convenience as (21a).

(21)   a. $S \rightarrow X^2, H/X^2$
        b.   S/NP
                    NP
                    S/NP

Nevertheless, it is not an admissible projection, given our definition of that notion. The FFP requires the **FOOT** feature specifications instantiated on the mother in any given local tree to be equal to the unification of the **FOOT** feature specifications that have been *instantiated* on the daughters. However, the **FOOT** feature specifications on the daughters in local trees compatible with this rule (and indeed with all such rules which introduce unbounded dependencies) are inherited from the licencing category in the rule. Consequently, they can never satisfy the FFP's requirements when the same **FOOT** feature specifications have been instantiated on the mother in a tree.

Consider now the possibilities for terminating a UDC within an NP. STM1 introduces null elements only as sisters of lexical categories. Thus a PP complement of an N^0, or an NP within such a complement may be realized as [+NULL]. This allows for the following topicalizations:

(22)   a.   Of that book, they published five reviews [*e*].
        b.   That book, they published five reviews of [*e*].

It is often thought that the impossibility of possessive null elements, as in (23), is due to a general constraint barring such elements from appearing on left branches.[5]

(23)   a.   *Leslie's, we liked [*e*] book.
        b.   *Leslie, we liked [*e*]'s book.

However, as pointed out by Grosu (1974), there is a general constraint in English (but not in several other languages discussed by Grosu) against the 'extraction' of possessive NPs, as is evidenced by the impossibility of gaps in postnominal possessives as well:

(24)   a.   I read a book of Kim's.
        b.   *Kim's, I read a book of [*e*].

These facts are entailed by our analysis. Prenominal possessives cannot be realized as traces because they are introduced by the following rule:

(25)   NP → NP[+POSS], H¹

Rule (25) is not a lexical ID-rule, and hence cannot undergo STM1. Moreover, postnominal possessives are introduced as sisters of N¹ in virtue of the rules below.[6]

(26)   N¹ → H, PP[+POSS]
(27)   P¹[+POSS] → H[41], NP[+POSS]

Since SLASH is a **HEAD** feature as well as a **FOOT** feature, this entails that [SLASH NP[+POSS]] can be instantiated on a sister of N¹ only if it is also instantiated on the N¹ head as well. This correctly rules out examples like (23b), where the only gap appears within the postnominal modifier. But in fact no NP[+POSS] constituents are ever introduced as sisters of lexical categories. Consequently, they can never receive a [+NULL] specification by virtue of STM1, and the [SLASH NP[+POSS]] cannot be legitimately discharged as a gap. As a result of these considerations, even though (28) is an admissible local tree, it is one that can never form part of a larger admissible terminated tree.

(28)   N¹/NP[+POSS]
         N¹/NP[+POSS]
         PP[+POSS]/NP[+POSS]

Similarly, because the rule expanding NP[+POSS] as NP followed by the possessive suffix *'s* is not a lexical ID-rule, it can never undergo STM1. This fact is responsible for the deviance of (23b) above and (29).

(29)   a. *Sandy, we read a book of [e]'s.
         b. *Sandy, we found the pictures of [e] of [e]'s.

Many constraints on the possible realizations of SLASH within NP are thus correctly predicted without the supposition of any ad hoc 'island conditions' (as indeed are various other constraints on UDCs discussed under this general rubric, which we will turn to in subsequent sections). Note finally that nothing said so far blocks the possibility of topicalization in embedded clauses where no UDC is involved. We therefore allow the examples in (30) (cited by Iwakura (1980, p. 59)).

(30)   a. Harry said that Max, Joan would never be willing to marry.
         b. The inspector explained that each part he had examined very carefully.

5   Missing-object constructions

Missing-object constructions have a paradoxical history in transformational grammar. On the one hand, the classic *easy to please/eager to please* contrast has played an important part in the rationale for assuming two distinct levels of syntactic structure. And, on the other, these constructions have consistently provoked ugliness and ad hocness in the transformational analyses actually suggested.[7] There is an analogy here with the *respectively* construction, which has similarly been a standard component of the pedagogic commercial for TG despite the fact that no remotely adequate transformational analysis of the construction was ever proposed (as was pointed out by Pullum and Gazdar (1982, p. 484)).

Our analysis of missing-object constructions consists of a single lexical ID rule which permits certain adjectives to have a slashed infinitive VP or S complement. This rule is shown in (31).[8]

(31) $A^1 \rightarrow H[42], V^2[INF]/NP[-NOM]$

The rule then accounts immediately for the sentences in (32).

(32)   a.   Kim is easy to please.
        b.   Kim is easy for us to please.
        c.   Kim is easy for us to make Sandy accept.

For historical reasons, it is worth exhibiting the two structures that our grammar assigns to the minimal pair in (33).

(33)   a.   Kim is eager to please.
        b.   Kim is easy to please.

This we do in (34) and (35), respectively.

(34)

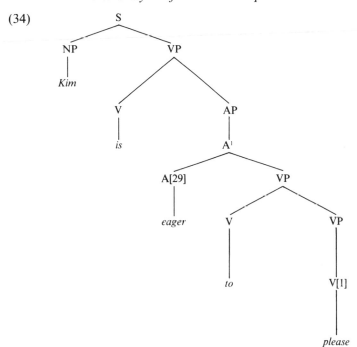

(35)

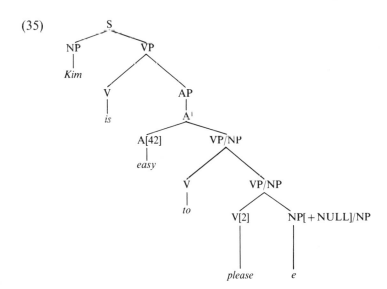

The [−NOM] specification takes care of the contrast in

(36)   a.   Mary is hard for me to believe John kissed.
         b.   *Mary is hard for me to believe kissed John.

Since the notion of case relevant here is just the traditional morphological one, and since the NP that follows an EQUI verb takes accusative morphology, not nominative, (31) will allow the grammar to generate (37) (from Nanni 1978, p. 111, cited in Schachter 1981, p. 440, n. 10).

(37)   John is hard for us to pretend to want to marry Nancy.

However, not every accusative 'subject' can terminate the projection path; thus STM1 will not supply the rules that would be necessary to generate (38).

(38)   *Kim is easy for __ to please Sandy.

Since the A^1 expanded by (31) is not itself slashed, it will have exactly the same distribution as any other complement-containing A^1. In particular, there is no reason to expect it to be 'restricted to contexts in which there is an overt subject NP' (Schachter 1981, p. 439). And so the examples in (39) (from Schachter 1981, p. 432) can be generated by exactly the same rules (modulo (31) itself) as are responsible for the examples in (40).

(39)   a.   Being lovely to look at has its advantages.
         b.   It pays to be lovely to look at.

(40)   a.   Being eager to learn has its advantages.
         b.   It pays to be eager to learn

The next examples show the predictions which are made by the interaction of (31) with various rules for unbounded dependencies.[9]

(41)   a.   How difficult for the students to solve do you think this problem will be?
         b.   How difficult do you think this problem will be for the students to solve?
         c.   This problem was difficult for us to think up and for the students to solve.
         d.   My problems were difficult, but yours were almost impossible, for the students to solve in an hour.

By itself, our analysis of missing-object constructions does not predict the grammaticality of (42).

(42)   a.   For which students will this problem be difficult to solve?
         b.   This problem will be difficult to solve, for the students who arrived late.

However, both these strings can be accounted for if we take the *for* phrase to be analyzable as a modifying adverbial.

6 WH constructions

Our treatment of WH constructions appeals to the **FOOT** feature WH, and to the feature WHMOR. Two of WHMOR's values, Q and R, serve to distinguish interrogative and relative pronouns, respectively. Typical examples of such pronouns are listed in the lexicon as indicated in (43):

(43) ⟨*what*, NP[WH NP[Q]], {}, . . .⟩
      ⟨*which*, NP[WH NP[Q]], {}, . . .⟩
      ⟨*which*, NP[WH NP[R]], {}, . . .⟩
      ⟨*which*, Det[WH NP[Q]], {}, . . .⟩
      ⟨*which*, Det[WH NP[R]], {}, . . .⟩
      ⟨*whose*, Det[+POSS, WH NP[Q]], {}, . . .⟩
      ⟨*whose*, Det[+POSS, WH NP[R]], {}, . . .⟩

From now on, we will use '+Q' and '+R' as abbreviations for the feature specifications [WH NP[WHMOR Q]] and [WH NP[WHMOR R]], respectively. The inheritance of WH works in just the same way as that of SLASH, except that (i) WH, unlike SLASH, is not a head feature, and (ii) FCRs impose severe limitations on the contexts in which WH can occur.

(44) FCR 20: ~([SLASH] & [WH])
      ГCR 21: A¹ ⊃ ~[WH]
      FCR 22: VP ⊃ ~[WH]

Thus WH gives rise to instantiations of the sort exemplified by the trees in (45)–(47):

(45)

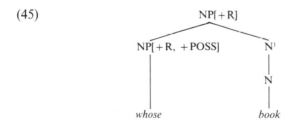

(46)

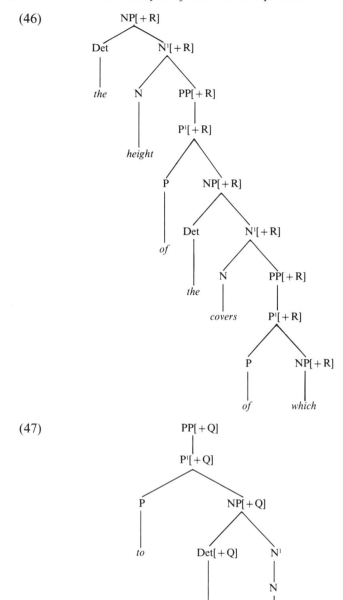

(47)

But the FCRs we have given will correctly block questions like (48).

(48)   a.   *Going to what party are you?
        b.   *Fond of whom are you?

Since the FCRs will not forbid the appearance of WH specifications on A^2, the occurrence of *wh* words in APs is restricted to the determiner position, as in examples like (49):

(49)   How fond of them are you?

The FCR which makes WH and SLASH mutually exclusive is motivated by the need to prevent examples like (50).

(50)   *Which books did you wonder whose reviews of had annoyed me?

The following ID rules will now serve to introduce relative clauses and embedded questions, respectively.

(51) $N^1 \rightarrow H, S[+R]$

(52)   a. $VP \rightarrow H[43], S[+Q]$
        b.   wonder, ask, inquire, ...
        c.   wonders who Lee likes

The sentential daughters in the rules just given are expanded by the two rules we have already introduced for expanding S, namely those in (53):

(53)   a. $S \rightarrow X^2, H[-SUBJ]$
        b. $S \rightarrow X^2, H/X^2$

The feature WH is a **FOOT** feature, as we have seen. Thus it will be instantiated by the FFP in exactly the same way as SLASH, provided, of course, that the resulting instantiations are consistent with the prevailing FCRs. This means that the rules in (53) will give rise to local trees like those in (54) and (55).

(54)   a. $S[+R]$
                $NP[+R]$
                VP

        b.   i. $S[+R]$
                    $NP[+R]$
                    S/NP
              ii. $S[+R]$
                    $PP[+R]$
                    S/PP
              iii. $S[+R]$
                    $AP[+R]$
                    S/AP

(55)   a.   S[+Q]
                 NP[+Q]
                 VP

       b.   i.   S[+Q]
                     NP[+Q]
                     S/NP

            ii.   S[+Q]
                     PP[+Q]
                     S/PP

            iii. S[+Q]
                     AP[+Q]
                     S/AP

These structures, none of which requires any special statement of any sort, combine with the structures induced by the rules in (51) and (52a) so as to generate all the examples in (56) and (57).

(56)   a.   The doctor who worked for Kim died.
       b.   i.   The doctor who Kim worked for died.
            ii. The doctor for whom Kim worked.
       c.   The doctor whose book Sandy had read gave a lecture.
       d.   The committee objected to all books the height of the covers of which the government had prescribed.

(57)   a.   Sandy wondered who worked for Kim.
       b.   i.   Sandy wondered which party Leslie was going to.
            ii. Sandy wondered to which party Leslie was going.
            iii. Sandy wondered how expensive the wine was.

Note that there is no exemplar for (56b.iii) in English, although some other languages permit adjectival relatives of this kind. Their absence in English is explained partly by FCR 21 (see (44)) and partly by the fact that the English lexicon contains no [+R] counterpart to the interrogative adjectival determiner *how*.

It is a surprising consequence of the present proposals that matrix subject relatives and constituent questions like those in (56a) and (57a) must have, and can only have, the simple NP–VP structures shown in (58) and (59).

(58)

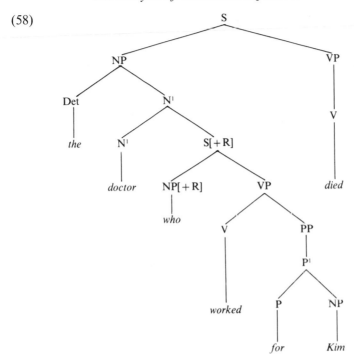

(59)

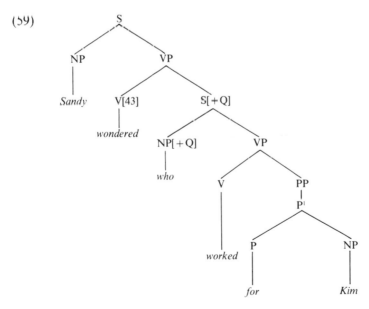

They must have this structure because of the existence of the 'S → X², H[−SUBJ]' rule and the principle that governs the way **FOOT** features work. And they can only have this structure, and not, say, one in which the *wh* NP is followed by a sentence with a missing subject, because no other rules are available. In particular, since STM1 is a metarule, it cannot apply to a non-lexical ID rule such as 'S → XP, H[−SUBJ]' rule so as to eliminate the subject. The present framework thus offers no counterpart to the string-vacuous movement analysis of such sentences standardly offered in transformational accounts.[10]

7   *It* clefts

In this section we will use [+ *it*] as an abbreviation for [AGR NP[NFORM *it*]]. Our analysis of the cleft construction comprises the following pair of rules (where V[44] introduces the verb *be*):

(60)   VP[+ *it*] → H[44], NP, S[+ R]

(61)   VP[+ *it*] → H[44], X², S[FIN]/X²

Given (60), all the examples in (62) will be generated.

(62)   a.   It is Kim that relies on Sandy.
        b.   It is Kim that Sandy relies on.
        c.   It is Kim who relies on Sandy.
        d.   It is Kim who Sandy relies on.
        e.   It is Kim on whom Sandy relies.
        f.   It is Kim in whose pockets were found the stolen jewels.

And given (61), all the examples in (63) will be generated.[11]

(63)   a.   It is Kim Sandy relies on.
        b.   It is Kim that Sandy relies on.
        c.   It is on Kim Sandy relies.
        d.   It is on Kim that Sandy relies.

Here (62c) will be assigned the tree shown in (64), and (63a) will be assigned that shown in (65).

(64)

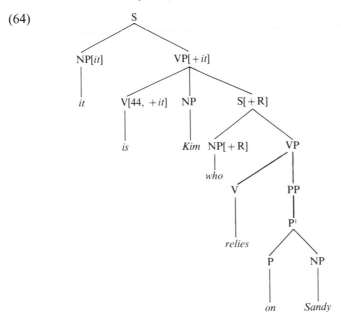

(65)

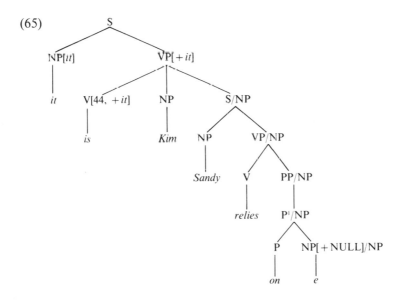

The rule in (61) does not constrain the instantiation of X^2. As Jim McCloskey has pointed out to us, there is some variation across dialects of English with respect to this. For example, in some varieties of Irish English X^2 can be AP, and strings like (66) are grammatical.

(66)   %It is very enthusiastic that Sean is.

Neither (60) nor (61) will permit any of the examples in (67) to be generated, however.[12]

(67)   a.   *It is Kim relies on Sandy.
         b.   *It is Kim on whom that Sandy relies.
         c.   *It is Kim on whom Sandy relies on.
         d.   *It is Kim on that Sandy relies.
         e.   *It is on Kim whom Sandy relies.
         f.   *It is on Kim on whom Sandy relies.

The cleft rules we have given are lexical ID rules, and, as such, are within the domain of metarule application. In particular, STM1 can apply to (60) and (61) resulting in the rules shown in (68).

(68)   a. $VP[+it] \rightarrow H[44], NP[+NULL], S[+R]$
         b. $VP[+it] \rightarrow H[44], X^2[+NULL], S[FIN]/X^2$

And these rules, in turn, will allow the grammar to generate examples such as those in (69).[13]

(69)   a.   I wondered who it was ___ who saw you.
         b.   I wondered who it was ___ you saw ___.
         c.   I was wondering in which pocket it was ___ that Kim had hidden the jewels ___.

8   Slash termination, Metarule 2

The reader will recall that we have, as yet, only provided half of our account of the bottom of UDCs, namely STM1. Although, as we have seen, a considerable amount follows from STM1, it does not, and cannot, provide an exhaustive account of slash termination. For example, given only what we have presented so far, the grammar will not contain a rule that permits the following sentence to be generated.

(70)   The doctor who we believe worked for Kim is dead.

The reason for this is simple: STM1 is a metarule, metarules apply only to lexical ID rules, the subject of an English declarative is not introduced by a lexical ID rule, therefore it cannot be eliminated by STM1.

We now introduce the second of the two metarules that allow for termination of slash chains.

(71) Slash Termination Metarule 2 (STM2)

$$X \rightarrow W, V^2[+SUBJ, FIN]$$
$$\Downarrow$$
$$X/NP \rightarrow W, V^2[-SUBJ]$$

This says that any rule which introduces a finite sentential complement has a corresponding rule where a VP[FIN] is introduced in place of that complement and where [SLASH NP] is introduced on the mother. Crucially, STM2, like STM1, can only apply to rules that specifically introduce a lexical category, i.e. the lexical ID rules. To show the effect it has, we exhibit in (72) a couple of the rules that result from the application of STM2.

(72) VP/NP → H[40], VP[FIN]
     VP/NP → H[9], (PP[*to*]), VP[FIN]

STM2 provides the grammar with the rule it needs to generate (70), and the grammar will then assign it the structure shown in (73).

(73)

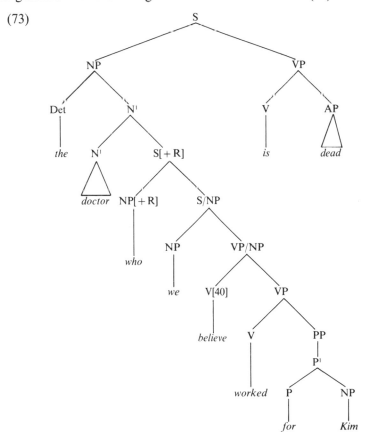

Notice that STM2 will not apply to rules which expand S[COMP *that*], S[COMP *for*], S[COMP *whether*] and S[COMP *if*], since these are not lexical ID rules. Thus our grammar makes exactly the right predictions regarding the 'complementizer-trace' facts illustrated by the following examples:

(74)   a.   The man that chased Fido returned.
       b.   *The man chased Fido returned.
       c.   The man that Fido chased returned.
       d.   The man Fido chased returned.

(75)   a.   *The man who I think that chased Fido returned.
       b.   The man who I think chased Fido returned.
       c.   The man who I think that Fido chased returned.
       d.   The man who I think Fido chased returned.

(76)   a.   *The man who I wondered whether chased Fido returned.
       b.   *The man who I wondered if chased Fido returned.
       c.   *The man who I wondered chased Fido returned.
       d.   *The man who I was eager for to chase Fido returned.
       e.   *The man who I was eager to chase Fido returned.

Some verbs, e.g. *complain*, subcategorize only for S[COMP *that*] in many varieties of English, and will not permit a simple tensed S. The STM2 will operate on the lexical ID rules responsible for introducing such verbs, but the resulting rules will introduce the category VP[[COMP *that*], [VFORM FIN]], which can never be instantiated in a manner which obeys the FCRs that are independently needed in the grammar of the English complementizer system. Thus for these varieties of English, we predict the grammaticality distribution shown in (77) in the case of a verb like *complain*.

(77)   a.   Who did you complain that you hated?
       b.   *Who did you complain you hated?
       c.   *Who did you complain that hated you?
       d.   *Who did you complain hated you?

9   Parasitic gaps

Among the local trees that the FFP permits from the rules used for exemplification in section 2 are the following:

(78)   S/NP
       NP/NP
       VP/NP

     VP/NP
       VP/NP
       PP[+ADV]/NP

     VP/NP
       V[3]
       NP/NP
       PP[*to*]/NP

     VP/NP
       V[17]
       NP/NP
       VP[INF]/NP

     VP/NP
       V[9]
       PP[*to*]/NP
       S[FIN]/NP

These structures have two things in common: (i) we have made no reference to any of them, nor have we invoked any of them in providing example sentences or trees, and (ii) they all introduce two phrasal daughters with a SLASH specification identical to that of the mother. But they exist, and they have consequences for what the grammar will generate. For example, they predict that the strings in (79) should all be grammatical.[14]

(79)   a.   Kim wondered which authors reviewers of __ always detested __.
     b.   Which articles did Dana file __ without reading __?
     c.   Kim wondered which models Sandy had sent pictures of __ to __.
     d.   Kim wondered which authors the editor wanted reviewers of __ to please __.
     e.   Kim wondered which authors the editor had told reviewers of __ that they should pan __.

And, somewhat surprisingly, they are all grammatical. Thus (79a), for example, will be assigned the structure shown in (80).

(80)

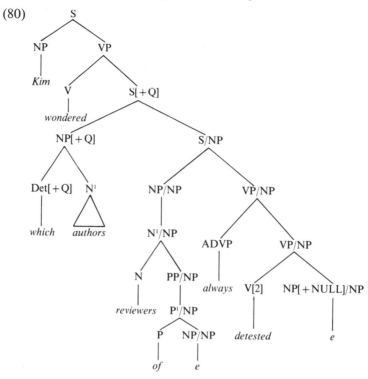

However, as Engdahl (1983) shows, the appearance of these 'parasitic gaps' is highly constrained. For example, they only show up in UDCs, and not by virtue of passive, equi, or raising constructions. Engdahl points out that this fact supports a distinction between local and nonlocal dependencies, a distinction which is expressed in terms of slashed categories in the present framework. The grammaticality of the examples shown above follows from the operation of the FFP on SLASH specifications required by the UDCs involved. Passive, equi, and raising constructions are not UDCs nor can they be properly analyzed as such, and thus they cannot, in themselves, legitimate the appearance of parasitic gaps.[15]

Furthermore, the analysis we have presented does not sanction local trees like the following:

(81)   a.   S/NP
                  NP/NP
                  VP

        b.   VP/NP
                  VP
                  PP/NP

These structures violate the HFC. SLASH is a **HEAD** feature whose specification on the mother has failed to be instantiated on the head daughter. For this reason we do not derive examples like those in (82).

(82)   a.   *Kim wondered which authors reviewers of ___ always detested meeting deadlines.

        b.   *Which articles did Dana file dossiers without reading ___?

Thus our assumption that SLASH is both a **HEAD** feature and a **FOOT** feature, taken together with independently motivated principles of feature instantiation, correctly predicts that certain gaps are 'parasitic' on the appearance of another gap within the head of a given constituent. This is precisely in accord with Engdahl's observations.

Engdahl also provides data bearing on an altogether more subtle constraint illustrated in the example below, which is taken from her paper.

(83)   *Who did you say ___ was bothered by John's talking to ___?

This example clearly involves UDCs, and yet parasitic gaps are not possible. The theory of UDCs outlined in this chapter is in the enviable position of not needing to say anything about such examples or, indeed, the examples in (79). The latter will be generated, those like (83) will not. Since this fact is not immediately obvious, we will briefly pursue the topic.

Consider the subject gap in (83). This can only be induced by the rule shown in (84a).

(84)   a.   VP/NP → H[40], VP[FIN]
        b.   VP/NP
              V[40]
              VP[FIN]/NP
        c.   VP → H[??], VP[FIN]

Inspection of (72) will confirm that (84a) is indeed in the grammar, thanks to STM2. However, (84a) will not allow us to generate (83) because the VP it introduces is not slashed, and the VP in (83) must be slashed since it has a gap in it which is not legitimized by any UDC internal to the VP. To get (83), we would need the local tree shown in (84b), but this is not an admissible structure. It cannot arise through instantiation of (84a), because the FFP requires that any SLASH specifications instantiated on a daughter in a local tree also be instantiated on the mother, not inherited by the mother from the licencing category in the rule. It could arise through instantiation of (84c), but the latter is not, and must not be, in the grammar. If it were, then we would be claiming that strings like (85) were grammatical standing on their own.

(85)   *You said was bothered by Sandy.

Consider now the following sentence.

(86)   Which caesar did Brutus imply ___ was no good while osten-
         sibly praising ___?

Engdahl notes that this example, due originally to Alan Prince, is
grammatical, even though, at first sight, it appears to be similar to the
ungrammatical (83). But there is an important structural difference
between them, and this difference means that the present analysis correctly
predicts the grammaticality of the example. Crucially, the adverbial
phrase modifies the VP *imply ___ was no good*, not the VP *was no good*. The
former is slashed, but the latter is not. The parasitic gap thus gets into (86)
in virtue of the local tree in (87b). This is admissible by the FFP from the
rule in (87a).

(87)   a.   VP → H, ADVP
         b.   VP/NP
              VP/NP
              ADVP/NP

There is one class of example where the FFP would lead us to expect
grammaticality, but which Engdahl claims to be ungrammatical.

(88)   a.   ?Who do you seldom talk to ___ about ___?
         b.   Which neighbours did you complain to ___ about ___?

Reaction to oral presentations of this material to audiences of native
speakers of English suggests, however, that a number of speakers do find
them acceptable. Example (88b), a variant of one of Engdahl's which
seems grammatical to us, was suggested by such a speaker (Maggie
Tallerman). The construction is that in which a verb subcategorizes for
two PPs. In this construction the FFP gives rise to structures which will
permit both prepositions to be stranded. Interestingly, Engdahl notes that
the equivalent of (88a) is acceptable in Swedish. We have no syntactic
explanation to offer for the widespread unacceptability of the English
examples, and we suspect that Engdahl's hypothesis that the correct
explanation is tied into language-particular conditions on coreferential
proforms is correct. And, like Engdahl, we also need to make appeal to
such constraints to explain the unacceptability of examples like (89),
which are generated by the syntactic principles we have outlined.

(89)   *Which slave did you give ___ to ___?

This, we believe, is the correct position to take on such cases. Hence we
have an account of parasitic gaps which is as close to optimal as any we
know of, although we make no special statement to deal with them in our

grammar. The properties of parasitic gap sentences are a consequence of the general character of our treatment of unbounded dependencies.

Notes

1 We use 'type' informally here to mean syntactic category, of course, not semantic type of corresponding intensional logic translations.

2 In Wasow 1972 and in Chomsky 1973 it was postulated that movement rules in a transformational grammar should deposit invisible (i.e. inaudible) pronouns at the site from which a (noun) phrase was moved, in order that constraints on allowable positions for such sites could be captured in terms of the resulting structures. The general idea grew out of earlier suggestions, particularly by J. R. Ross, that certain rules should be treated as copying operations rather than 'chopping' (i.e. straight movement) rules. The idea has assumed steadily growing importance in more recent transformational work.

3 We will use the term 'slash category' informally to designate any category which contains a specification for the feature SLASH.

4 An example of a verb of category V[45] is *approve*, as in *They don't approve of that sort of thing.*

5 Such a constraint is suggested by Ross (1967) and revived by Gazdar (1981b).

6 It is tempting to suppose that POSS is a **FOOT** feature. This idea has been explored in unpublished work by Dan Flickinger.

7 See Schachter 1981 and Jones 1983.

8 Following Schachter (1981), we assume that contrasts such as those illustrated in (i) and (ii) are to be explained in the semantics (or pragmatics), not in the syntax of the construction.

    (i)   a.   Kim is pretty to look at.
           b.   *Kim is pretty to work for.
    (ii) a.   *Kim is tyrannical to look at.
          b.   Kim is tyrannical to work for.

9 Nanni (1980) claims that (i) but not (ii) should be asterisked, and argues from this putative fact that *for the children to please* does not form a constituent with *easy*.

    (i)   How easy for the children to tease is John?
    (ii) How easy is John for the children to tease?

The difference between the two examples seems negligible to us.

10 For some relevant discussion of the NP–VP analysis, see Gazdar 1981b, pp. 171–2, nn. 22, 23), Dowty 1982b, p. 115, Chung and McCloskey 1983, Fodor 1983b, and Schachter 1984.

11 Notice that (62b) is identical to (63b), i.e. both (60) and (61) will assign a structure to this string. However, no detectable semantic difference accompanies this structural ambiguity.

12 We suspect that there are varieties of English in which (67a) is grammatical. On examples of the (67f) type, see Higgins (1976, p. 26) and reference therein.

13 Examples of this kind were drawn to our attention by Stan Peters. Note that the FFP can also interact with the rules in (60) and (61) so as to induce trees for examples such as (i).

(i)   ?*Which books was it reviews of __ which caused the author to take her own life.

Alternative theories, so far as we are aware, make no predictions whatsoever about such cases. The string in (i) exemplifies the descriptive generalization which Kuno called the clause nonfinal incomplete constituent constraint (Kuno 1973, p. 381). Notice that, under our analysis, the examples in (62) and (63) are consistent with this generalization since the incomplete constituent in each case is a clause final VP.

14 The existence of examples of this kind was noted by Ross (1967), but they were almost entirely neglected from then until Engdahl's important (1983) paper which thoroughly explored both the facts and their theoretical implications. Most of the examples below are adapted from ones to be found in her paper. An earlier GPSG analysis of her data is to be found in Sag (1983).

15 Of course, such constructions may be embedded in UDCs, and thus have parasitic gaps within them in virtue of the UDC in which they appear, as in *Which mafiosi do you expect relatives of to eliminate?*

8

The syntax of
coordination

1 Introduction

In the earliest work in GPSG, for example Gazdar (1982, written in 1979/80), heavy use is made of rule schemata and variables over categories. In treating coordinate conjunction and disjunction (henceforth, coordination), for example, the cross-categorial aspect of coordination was handled by means of schemata containing variables that could be instantiated as any category employed in the grammar, complete with all its feature structure. That is not the approach that will be adopted in this book. In this chapter we will begin to exploit seriously the potential of underspecified categories, and we will see that much of the need for schematization drops away.

All languages, as far as we know, make use of coordinate constructions.[1] This apparently innocent claim implicitly embodies an important metatheoretical assumption to the effect that there is a unitary notion of coordination, one that abstracts away from the evident differences between the coordinate constructions of Dyirbal, English, Hausa, Japanese, Latin, Swahili, and so on.

It is worth observing that transformational grammar has never been able to capture such a unitary notion of coordination, for reasons that were endemic to the framework. Consider the following examples.

(1) a. Kim sang and Sandy danced.
     b. Kim and Sandy met.
     c. Kim sang and was accompanied by Sandy.

Examples (1a) and (1b) would have been, and could only have been, generated directly by base rules. But example (1c) had to be derived in a completely different way, via a transformation of Conjunction Reduction, in any grammar that handled passive constructions transformationally. Analogous triads of examples can be constructed for almost every transformation ever proposed. The rule of Conjunction Reduction, though more often assumed than defined in the transformational literature, had to be formulated in such a way as to produce structures that were isomorphic to those that would have been produced if everything had been base-generated in the first place. Thus obvious generalizations, such as the fact that VPs participate in coordinate constructions of just the same sort as NPs and Ss (*and* precedes the last VP in the coordinate structure, for instance, rather than following it or being infixed into it) failed to be expressed. The structures needed could be generated by brute force, but the similarity of coordinate structures across categories was not thereby explained.[2]

The theory of coordination presented in this book is able to locate all the parochial aspects of coordinate constructions in the components of the grammar that constitute natural repositories for parochial facts, namely the rules responsible for the realization of specific morphosyntactic features, and the rules which determine linear precedence among constituents. The rest of the work is done by rule schemata that are abstract enough to be candidate universals, and by very general feature instantiation principles – especially the HFC – which are motivated by considerations independent of coordination.

The essence of our theory of coordination is the claim that coordinate constructions are simply multidaughter constructions in which every daughter is a head. To the extent that such constructions have the properties standardly attributed to them, they have those properties in virtue of their multiheadedness.[3]

2   Rule schemata

From now on we will be referring to items like *and, or, but, either, neither,* and *nor* as conjunctions, and the phrases they link (to put it informally) as conjuncts. Despite the fact that, for example, *or* corresponds to logical disjunction rather than conjunction, there seems little chance of confusion arising through this usage.

We distinguish two sorts of coordinate construction that have seldom been appropriately distinguished in the literature. In one, there can be only two conjuncts. In the other, there is no limit to the number of conjuncts permitted.[4] We conjecture that there are only these two specified lengths for coordination rules, and that no language can have, say, a three-place conjunction morpheme. If there were one in English, pronounced *triand*, we would find *Kim, Sandy, triand Lee* grammatical, but not **Kim triand Sandy* or **Kim, Sandy, Lee, triand Tracy*. We know of nothing like this in any attested language.[5] The restriction to two subconstituents with certain coordinating words is quite real, however, as is the arbitrary-length type. We postulate two rule schemata, one for each type of coordination. These schemata are exhibited in (2) and (3). The first is for the arbitrary-length coordinate structures, and the second for the binary ones. Note that the values that the CONJ feature can have in English for the two constructions differ (actual occurrence of coordination morphemes being a highly parochial matter).[6]

(2)   Iterating coordination schema (CS$^+$)
        X → H[CONJ a_0], H[CONJ a_1]$^+$
        where $a \in \{\langle and,$ NIL$\rangle, \langle$NIL$, and\rangle, \langle neither, nor\rangle,$
        $\langle or,$ NIL$\rangle, \langle$NIL$, or\rangle\}$

(3)   Binary coordination schema (CS^2)
        X → H[CONJ a_0], H[CONJ a_1]
        where $a \in \{\langle both, and\rangle, \langle either, or\rangle, \langle$NIL$, but\rangle\}$

The ID rules for expanding a category with a value for CONJ are shown in (4):

(4)   a.   X[CONJ NIL] → H
        b.   X[CONJ a] → {[SUBCAT a]}, H
               where $a \in \{and, both, but, neither, nor, or\}$

Among the possible values for CONJ mentioned in these schemata is NIL. Whereas NP[CONJ *and*] dominates strings such as *and their dog*, NP[CONJ NIL] dominates strings like *their dog*. In English, LP rules have the effect of reserving this for nonfinal conjuncts, but there are languages, as mentioned in note 1 of this chapter, in which all conjuncts take [CONJ NIL] in a coordinate structure.

The rules given above are schemata only by virtue of the fact that they range over different values for CONJ. The symbols X and H are not variables. Rather, they are extreme instances of an underspecified category.[7]

Notice that the only variables involved are those which range over the list of specific morphemes that can mark conjuncts. In all previous proposals for coordination schemata that we know of, the coordination was stated on variables ranging over categories which enforced categorial identity across the conjuncts, by means of a uniform substitution principle (mainly left implicit in earlier proposals). For instance, there is some discussion of the semantics for coordination schemata in Cooper 1979, Gazdar 1980, Keenan and Faltz 1978, Partee and Rooth 1983, and Rooth and Partee 1982, and all of them, as far as we can tell, assume variables across categories. The present proposal does not. X in the above rules is not a variable over the set of categories, but a category – a minimally specified one, compatible with any category in the grammar in respect of feature structure. And X[CONJ NIL] is a category with a feature composition such that it will unify with any category that has NIL as its value for CONJ. If we abstract away from the details concerning the values for the CONJ feature, all that (2) and (3) say is that the mother is a category, that the daughters are categories, and that the daughters are all heads. If completely free feature instantiation were permitted (which of course it is not), then (2) would in principle be consistent with, for example, a coordinate structure in which a preposition expanded as an AP conjoined with an NP and a couple of adverbs. The only information that the two schemata contain concerns the distribution of CONJ and the possibility of iteration.

A consequence of this is that the schema in (3) collapses exactly three English coordination rules, namely those arrived at by substituting in the three possible value pairs for a_0 and a_1. These three rules will correspond to numerous distinct local subtrees defined by feature instantiation, but they are not schemata over a set of fully specified rules corresponding directly to those instantiations. We are stressing this point because it has empirical consequences to which attention will be drawn subsequently. In particular, the approach we have adopted, abjuring variables over fully specified categories, does not entail that every conjunct be categorially identical to each of its sisters, although near-identity usually follows from the categorial requirements imposed by other ID rules and from their interaction with the various principles of feature instantiation.[8]

One further parochial component to our analysis of coordination is needed in order for us to be able to explore the claims it makes concerning the structure of English. We need LP statements to express the ordering constraints that hold across the various types of conjunct characterized by distinct values for the feature CONJ. These LP statements can be collapsed into a single schema.

(5)   Coordination LP schema (CS^{LP})
       [CONJ a_0] $<$ [CONJ a_1]
       where a_0 is in {*both, either, neither*, NIL},
       and a_1 is in {*and, but, nor, or*}.

The various coordination schemata interact to make a very wide range of detailed predictions concerning possible and impossible coordinate structures in English. We will illustrate these predictions by reference to examples involving coordinate VPs, and concern ourselves only with the predictions made with respect to iterability, ordering, and the choice of conjunction morpheme, since these are the issues that (2) through (5) address. The categorial identity, or lack of it, between mother and conjunct, and between conjunct and conjunct, is a topic that we leave to the next section. Here we will simply assume that constituents of the same category can conjoin to form a coordinate constituent of that category.

Since there are eight distinct values for CONJ in English, it follows that there are 64 logically possible two-conjunct coordinate structures. However, only six of these 64 possibilities are, in fact, grammatical, namely the six illustrated in (6).

(6)   a.   made a speech and stuttered
        b.   made a speech or stuttered
        c.   neither made a speech nor stuttered
        d.   both made a speech and stuttered
        e.   neither made a speech or stuttered
        f.   made a speech but stuttered

CS^+ and CS^{LP} interact to admit the relevant local subtrees corresponding to (6a, b, c) and no others. CS^2 and CS^{LP} interact to admit the relevant local subtrees for (6d, e, f) and no others. Thus the schemata we have given induce all and only the six grammatical English two-conjunct coordinate structures.[9]

We now turn our attention to three-conjunct examples with flat constituent structure.[10] Here there are 512 logical possibilities. Of these, five are grammatical. They are illustrated in (7).

(7)   a.   whimpered, shouted, and screamed
        b.   whimpered and shouted and screamed
        c.   whimpered, shouted or screamed
        d.   whimpered or shouted or screamed
        e.   neither whimpered nor shouted nor screamed

CS^2 is irrelevant for the flat structures of these examples. However, CS^+ interacts with CS^{LP} to admit structures for these five types of coordinate constituent, but not for any of the other 507 possibilities.

Finally, consider flat four-conjunct constructions. Here there are 4096 logical possibilities for assigning conjunctions to the conjuncts, but again only five are grammatical, and just those five are legitimated by the interactions of the CS^+ and the CS^{LP}:

(8)   a.   moaned, whimpered, shouted and screamed
        b.   moaned and whimpered and shouted and screamed
        c.   moaned, whimpered, shouted or screamed
        d.   moaned or whimpered or shouted or screamed
        e.   neither moaned nor whimpered nor shouted nor screamed

There is some variation among speakers of English with respect to *either* and *neither*. More liberal varieties than our own allow the examples in (9).

(9)   a.   either whimpered or shouted or screamed
        b.   either moaned or whimpered or shouted or screamed

That is, they flout the familiar prescriptive injunction not to use *either ...
or* with more than two disjuncts. There may also be people who are less
liberal than us with respect to *neither ... nor*, and are not prepared to use
it iteratively. Such varieties are straightforwardly described by making
minor changes to the parochial components of CS$^+$ and CS^2. Thus, to
increase liberality with respect to *either ... or* one simply mentions it in the
value specifications for CS$^+$ rather than CS^2, and to decrease liberality
with *neither ... nor* one makes the relevant move in the opposite
direction.[11]

3 Conjuncts as heads

The coordination schemata that we have introduced in the preceding
section deal only with the distribution of the coordination morphemes and
with the possibility of the iteration of conjuncts. Nothing has been said
about the categorial status of conjuncts, or about the category of the
mother given the categories of conjunct daughters. The conventional
wisdom on this topic has it that conjuncts must all be of the same
category, say *C*, and that the mother of these conjuncts will also be of
category *C*. But the conventional wisdom is wrong, in ways that are fairly
widely known. However, in the absence of any other candidate analyses, it
has not so far been replaced.

There are two classes of phenomena that show that the requirement of
categorial identity is incorrect. First, the case, person, number, and gender
of coordinated NPs do not behave in the manner it would lead one to
expect. Thus, for example, a singular NP can conjoin with a plural NP (or
with another singular NP) to form a plural NP. Until very recently
(Farkas and Ojeda forthcoming, Karttunen 1984, Sag et al. forthcoming),
the literature on coordination had provided no formal solutions to this
nest of problems, and we shall not pursue the matter here.

The second class of phenomena concerns examples such as the following:

(10)   She walked slowly and with great care. (Adv & PP)

(11)   His father ... was well known to the police and a devout
        catholic.[12] (AP & NP)

Two questions immediately arise: what is the category of the mother of the
conjuncts in such cases? And why is the coordination of AP with NP seen
in (11) not possible in (12)?

(12) a. *The [well known and a catholic] man was my father.
      b. *Soon [well known and a catholic] started shouting again.

The theory outlined here addresses both these classes of problems.

Consider the reduced form of the HFC ((45) in chapter 5) for the case of multiply headed constructions (the form which the general definition reduces to in the absence of any source of inconsistent feature specifications):

(13) $\phi(C_0)|\textbf{HEAD} = \bigcap_{C_i \in W_H} \phi(C_i)|\textbf{HEAD}$

The copular verb *be* syntactically selects an X^2 complement with the feature specification $\langle \text{PRD}, + \rangle$ (predicative). It imposes no other restrictions on the category status of that X^2. It may be an NP, a VP, an AP, or a PP, as seen in *is a sick man, is suffering from fever, is very sick*, and *is in poor health* respectively. If we construct a coordinate phrase with conjuncts of unlike category, e.g. *is a sick man and suffering from fever*, we find that it is possible to admit the structure involved. Looking just at the **HEAD** features, N, V, PRD and BAR, we have:

(14)   Features of NP: $\{\langle \text{BAR}, 2 \rangle, \langle N, + \rangle, \langle V, - \rangle, \langle \text{PRD}, + \rangle\}$
       Features of VP: $\{\langle \text{BAR}, 2 \rangle, \langle N, - \rangle, \langle V, + \rangle, \langle \text{PRD}, + \rangle\}$
       Intersection of above: $\{\langle \text{BAR}, 2 \rangle, \langle \text{PRD}, + \rangle\}$
       Required by copula: $\{\langle \text{BAR}, 2 \rangle, \langle \text{PRD}, + \rangle\}$

Since the copula permits a partially specified complement, and since the intersection of the instantiated head features of the two categories conjoined in this example yields something compatible with the partial specification that the copula requires, a sentence like *Lee is a sick man and suffering from fever* is predicted to be grammatical by (13), above. Analogous reasoning deals with *His father was well known to the police and a devout catholic* (AP conjoined with NP) and so on. Yet ill-formed examples like *A sick man and suffering from fever needs rest* are not sanctioned. A verb like *needs* must have a subject NP. If *a sick man and suffering from fever* is analyzed as an NP, the HFC will be violated, since *suffering from fever* will be a VP daughter of an NP mother, and the mother, which has to be an NP, will not have as its **HEAD** features the intersection of the **HEAD** features of the daughters:

(15)   **HEAD** features of NP: $\{\langle \text{BAR } 2, \rangle, \langle N, + \rangle, \langle V, - \rangle, \ldots\}$
       HEAD features of VP: $\{\langle \text{BAR}, 2 \rangle, \langle N, - \rangle, \langle V, + \rangle, \ldots\}$
       Intersection of above: $\{\langle \text{BAR}, 2 \rangle, \ldots\}$
       Features needed on mother: $\{\langle \text{BAR}, 2 \rangle, \langle N, + \rangle, \langle V, - \rangle, \ldots\}$

Not all multiply headed constructions are covered by the reduced form of the HFC shown in (13) since potential sources of feature specification inconsistency can arise in such constructions, just as they do in single-headed constructions. Consider the rule shown in (16):

(16) a. VP → H[48], H[CONJ *and*]
      b. come, go, . . .
      c. went and bought a parrot.

This rule is multiply headed and the mother is specified as $\{\langle\text{BAR}, 2\rangle,$ $\langle\text{SUBJ}, -\rangle, \langle\text{N}, -\rangle, \langle\text{V}, -\rangle\}$. The (nonreduced form of the) HFC will force all these features onto the head marked [CONJ *and*], since nothing prevents them being forced onto it, and it will force all of them *except* $\langle\text{BAR}, 2\rangle$ onto the lexical head ($\langle\text{BAR}, 2\rangle$ is inconsistent with $\{\langle\text{SUBCAT}, 48\rangle, \langle\text{N}, -\rangle, \langle\text{V}, +\rangle\}$ by FCR 7, as given in section 5 of chapter 2). Any useful instantiation of (16a) will also contain a VFORM specification on the mother, and the HFC will ensure that both daughters in (16a) will get instantiated with the *same* value for VFORM (i.e. that on the mother). This predicts the following pattern of grammaticality:[13]

(17) a. She went and bought a parrot.
      b. She goes and buys a parrot.
      c. She has gone and bought a parrot.
      d. She will go and buy a parrot.
      e. *She has gone and buy a parrot.
      f. *She will go and buys a parrot.
      g. *She will go and bought a parrot.
      h. *She went and buy a parrot.

4 Across the board phenomena

As the construction we have just been considering well illustrates, it is not always the case that all the heads in a multiply headed construction are simply extensions of the mother category (although this is certainly the usual case). As we have noted in earlier chapters, SLASH is both a **HEAD** feature and a **FOOT** feature. Since its behavior is therefore constrained by both the HFC and the FFP, it is matter of some interest to determine exactly how it gets distributed in multiply headed constructions.

Consider first the rule in (16a), above. Let us suppose that [SLASH NP] instantiates on the mother. Then the FFP will require the presence of that specification on at least one daughter, and the absence of any distinct SLASH specification on any other daughter. The HFC, on the other hand, will require the presence of [SLASH NP] on *every* daughter on which it can legitimately fit. As it happens, in this construction there is exactly one daughter on which it may legitimately fit, namely the head which is marked [CONJ *and*]. It cannot appear on the lexical head since its appearance there would violate FCR 6 (see section 3 of chapter 2), and result in an illegal extension of the category. Thus all the local trees that we get from instantiating [SLASH NP] on (16a) will have the form shown in (18):

(18)   VP/NP
       V[48]
       VP[CONJ *and*]/NP

Such local trees will permit examples such as that shown in (19).

(19)   What did she go and buy?

But the case we have just been considering is not the normal case. In the common multiply headed constructions, such as those defined by CS^+ and CS^2, no feature specification conflict arises, and the HFC applies in its reduced form shown again as (20), for convenience:

(20) $\phi(C_0)|\textbf{HEAD} = \bigcap\limits_{C_i \in W_H} \phi(C_i)|\textbf{HEAD}$

The applicability of this reduction to the normal case of a multiply headed construction leads to a prediction of some interest. It predicts essentially all the facts discussed by Ross (1967) under the rubric of the Coordinate Structure Constraint and the Across-the-Board exceptions to it.

SLASH is both a **HEAD** feature and a **FOOT** feature. Consider it first as the latter. Neither CS^+ nor CS^2 make any SLASH specification. It follows that any such specification will have to be by instantiation. But if it is by instantiation, then the FFP will require that it be on the mother (and on at least one daughter). Now consider SLASH as a **HEAD** feature. We have seen that the SLASH specification, if it is present at all, must be on the mother. But, by the HFC reduction shown in (20) above, if it is on the mother, then it must be in the intersection of all the daughters, since all the daughters are heads. And, if it is in the intersection of all the daughters, then it must be on every daughter.

Thus we have an account for the contrasts in (21) and (22).

(21)   a.   The doctor who Kim worked for and Sandy relied on died.
       b.   *The doctor who Kim worked for and Sandy relied on Lee died.

(22)   a.   The doctor for whom Kim worked and Sandy ran errands died.
       b.   *The doctor for whom Kim worked and Sandy liked died.

Example (21a) is a coordination of S/NP with S/NP which is permissible under the HFC and FFP, whereas (21b) is an attempt to coordinate an S/NP with an S, and this is not consistent with the HFC and FFP. Example (22a) involves the legitimate coordination of S/PP[*for*] with S/PP[*for*], whereas (22b) is an illegitimate attempt to coordinate an S/PP[*for*] with an S/NP. Thus the facts which motivated Ross's (1967) Coordinate Structure Constraint (CSC) and Williams's (1978) Across-the-Board (ATB) Convention can be seen to follow directly from the FFP and the HFC.

More subtle predictions also follow. Consider the examples in (23) ((23a)–(23c) are from Williams 1978, p. 34, and the relevance of (23d) was pointed out by Paul Hirschbühler).

(23)   a.   I know a man who Bill saw and Mary liked.
       b.   I know a man who saw Bill and liked Mary.
       c.   *I know a man who Bill saw and liked Mary.
       d.   I know a man who Mary likes and hopes will win.

There is some controversy about these facts; MacKaye (1982) has questioned the data (it seems that sentences like (23c) are sometimes encountered in conversation) and criticized the analysis given in Gazdar 1981b, and Anderson (1984) presents some psycholinguistic results suggesting an explanation for the unacceptability of (23c) in terms of processing confusion due to similarity to ungrammatical strings. Under the analysis we have given here, examples (23a), (23b), and (23d) involve the coordination of two S/NPs, two VPs and two VP/NPs, respectively. All three are consistent with the FFP and HFC. But given STM1 and STM2, (23c) can only be viewed as an attempt to coordinate an S/NP with a VP, or to coordinate a VP/NP with a VP, and neither possibility is sanctioned, so our prediction is that it is not just unacceptable but ungrammatical.

Finally, we note that the feature NULL has ~[NULL] as its default, and that STM1 and STM2, like every other metarule, are restricted in their application to the lexical ID rules, which means that none of the following examples can be generated (cf. Gazdar, Pullum, Sag, and Wasow 1982):

(24)   a.   *I wonder who you saw [[*e*] and [*e*]]?
       b.   *I wonder who you saw [[*e*] and [a picture of [*e*]]]?
       c.   *I wonder who you saw [[a picture of [*e*]] and [*e*]]?

In many versions of theories that have full constituents (traces) at gap locations in sentences with unbounded dependencies, the problem of blocking constituents like [*e*] *and* [*e*] or [*e*] *and a picture of* [*e*] has not even been addressed, let alone solved; but such facts do not pose any problem for the account of unbounded dependencies presented in chapter 7.

Notes

1 We include here not only languages like English, Japanese, and Latin in which there are specific morphemes reserved for logical conjoining and disjoining of statements, but also languages like Dyirbal (Dixon 1972; see e.g. p. 154) in which coordinate constructions appear without overt conjunction morphemes like English *and*. Note also that some languages use an overt coordinating morpheme for NPs but not for clauses; Hausa is an example: see Abraham (1941, p. 92), Kraft and Kraft (1973, p. 330). Realization of coordinating morphemes is a highly parochial matter. This chapter concentrates more on matters that we believe are much less parochial, and in many cases probably universal.

2 Gazdar, Pullum, Sag, and Wasow (1982) develop a critique of the modified transformational theory of coordination found in Williams (1978) and defended in Williams (1981), which abandons tree-representable phrase-markers in favor of objects for which he does not supply a coherent interpretation. Another recent transformational account of coordination, in George (1980), seems to us a revealing *reductio ad absurdum* of the approach that derives everything but sentential coordination by deletion from larger paraphrases. Still more recently, Goodall (1983) has proposed a treatment of coordination involving sentence (actually phrase-marker) unions that he claims are not two-dimensionally expressible, and realizes conjuncts linearly in the phonological component (see p. 146: 'the question of how the phonology interprets union of sentences'). Since at least the syntax of constituent order and agreement interact with the linearization of conjuncts (Goodall derives *John drinks beer and Mary whisky* from the same source as *John and Mary drink beer and whisky* as alternative phonological interpretations; see his examples (9a), (9b), (9′)), it is clear that from Goodall's perspective, much of the present book deals with phonological matters. What strikes us most about all these three proposals is the extent to which the formal details and their consequences for other aspects of the grammar simply have not been worked out in a serious way.

3 Our claim entails that certain comparative and equative constructions are coordinate (cf. Pinkham 1983).
   The present theory has its roots in talks given at Stanford and elsewhere by Tom Wasow in 1981. Wasow saw that the counterexamples to the standard claim that conjuncts must be of the same syntactic category would be eliminated if one revised the claim to require merely that each conjunct contain a superset of the featural information present on the mother. This idea was subsequently implemented in the 'Conjunct Realization Principle' of Gazdar, Klein, Pullum, and Sag (1982). Subsequently, Farkas et al. (1983) eliminated this principle in favor of the HFC. This proposal is adopted, and considerably elaborated, in Sag et al. forthcoming, whose analysis we present in essence below. Cf. also Dowty 1982a.

4 Langendoen and Postal (1984) argue that not even a limit to finite length should be assumed.

5 Cf. Gazdar and Pullum 1976 for some related discussion.

6 Since α is a variable ranging over ordered pairs, we use 'α_0' to denote the first element of the pair, and 'α_1' to denote the second member of the pair.

7 As noted in chapter 2, we use X to represent the empty set of feature specifications. Thus X[CONJ *and*] denotes the union of {} and {⟨CONJ, *and*⟩}, which is {⟨CONJ, *and*⟩}.

8 Notice that none of the ID rules induced by the various coordination schemata above is a lexical ID rule, under the definition of the latter given in section 4 of chapter 3. Although the head daughters in the local trees induced by (2), (3), and (4) may be extensions of [SUBCAT] categories, the heads given in the rules are not. Hence no conflict arises between the infinite cardinality of the set of rules denoted by (2) and the finite closure of metarule application discussed in chapter 4. The coordination rules, like 'S → XP, H[− SUBJ]', and every other nonlexical ID rule, are outside the domain of metarules.

9 However, *but* cannot be used to coordinate [+ N, − V] categories (**Kim but Sandy stuttered*), and *both* cannot be used to coordinate full sentences that lack complementizers (**Both Kim sang and Sandy danced*). Such idiosyncratic facts can readily be handled by means of FCRs. We do not dwell on them here because they do not, as far as we can tell, illustrate anything interesting about the principles underlying coordination.

10 Obviously, there are three-conjunct examples that involve a two-conjunct structure with a further constituent conjoined to it, and so on. To some extent semantic and intonational tests can be used to determine which structure we would want to assume for a given string used in a given context. The question we are addressing is how to account for the flat structure which is not grouped hierarchically into pairs.

11 A more serious revision to our account will be necessitated if we attempt to deal with a judgement Ed Keenan has reported to us. We allow for *neither heat, nor frost, nor thunder* (Coleridge, *Christabel*, 1. 424), but not for structures such as *?neither heat, frost, nor thunder*, with three different CONJ values (*neither, nor*, and NIL). Keenan and other informants find these grammatical. Our own judgements are uncertain. The brute force way to describe this kind of constituent, or its non-negative analog *either heat, frost, or thunder*, would be to set up an third schema, CS³, involving a 3-tuple of CONJ values. Notice that the orders required by CS^{LP} are consistent with Keenan's data.

A more radical and potentially much more elegant strategy is to abandon CS² altogether in favor of modifications to CS$^+$, and use LP statements such as

(i)   [CONJ *either*] ≺ [CONJ *either*]

to enforce the unique occurrence of the noniterating conjunct types. We have not worked out such an account in detail, but we think it would be interesting to attempt to do so.

12 From the Monty Python sketch 'The Piranha Brothers'.

13 The analysis just outlined provides no explanation for the marginal acceptability of (i).

(i)   ?She was going and buying a parrot.

Note also that the HFC, *eo ipso*, will not require the two heads of a [VFORM FIN] instantiation of (16a) to share the same tense. So the syntax will permit (ii) and (iii).

> (ii)　?She goes and bought a parrot.
> (iii)　?She went and buys a parrot.

However, the HFC will not allow the structures which legitimate these strings to have a tense specification on the mother VP (since the intersection of $\{\langle \text{PAST}, -\rangle\}$ with $\{\langle \text{PAST}, +\rangle\}$ is the empty set). If tense has to be interpreted semantically at VP or S nodes, rather than at V nodes, as proposed in chapter 10, section 5, then there would be an independently motivated semantic explanation for the anomaly evident in (ii) and (iii).

9

Preliminaries to
semantic interpretation

1 Introduction

The initial appeal of transformational syntax owed much to the
impression that it could explain semantic relatedness between sentence
types. One familiar example is the Passive transformation. The truth-
conditional equivalence of pairs such as

(1)   Kim seduced Lee.
        Lee was seduced by Kim.

was held to follow from the common semantic properties of the respective
'deep structures' of these sentences. Many other transformations were
motivated in part, though often only implicitly, by purporting to account
for semantic facts: Raising, Equi, Topicalization, Conjunction Reduction,
to name but a few.

This situation was changed radically by the advent of Montague's
model-theoretic approach to natural language semantics in the early
1970s. It became clear that many kinds of semantic relatedness between
sentence types could be accounted for in purely semantic terms, without
having recourse to an abstract level of syntactic structure. This line of
attack was particularly prominent in the fragments developed by
Thomason (1976 a,b). Thomason argued strongly that the systematic use
of meaning postulates could lead to 'striking simplifications in the syntax'.
Examples of this strategy will be discussed later in the chapter. The
development of restrictive theories of syntax such as generalized phrase
structure grammar have to a large extent been made possible by a division
of labor in which the semantic component of the grammar does substantial work in capturing significant generalizations. The main thrust of this
and the next chapter is to show in more detail how syntax and semantics
interact in our grammar.

Montague semantics has achieved the status of a paradigm within truth-conditional approaches to natural language semantics. Montague's (1974) contention that natural languages are susceptible to the same kind of semantic analysis as artificial languages has proved to be enormously influential among linguists, and the theoretical foundation established by Montague has been successfully extended to wider and wider fragments of natural language. This success has been marked by the appearance of an excellent textbook, Dowty, Wall and Peters 1981. There is now a body of shared assumptions about what constitutes the central data of natural language semantics, about the level of mathematical precision which is appropriate, and even about certain analyses. Yet it is also widely held that Montagovian orthodoxy is seriously inadequate in its treatment of certain natural language phenomena, most notably propositional attitudes and anaphora. Montague semantics has also been attacked on both philosophical and psychological grounds for its excessively elaborate ontology. Some important recent innovations are situation semantics (Barwise and Perry 1983), Boolean semantics (Keenan and Faltz 1978, forthcoming) and discourse representation semantics (Kamp 1981). These new approaches have proved capable of shedding new light on old problems and of bringing into focus fresh bodies of data.

We shall adopt a somewhat conservative stance *vis-à-vis* such recent theoretical developments. The semantic analyses we will develop are all couched within the framework of Montague's possible world semantics. One reason is that we are concerned with the close interaction between syntactic and semantic rules. It still seems to us that the most precise and detailed analysis of syntax/semantics interaction are those which have been developed within extended Montague grammar. The second reason follows from the paradigm status of Montague semantics. We consider it important that the reader should grasp, at least in outline, how the task of capturing linguistic generalizations is divided between syntax and semantics in generalized phrase structure grammar. Although formal semantics is often considered 'difficult' by linguists, knowledge about the techniques and formalisms of Montague semantics is becoming more widely diffused, and there now exist introductory texts which render the subject reasonably accessible to even those students who lack a training in mathematics or formal logic. In the subsequent exposition, we shall in fact assume that the reader has worked through Dowty, Wall and Peters 1981. In chapter 10, we shall present a fairly detailed treatment of the compositional semantics of most of the syntactic constructions discussed in the earlier chapters of this book. The present chapter has the goal of explaining and motivating certain modifications of Montague semantics which play a crucial role in our theory.

2   Types

One of the fundamental tasks of a semantic theory for a language is to recursively determine the semantic interpretation of well-formed expressions of the language. In a model-theoretic semantics of the sort developed by Montague, this can be broken down into two smaller tasks:

(i)   specifying the possible denotations of each syntactically determined category of expression, and

(ii) specifying the manner in which the denotations of complex expressions are produced as a function of the denotations of their constituents.

For a simple example, consider how we might determine the interpretation of the following (analyzed) expression:

(2) $[_S[_{NP}$ Kim$]$ $[_{VP}$ walks$]]$

We assume that this will receive an interpretation relative to a model for English. According to (i), we have to decide what kinds of things can be denoted by Ss, NPs and VPs. Let us assume that there is a function *Den* such that whenever a is a syntactic category, *Den*(a) is the set of possible denotations in the model which are associated with expression of category a. Thus, the domain of *Den* is the set of categories of the grammar. The range of *Den* is the collection of set-theoretic structures which are provided by the model. For present purposes, it does not matter too much how we define *Den*(NP) and *Den*(S). We shall take *Den*(S) to be the set $\{0, 1\}$ of truth values. *Den*(NP) will be the set of characteristic functions of sets of sets of individuals. Since *Kim* is of category NP, this means that *Kim* will denote a member of *Den*(NP). In fact, given any world w, it will always be the characteristic function of the set containing every set to which Kim belongs in w.

The problem of determining *Den*(VP) cannot be approached without considering the requirement (ii) mentioned above. In this particular case, we need to specify how the denotation of an NP combines with the denotation of a VP to produce an S-denotation. Following Montague, we will restrict our attention to only one mode of combination, namely function–argument application. Then two options are open to us: either *Den*(NP) is applied as a function to *Den*(VP), or else *Den*(VP) is applied as a function to *Den*(NP).[1] Although the first option is the one that is traditionally adopted in Montague semantics, we shall take the second (for further discussion, see section 3 below). This means that the set of denotations associated with VPs is completely determined by those of S and NP: it is the set of functions from *Den*(NP) to *Den*(S). Consequently,

Den(VP) will be the set of all functions from characteristic functions of sets of sets of individuals to truth values.

While it is feasible to proceed directly from syntactic categories to sets of possible denotations, as we have just done, Montague found it more convenient to proceed indirectly, through the mediation of an artificial language, Intensional Logic (henceforth IL). This strategy, of translating expressions of natural language into a logical calculus of some kind, is familiar to linguists. The aspect of Montague's approach which requires emphasizing is that translation into IL is not itself the primary goal of the semantics. Rather, it is a useful but dispensable aid to carrying out the tasks (i) and (ii) which we presented above. In line with this theoretical orientation, we adopt the position that the expressions of IL which serve as translations of English expressions do not constitute a level of representation in the grammar. On the other hand, we will later claim that the semantic properties associated with syntactic categories – such as the fact that VPs denote functions from *Den*(NP) to *Den*(S) – do have grammatical significance. While these semantic properties are properly expressed in terms of the model theory, they can also be represented by IL-translations, since the relation between IL and the model-theoretical interpretation is designed to be transparent. In particular, the *semantic types* of IL will be exploited as a means of representing the semantic role of the various syntactic categories in the grammar.

In Montague's approach, the types of IL are in fact the syntactic categories of the logical language. It may be helpful at this point if we remind the reader of some of Montague's definitions. The formation rules of IL typically have the following form:

(3)   If α is of type a and β is of type b, then $F_i(\alpha, \beta)$ is of type c.

That is to say, the syntactic rules of IL conform to the general pattern of such rules as elaborated by Montague in his UG ('Universal Grammar' in Montague 1974): given input expressions of specified categories, an output expression of some further specified category is produced when α and β are combined by the syntactic operation F_i.

The basic types of IL are e and t, and complex types are defined inductively:

(4)   If a is any type then so is $\langle s, a \rangle$
        If a and b are any types, then so is $\langle a, b \rangle$.

The most general and, for our purposes, the most important syntactic rule of IL is the following:

(5)   If α is of type $\langle b, a \rangle$, and β is of type b, then $\alpha(\beta)$ is of type a.

In this case, the operation F_i is simply functional application. To illustrate (5), let us use x, y, z as individual variables of IL: they will be of type e. We will generally use P and Q to stand for one-place predicate variables: they are of type $\langle e, t \rangle$. So, according to (5), the expression of $P(x)$ is of type t.

We mentioned earlier that the range of *Den* was determined by the relevant class of models for a language. Rather than talk of sets of possible denotations in this context, we shall use the term *domains* of the model. Like the types of IL, these too are defined inductively. The basic domains are E (the set of entities), $\{0, 1\}$ (the set of truth values), and W (the set of possible worlds). Complex domains are defined as follows (where for any sets X and Y, X^Y denotes the set of all functions from Y to X):

(6)   If X is a domain, then X^W is a domain.
       If X and Y are domains, then X^Y is a domain.

Let D be a function from types to domains, defined as follows:[2]

(7) $D_e = E$
       $D_t = \{0, 1\}$
       For any type a, $D_{\langle s, a \rangle} = D_a{}^W$
       For any types a and b, $D_{\langle a, b \rangle} = D_b{}^{D_a}$

Once we know the type of an expression in IL, we know what kind of thing it will denote. So, for example, an expression of type e has E as its range of possible denotations. This means that it will denote some object in E, that is, an entity. An expression of type $\langle e, t \rangle$ will denote a member of the domain $D_t{}^{D_e} = \{0, 1\}^E$, that is, a function from entities to truth values.

Suppose now that *TYP* is a function whose domain is the set of syntactic categories, and such that whenever X is a category, $TYP(X)$ is a type of IL. The rules for translating expressions of English into IL will operate in such a way that if α is an expression of category X, then the translation of α, which we will refer to as α', will be an IL expression whose type is $TYP(X)$. We have already seen that D will map $TYP(X)$ into a domain of the model. Consequently the composition of D with TYP, $D \circ TYP$,[3] is a function from the set of categories into the set of semantic domains. That is, for any category X, $D \circ TYP(X)$ is the set of possible denotations associated with expression of category X. It should be obvious now that the function *Den* which we introduced earlier is equivalent to $D \circ TYP$. Given this apparatus, once we know the type which is assigned to a given category X, we also know what kind of thing can be denoted by an arbitrary expression of that category. In other words, the type associated with X provides information about certain semantic properties of X, since it gives a concise coding in function–argument terms of the combinatorial potential of Xs. As an illustration, recall that we claimed that *Den*(VP) was the set of functions from *Den*(NP) to *Den*(S). This is equivalent to saying that $D \circ TYP$(VP) is $D \circ TYP(\text{S})^{D \circ TYP(\text{NP})}$. Working backwards, we see that TYP(VP) must be

$\langle TYP(\text{NP}),\ TYP(\text{S})\rangle$. Although, strictly speaking, categories of English do not have types in the same way that expression of IL do, our appeal to the type-theoretical properties of categories will be so frequent that we will talk of 'the type of a category X' as a shorthand for 'the type associated with X by TYP'.

The categorial syntax adopted by Montague in *PTQ* ('The proper treatment of quantification in ordinary English', in Montague 1974) allowed the set of categories to be defined by rules of the following kind:

(8) e and t are categories.

   If A and B are categories, then $A/_nB$ is a category (for $n \geq 1$).

This in turn allowed Montague to define TYP as a homomorphism from his syntactic categories into types in the following manner:

(9) $TYP(e) = e$

   $TYP(t) = t$

   $TYP(A/_nB) = \langle\langle s,\ TYP(B)\rangle,\ TYP(A)\rangle$

The advantage of this approach is that the structural complexity of the syntactic categories corresponds in a uniform fashion to the functional complexity of the associated denotation domain. As the reader will be well aware, syntactic categories are complex objects in our theory, despite the fact that we do not use a categorial syntax. However, this complexity does not mirror their semantic structure: on our approach, TYP is not a homomorphism from the set of categories into the types of IL. By and large, the values of TYP must be simply listed, and this stands in contrast to the simple mapping (9) given by Montague.

In an obvious sense, this renders our grammar less general. The postulation of a homomorphism from categories into denotations amounts, in practice, to the claim that there are no autonomous syntactic generalizations about categories. Generalizations about syntactic categories turn out to be generalizations about the associated denotation sets.[4]

While this is certainly an interesting claim, we are skeptical about the possibility of sustaining it. As far as we are aware, no pure categorial grammar has been developed for a fragment that is as complex and detailed as the one studied here. It is difficult to make adequately fine-grained distinctions in a grammar which is restricted to, in effect, one kind of feature in its categories; i.e. the categorial 'slash'. It is also the case that certain of the claims made in categorial syntax can still be expressed in generalized phrase structure grammar (see, for example, the discussion of grammatical relations and control in subsequent sections). This is possible because the function–argument relations which are encoded in categorial categories can be restated in terms of the semantic types which are associated with the corresponding categories in a PSG. On the other hand, it also seems to be true that categorial syntax allows the succinct expression of properties of categories that are not easily captured in our current theory of features. Work by Shieber et al. (1983) and Pollard (1984) suggests that a suitably enriched categorial syntax might be seen as a natural progression from our current theory of grammar.[5]

3   Nonlexical type assignments

The lexical types of the grammar are those types which are assigned by *TYP* to lexical categories. We shall temporarily ignore these, and turn our attention first to nonlexical types, the types assigned to categories of bar level 1 or more. We will go through the major categories of the grammar, and discuss the types with which they are associated, pointing out the way in which our approach is related to previous work in Montague semantics. Following PTQ, we shall use primed variants of English words to stand for nonlogical constants of IL.

Noun phrases

In PTQ, a phrase like *some unicorn* receives the following sort of translation:

(10) $\lambda P \exists x[\textbf{unicorn}' (x) \wedge P\{x\}]$

The variable x is here taken to be of type $\langle s, e \rangle$, while P is a variable of type $\langle s, \langle \langle s, e \rangle, t \rangle \rangle$, i.e. it ranges over properties of individual concepts. The type of the whole phrase is $\langle \langle s, \langle \langle s, e \rangle, t \rangle \rangle, t \rangle$. We shall follow the lead of numerous writers (cf. Dowty, Wall and Peters 1981) in excluding individual concepts from the semantics. Consequently, as we mentioned before, we use x, y, z as variables of type e, ranging over individuals. In addition, Thomason (1976b) has argued that no useful purpose is served by making noun phrases denote sets of properties of individuals – it is sufficient if they denote sets of sets of individuals. Hence, we let the variable P in (10) be of type $\langle e, t \rangle$ (rendering the brace notation redundant in this case). On the other hand, we shall slightly complicate the denotation of NPs so that they are always intensional. The motive for this is uniformity: at least some compositional rules require functions to apply to the intensions of NP arguments, and we do not wish to specify such rules case by case. As a result of these modifications, our translation of *some unicorn* is equivalent to (11a), and its type is (11b).

(11)   a. $^{\wedge}\lambda P \exists x[\textbf{unicorn}' (x) \wedge P(x)]$
        b. $\langle s, \langle \langle e, t \rangle, t \rangle \rangle = TYP(\text{NP})$

Modulo the abandonment of individual concepts, we will treat N¹s in the same way as CNs in PTQ: they will be of type $\langle e, t \rangle$. Consequently, determiners will be of type $\langle TYP(\text{N1}), TYP(\text{NP}) \rangle = \langle \langle e, t \rangle, \langle s, \langle \langle e, t \rangle, t \rangle \rangle \rangle$.

Verb phrases

We pointed out earlier that we treat VPs as denoting functions from *Den*(NP) to *Den*(S).[6] This contrasts with PTQ, where NPs denote functions from *Den*(VP) to truth values. The VP-as-functor analysis is adopted by Montague in UG, and is also advocated by Thomason (1976b), Keenan and Faltz (1978) and Bach (1980b.) Within the syntactic framework of categorial grammar, such an analysis is implemented by modifying the syntactic category of VP – it means that VP is analyzed as *t*/NP (the category of functions from VP denotations to things of type *t*). In our framework, the syntactic category VP is not affected, but we have to specify the type of VP to be $\langle \langle s, \langle \langle e, t \rangle, t \rangle \rangle, \langle s, t \rangle \rangle$. As we will often have occasion to refer to types of this complicated kind, it is useful to have an abbreviatory notation. We shall adopt the convention that a category label *X* denotes $TYP(X)$ when it occurs in an unambiguous context. So, for example, instead of writing the type of VP as $\langle \langle s, \langle \langle e, t \rangle, t \rangle \rangle, \langle s, t \rangle \rangle = \langle TYP(\text{NP}), TYP(\text{S}) \rangle$, we shall simply represent it as $\langle \text{NP}, \text{S} \rangle$. And, indeed, instead of writing $\langle s, \langle \langle e, t \rangle, t \rangle \rangle$ we shall simply write NP.

A number of arguments can be advanced for treating VPs as functors on NPs. We shall outline the two which are most relevant to our concerns.

(i) *Intensionality of subject position.*[7] Let us assume, temporarily, that NPs are functors on VPs. A PTQ-style analysis tree for NP VP structures will look like (12a). (12b) is the associated semantic tree.[8]

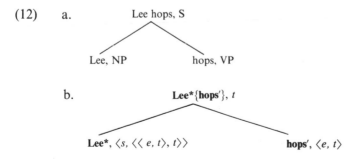

(12) a.   Lee hops, S
          Lee, NP   hops, VP

     b.   **Lee*{hops′}**, *t*
        Lee*, $\langle s, \langle \langle e, t \rangle, t \rangle \rangle$ **hops′**, $\langle e, t \rangle$

Suppose now that head of the VP is a modal like *may, must,* or a tense auxiliary like *have, will,* or a raising verb like *seem, tend.* It is reasonable to suppose that all these cases should be treated as in (12), with a single syntactic and semantic rule. In other words, the syntax and the compositional semantics should be formulated in a way which obviates having to specify the identity of the head of the VP. It is also plausible to assume that the auxiliaries and raising verbs listed above play the semantic role of propositional operators. These assumptions suggest that a sentence like (13) should have a semantic analysis like (14):[9]

(13)   Lee may hop.

(14)

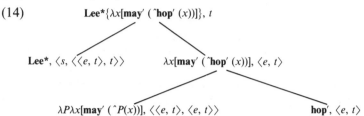

The top line in (14) is logically equivalent to (15). (We make the standard assumption that individual constants like **Lee′** are interpreted as rigid designators).

(15)   **may′ (ˆhop′ (Lee′))**

However, if the subject NP is quantified, a semantic problem arises. For example, all the following examples will be predicted to carry existential entailments:

(16)   A solution may turn up.
        An infant savior will be born.
        A unicorn seems to be in the garden.

In fact, all the above sentences have 'non-specific' readings. Given standard assumptions in Montague semantics, this requires that the subject NP be assigned narrower scope than the first element in the VP. That is, a uniform treatment along the lines of (12) will only give rise to translations like those in (17a). Yet we also want to allow translations like those in (17b):

(17)   a. $\exists x[\textbf{solution}'\ (x) \land \textbf{may}'\ (ˆ\textbf{turn-up}'\ (x))]$
              $\exists x[\textbf{infant}'\ (x) \land \textbf{savior}'\ (x) \land \textbf{will}'\ (ˆ\textbf{be-born}'\ (x))]$
              $\exists x[\textbf{unicorn}'\ (x) \land \textbf{seem}'\ (ˆ\textbf{be-in-the-garden}'\ (x))]$
        b. $\textbf{may}'\ (ˆ\exists x[\textbf{solution}'\ (x) \land \textbf{turn-up}'\ (x)])$
              $\textbf{will}'\ (ˆ\exists x[\textbf{infant}'\ (x) \land \textbf{savior}'\ (x) \land \textbf{be-born}'\ (x)])$
              $\textbf{seem}'\ (ˆ\exists x[\textbf{unicorn}'\ (x) \land \textbf{be-in-the-garden}'\ (x)])$

PTQ solves the semantic problem by abandoning the principle that there should be a uniform syntactic and semantic analysis for NP–VP structures: each tense auxiliary requires a distinct syntactic and semantic rule. Another alternative is to abandon the idea that NPs are functors on VPs.

Suppose, then, that VPs are functors on NPs. The semantic tree in (12) will now look like this:

(18)

$$\text{hop}'\ (\text{Lee*}),\ S$$

hop', $\langle$NP, S$\rangle$ Lee*, NP

The interpretation of an auxiliary such as *may* can be given as (19). Here $\mathscr{P}$ is a variable over *Den*(NP), i.e. it is of type $\langle s, \langle\langle e, t\rangle, t\rangle\rangle$, while V is a variable over *Den*(VP), i.e. it is of type $\langle$NP, S$\rangle$. Since we have chosen to treat NP as an intensional type, we have ended up by claiming that *may* is intensional in subject position.

(19) $\lambda V\lambda\mathscr{P}\ [\textbf{may}'\ (V(\mathscr{P}))]$

This will allow us to build up translations in the following manner:

(20)

$$\textbf{may}\ (\textbf{turn-up}'\ (\hat{}\lambda P\exists x[\textbf{solution}'\ (x)\ \wedge\ P(x)])),\ S$$

$\lambda\mathscr{P}[\textbf{may}'\ (\textbf{turn-up}'\ (\mathscr{P}))],\ \langle$NP, S$\rangle$ $\hat{}\lambda P\exists x[\textbf{solution}'\ (x)\ \wedge\ P(x)],$ NP

$\lambda\ V\lambda\mathscr{P}[\textbf{may}'\ (V(\mathscr{P}))],\ \langle$VP, VP$\rangle$ turn-up', VP

Of course, the top line of (20) is still not quite the same as (17b), since the NP in the former is also within the scope of the VP *turn up*. However, in this case we can apply a meaning postulate which guarantees that verbs like *turn up* are extensional in subject position (cf. Thomason (1976a, p. 48)):

(21) $\forall\mathscr{P}\square[\textbf{turn-up}'\ (\mathscr{P})\ \leftrightarrow\ \mathscr{P}\{\textbf{turn-up}\dagger\}]$

That is, while **turn-up**' is a constant of type $\langle$NP, S$\rangle$, it can be reduced to a first-order constant **turn-up**† of type $\langle e, t\rangle$. Hence the top line of (20) is rendered equivalent to (22).

(22) $\textbf{may}'\ (\hat{}\exists x[\textbf{solution}'\ (x)\ \wedge\ \textbf{turn-up}\dagger(x)])$

(ii) *Generalization across verb types.*[10] If VPs are of type $\langle e, t\rangle$, then intransitive verbs will also be of that type. However, transitive verbs are assumed to be of type $\langle$NP, $\langle e, t\rangle\rangle$, and thus seem to be functions with quite a different domain. This runs counter to the traditional view of linguists and logicians that the essential difference between these two kinds of verbs lies in the number of NP arguments they allow. Keenan has also argued that morphological agreement patterns in natural language follow a simple semantic principle. Expressed rather crudely, the principle is that functors may agree with their arguments.[11] It is well known that transitive verbs in numerous languages agree with their direct objects, and of course subject–verb agreement is a wide-spread phenomenon. But this semantic generalization can only be stated if VPs are treated as functions on their subjects.

More generally, one would like the semantic analysis of any verb which allows NP arguments in its subcategorization frame to reflect the fact that such a verb will typically also allow the same kind of argument in subject position. Various constructions such as passive, raising, and equi modify the argument structure of verbs of different polyadicity. If there is no uniform correspondence between the category of a syntactic argument required by a verb (i.e. NP in this case) and the kind of semantic argument required by the function which the verb denotes, then it becomes extremely difficult to give any uniform statement of the semantic operations across the different types of verbs. (Some of the issues involved here should become clearer when we discuss the interpretation of these below.)

Adjective phrases

It is plausible to distinguish between two sorts of AP, according to whether they occur in predicate position or in prenominal position, assigning them the categories AP[+PRD] and AP[−PRD] respectively. There is a corresponding distinction in semantic type. As the name suggests, AP[+PRD]s are interpreted as predicates, and consequently denote functions into the truth values $\{0, 1\}$. This still leaves us with a choice. One possibility is to assimilate them to N¹s by assigning them type $\langle e, t \rangle$. Since the VP in a copular sentence will have the same type as other VPs, we will require the copula itself to raise the type of AP[+PRD]s from $\langle e, t \rangle$ to $\langle NP, S \rangle$. The alternative is to treat AP[+PRD]s like VPs, as having type $\langle NP, S \rangle$. The second option is the one which we shall adopt. In English, AP[+PRD]s resemble VPs most closely in the way they enter into control and agreement patterns. Moreover, crosslinguistic considerations suggest that predicate APs are grammatically closer to VPs. In languages like Japanese and Akan, the two categories are not distinguished. Second, even where a grammatical distinction is drawn, the copula is omitted before predicate APs in many languages. This would be rather surprising if the copula were required to raise the type of AP[+PRD]s in the manner suggested above.

The class of expressions that can occur as prenominal modifiers is wider and more heterogeneous than the AP[+PRD]s. Moreover, a compositional semantics cannot interpret them as predicates in any straightforward or general fashion. We shall analyze them in a way that has become standard in recent years, namely as functions from N¹ intensions to N¹ extensions. Thus the type of AP[−PRD] is $\langle \langle s, N^1 \rangle, N^1 \rangle$. Though we are well aware that the grammar should offer some account of the complex semantic relationships which hold between the two sorts of AP, we shall not attempt to deal with this issue here.

Prepositional phrases

Semantic and syntactic considerations combine to suggest that prepositional phrases have to be divided into subcategories. To begin with, we must isolate PPs which are marked with terminal symbol features like [PFORM *to*] and [PFORM *by*] and which act semantically as NP arguments of a verb. This subcategory will be identified as PP[PFORM]. Since they are semantically interchangeable with ordinary NP arguments, we set $TYP(\text{PP[PFORM]}) = TYP(\text{NP})$. One consequence of this is that, for example, the preposition *to* which occurs as head of a PP[PFORM *to*] will not have the semantic content of the homophonous item *to* which occurs in $\sim$[PFORM] directional PPs. In fact, it will denote the identity function on *Den*(NP), and will be of type $\langle \text{NP}, \text{NP} \rangle$.

The $\sim$[PFORM] PPs bifurcate in a manner which is reminiscent of APs. First, there is the class of phrases which act as adverbial modifiers. Although there are certain problems involved here, we shall set the type of this subcategory to be $\langle \text{VP}, \text{VP} \rangle$ (cf. Dowty 1979b, Keenan and Faltz 1978). The second class consists of those phrases which occur in postnominal modifiers, i.e. in the same position as relative clauses and certain APs. These will have type $\langle \text{NP}, \text{S} \rangle$. Again, there numerous problems in interrelating the interpretation of these different subclasses of PPs which we cannot enter into here. However, we briefly touch on the topic of postnominal modifiers in chapter 10.

By way of conclusion, in (23) we summarize the type assignments that we have arrived at so far.

(23)   Nonlexical Type Assignments

$TYP(\text{S})$	$= \langle s, t \rangle$		
$TYP(\text{NP})$	$= \langle s, \langle \langle e, t \rangle, t \rangle \rangle$		
$TYP(\text{N}^1)$	$= \langle e, t \rangle$		
$TYP(\text{Det})$	$= \langle \text{N}^1, \text{NP} \rangle$		
$TYP(\text{VP})$	$= \langle \text{NP}, \text{S} \rangle$		
$TYP(\text{AP[+PRD]})$	$= TYP(\text{A1[+PRD]})$	$= \langle \text{NP}, \text{S} \rangle$	
$TYP(\text{AP[-PRD]})$	$= TYP(\text{A1[-PRD]})$	$= \langle \langle s, \text{N}^1 \rangle, \text{N}^1 \rangle$	
$TYP(\text{PP[PFORM]})$	$= TYP(\text{P1[PFORM]})$	$= TYP(\text{NP})$	
$TYP(\text{PP[}\sim\text{PFORM]})$	$= TYP(\text{P1[}\sim\text{PFORM]})$	$= \langle \text{VP}, \text{VP} \rangle$	

One final comment remains to be made. It has generally been assumed that the grammar will only assign one semantic type to each syntactic category. We have already slightly relaxed this condition by letting the type assignment be sensitive to minor feature distinctions like $[\pm PRD]$, and we also allow some indeterminism in the assignment of types to lexical categories, as we show in the following chapter. Recent work by Partee (1984), Partee and Rooth (1983), and Rooth and Partee (1982) suggests that there may be justification for extending 'type ambiguity' much more radically. Although we shall not explore this option here, it is worth observing that such an approach could be integrated very readily into the mechanism for inducing semantic interpretations that we present in chapter 10.

4   Lexical type assignments

We saw before that the type associated with VP was determined by types associated with NP and S, once it had been decided that *Den*(VP) applied as a function to *Den*(NP), yielding *Den*(S) as value. In a similar manner, the type of a lexical head C_i will depend on the type of its complements and the type of its mother category C_0. The reason is that we always interpret a lexical head as denoting a function which takes the denotations of its complements as arguments. Its value for those arguments will be a member of *Den*(C_0). Consider for example the VP expansion rule below:

(24)   VP → H, NP

(SUBCAT values and other feature details are omitted as an expository simplification.) According to what we have just said, there is only one possible type that can be assigned to H, namely

(25)   ⟨NP, VP⟩

That is to say, given this type, H must denote a function which takes a *Den*(NP) as argument, and yields a *Den*(VP) as value. However, although the type of a lexical head will always depend on the types of its sisters and mother, it is not always unambiguously determined by them. This point can be illustrated with respect to a rule like the following:

(26)   VP → H, NP, S

There are two possible types that could be assigned to H in this rule:

(27)   ⟨NP, ⟨S, VP⟩⟩
         ⟨S, ⟨NP, VP⟩⟩

That is to say, *Den*(H) will be a set of functions of which some combine first with a *Den*(NP) and then with a *Den*(S), and others combine first with a *Den*(S) and then with a *Den*(NP). The same issue will arise when we consider any expansion rule in which the lexical head takes more than one complement.

It might seem at first that this is a matter of little consequence, but as we shall see later in the chapter, the order in which a function combines with its arguments plays a fundamental role in our treatment of both grammatical relations and of control. In the case of a rule like (26), therefore, the grammar must provide some means of choosing between the two possible types. This point will be further discussed in the next section.

5 Grammatical relations

The recent history of generative grammar has been marked by persistent attempts to find an appropriate characterization of grammatical relations. It has frequently been pointed out that the structural definition of subject and direct object in Chomsky 1965 is incapable of providing a universal account of these notions, assuming one adheres to a reasonably concrete syntax. One proposal has been to take grammatical relations as theoretical primitives. Different implementations of this idea can be found in relational grammar (Perlmutter 1983, 1984) and lexical-functional grammar (Bresnan 1982b). Another line of attack is to define grammatical relations in terms of something other than phrase marker configurations. This is the approach we shall adopt, following Dowty (1982b, 1982c).

Dowty's proposals are couched within the framework of Montague's theory of syntax and semantics. He offers the following 'principle of grammatical relations' (1982b, p. 84):

a verb that ultimately takes *n* arguments is always treated as combining by a syntactic rule with exactly one argument to produce a phrase of the same category as a verb of $n - 1$ arguments.

In order to illustrate this principle, we will temporarily adopt a notation suggested by Bartsch (1976), Keenan (1980) and Dowty (1982c) which encodes into verbal categories the number of arguments that phrases of that category can combine with. (A 'verbal category' here means the same as a projection of V in X-bar theory.) In general, we take V_n to be the category of a verb phrase which combines with *n* arguments. That is, V_2 is the category of transitive verb phrases, V_1 is the category of intransitive verb phrases, while V_0 is the category of sentences. By Dowty's principle, a V_1 will combine with an argument to produce a V_0. The analysis tree below shows how such phrases would be built up.

(28)

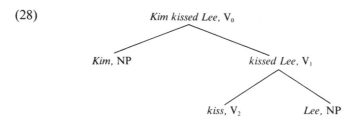

Dowty points out that Montague separated syntactic rules into three components: (i) the categories of expressions which form the input to the rule, (ii) the categories of output expression of the rule, and (iii) the syntactic operation which combines the output expressions to form the output expression. This tripartite division is illustrated in the following two rules:

(29)   S1: $\langle F_1, \langle V_1, \text{NP} \rangle, V_0 \rangle$ [Subject–Predicate Rule]
          S2: $\langle F_2, \langle V_2, \text{NP} \rangle, V_1 \rangle$ [Verb–DO Rule]

S1 says that some operation F_1 combines a V_1 and an NP to make a V_0, while S2 says that some operation F_2 combines a V_2 with an NP to make a V_1. Following the general pattern of Montague grammar, each of these syntactic rules will have a corresponding semantic rule. A V_n will always be of type $\langle \text{NP}_1, \langle \ldots \langle \text{NP}_n, t \rangle \ldots \rangle \rangle$. The required semantic rules will thus both be instances of the following schema:

(30)   If a is a V_n, β is an NP, and a, β translate into a', β' respectively, then $F_i(a, \beta)$ translates into $a'(\beta')$.

Dowty hypothesizes that, up to identity of the operations, the rules in (29) are universal across natural languages. That is, all languages will have rules S1 and S2 (plus the corresponding semantic rules), and they will only differ according to the nature of the operation. In English F_1 and F_2 might be the following concatenation operations (ignoring the precise realization of agreement and case marking):

$$F_1(a, \beta) = \beta^\frown a$$
$$F_2(a, \beta) = a^\frown \beta$$

This would lead to an analysis tree like that in (28). By contrast, the operations in a VSO language like Welsh would be something like this:

$$F_1(a, \beta) = \text{the result of inserting } \beta \text{ after the head of } a$$
$$F_2(a, \beta) = \beta^\frown a$$

The following tree illustrates:

(31) 'read   Siôn the book'

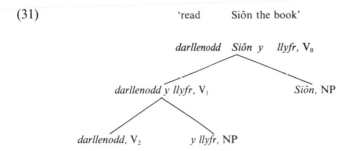

One major advantage of this approach, according to Dowty, is that it allows a universal definition of grammatical relations:

> we will define any term phrase in any language that is combined with [a V_1] via S1 as a subject term, and any term phrase that is combined with [a V_2] via S2 as a direct object ... (1982b, p. 87)

Indirect objects can also be dealt with in a similar manner, provided that we slightly complicate the formulation of the operation F_2 in rule S2. Consider, for example, the sentence (32):

(32)   Lee gave the cabbage to Jody.

Since *the cabbage* is the direct object of *give*, we want it to combine with a V_2 by means of S2 to produce a V_1, *give the cabbage to Jody*. This means that the required V_2 is *give to Jody*, and the operation F_2 must have the effect of inserting the term *the cabbage* immediately after the head verb in this V_2. Consequently, the rule for indirect objects should be of the following form:[12]

(33)   S3: $\langle F_3, \langle V_3, PP[PFORM\ to]\rangle, V_2\rangle$ [Verb–IO rule]
       $F_3(\alpha, \beta)$ = the result of inserting β after the head of α

The analysis tree in (34) illustrates:

(34)   *Lee gave the cabbage to Jody*, V_0

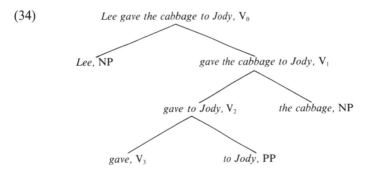

As noted earlier, every syntactic rule which combines an expression α of category V_n with a term β to form an expression category V_{n-1} will have a corresponding semantic translation rule in which α', the translation of α, is applied as a functor to β', the translation of β. Thus, we can construct a semantic analysis tree which parallels (34).

(35)

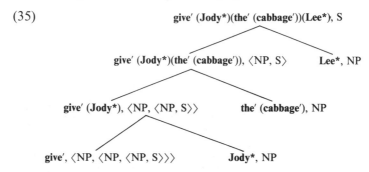

The order of the argument expressions in the final translation accurately reflects the order in which the corresponding terms were incorporated into the syntactic analysis tree (35).

Given the theory of phrase structure syntax advanced in this book, it is not possible for us to adopt Dowty's principle (quoted above) as it stands.

The syntactic operation invoked in S3 has no phrase structure analog, and consequently, it is not possible to adhere to the policy of 'one argument at a time'. Another way of putting it is that our syntactic framework does not allow us to abstract away from the details of the operation involved in particular syntactic rules, and thus we cannot attempt to give a language universal definition of such things as a 'Subject–Predicate Rule'. Nevertheless, it is still possible for us to formulate a universal characterization of grammatical relations which is very close to that suggested by Dowty. Dowty's approach makes reference to the order in which terms are incorporated in the analysis tree. That is, his account of grammatical relations could be expressed in the following manner:

(36)   (i)   The subject is that term which combines last of all with a verbal phrase to make a sentence.
        (ii) The direct object is that term which combines with the verbal phrase immediately before the subject term.
        (iii) The indirect object is that term which combines with the verbal phrase immediately before the direct object term.

As we noted above, the order in which terms are syntactically combined is reflected in the function–argument structure of the corresponding translation rule. This suggests that a semantic version of (36) can be formulated. In order to do so, we must first introduce some definitions.

(37)   NP Argument Position
a.   Suppose that α and β are IL-expressions of type $\langle a_n, \langle \ldots \langle a_1, t \rangle \ldots \rangle \rangle$ and a_n respectively. Then β is the n-argument in $\alpha(\beta)$.

This yields the following results:

(38)   **Jody*** is the 3-argument in **give′ (Jody*)**
the′ (cabbage′) is the 2-argument in **give′ (Jody*)(the′ (cabbage′))**
Lee* is the 1-argument in **give′ (Jody*)(the′ (cabbage′))(Lee*)**

It will be useful to generalize definition (37) to those cases where the argument in question is not the last argument of the whole expression. Thus, we supplement (37) as follows.

(39)   If β is the n-argument in $\alpha(\beta)$, where α and β are as in (37), and $\gamma_1, \ldots, \gamma_m$ are compatible arguments, then β is the n-argument in $\alpha(\beta)(\gamma_1) \ldots (\gamma_m)$.

From (39) we get the result that in an IL-expression like **give′ (Jody*) (the′ (cabbage′))**, the translation we will derive for the verb-phrase *gives the cabbage to Jody*, **Jody*** is the 3-argument and **the′ (cabbage′)** is the 2-argument. The same is true in **give′ (Jody*) (the′ (cabbage))(Lee*)**, which is the IL-translation of the sentence *Lee gives the cabbage to Jody*.

On the basis of the above definitions, we could construct a characterization of the grammatical relations created by an ID-rule in terms of the argument position of constituents in the corresponding interpreted structure. The direct object of a VP would be any NP[−PRD] constituent whose translation is the 2-argument in the VP's translation; the indirect object of a VP would be any NP or PP[*to*] whose translation is the 3-argument in the VP's translation.

Note that the notion '1-argument of an S-translation' subsumes the translations of both subjects and topics ('topicalized' constituents) and hence provides a basis for the description of languages where both kinds of elements participate in syntactic processes such as agreement. This entails a slightly more complex definition of the notion 'subject of a sentence'. For our purposes, however, the notion 'n-argument' provides a sufficient basis for the discussion of the interaction between grammatical relations and linear precedence in the following chapter.

6 Obligatory control

The analysis of control and complementation which we will develop in the next chapter owes much to previous work within Montague semantics. At this point, we take the opportunity to sketch some of the relevant background assumptions.

It will be helpful to compare Montague's treatment of control and complementation with that usually adopted in transformational frameworks. There are two aspects to the relation of control, a syntactic one and a semantic one. The syntactic aspect involves agreement between the controlling NP and some subconstituent of the complement. So, for example, the controller in (40) is the NP *they*, and the reflexive in the complement must agree with the controller:

(40)   They tried to see themselves/*itself/*yourselves

The semantic side of control involves the intuition that *they* is the 'understood subject' of the infinitive *to see themselves*. For the time being, we will ignore the problem of agreement, and focus on the semantic side of control.

Under REST-style assumptions, the infinitive complement of (40) has a phonetically null pronominal subject:

(41)   They tried [$_s$ PRO to see themselves]

In general, pronominal elements are free to take antecedents outside the sentence in which they occur, but the reference of PRO is not free when it occurs as the subject of a complement of *try*. Rather, it must be construed with *they* as its antecedent. In this case, the matrix NP is said to (obligatorily) *control* the subject of the infinitival complement. The approach presupposes a general notion of control like that proposed by Bresnan (1982a, p. 372).

> *Control* refers to a relation of referential dependence between an unexpressed subject (the *controlled* element) and an expressed or unexpressed constituent (the *controller*); the referential properties of the controlled element, including possibly the property of having no reference at all, are determined by those of the controller.

We dwell on this definitional issue only to foreshadow the point that we will be adopting a somewhat different characterization of control in our own analysis.

The REST syntactic analysis of (40) is clearly not the only one possible. Brame (1976) has advocated an alternative treatment of 'equi' verbs which denied the existence of an 'abstract' S node dominating the infinitive, and claimed instead that the complement is simply a VP:

(42)   They tried [$_{VP}$ to see themselves]

From a syntactic point of view, (42) is the simpler analysis in so far as it involves less constituent structure. But in order to be a serious contender it must provide a basis for defining a control relation comparable to that defined over (41). The syntactic treatment of verbs like *try* in PTQ is essentially the same as (42) when translated into a phrase structure analysis. Montague's semantic treatment closely parallels the syntax by assigning subjectless infinitives the same type as VPs. Adjusting for the differences in type which we discussed in section 3, the semantic translation of a sentence like (43a) comes out as (43b):

(43)   a.   Kim tries to leave
        b.   **try′ (leave′)(Kim*)**

This is to say, *try* is interpreted as a relation between individuals and properties. In this case, it is a relation holding between Kim and the third-order property corresponding to the first-order property of leaving. (43b) says nothing explicit about Kim being the 'understood subject' of *leave*, and this might appear to be a deficiency. One way of overcoming it would be to ensure that (43b) is semantically equivalent to a formalization in which a *try*-relation (denoted here by **try**|) holds between Kim and the proposition that Kim leaves:

(44)   ☐[**try′ (leave′)(Kim*)** ↔ **try†(leave′ (Kim*))(Kim*)**]

It is just such a view that we accept. For persuasive arguments against the propositional treatment of infinitival complements and for a property-based account of the sort we adopt here, see Chierchia 1984 and Dowty forthcoming.

So far, we have made no mention of a significant difference between *try* and *seem*. In the case of the latter, we have syntactic motivation in a PSG for positing two lexical items with distinct semantic interpretations. The postulate in (45) states a semantic equivalence between the two items, whereby the subject of the 'raising to subject' *seem* is related to the subject of the complement of the 'propositional' *seem*.

(45)   ☐[**seem′ (V)(x*)(y*)** ↔ **seem†(V(y*))(x*)**]

Such an analysis illustrates well how a meaning postulate can capture the kind of semantic generalization which required a syntactic rule in transformational grammar. By contrast, the 'equi' verb *try* has no corresponding 'propositional' *try* item which takes finite S complements:

(46)   *Kim tried that he left

Consequently, there is no syntactic motivation for positing the constant **try**† which occurs in (44). The proposal that there should be such a constant is not novel. Thomason (1976b, p. 49) presents a schematic postulate which has (45) as an instance, *modulo* some type differences, but he does not attempt to meet the point we have just raised.

The best argument, we believe, in favor of postulating equivalences like (44) in Montague semantics is that it provides the basis for a unitary account of the semantic aspect of control. The position can be expressed roughly as follows: although the infinitival complement of a control verb is simply interpreted as a property in the compositional semantics, it is involved in a semantic entailment whereby this property is predicated of the controlling NP argument. The notion of 'understood subject' is captured by defining appropriate semantic equivalences for the relevant classes of control verbs. These equivalences can be captured in a variety of ways. In Thomason (1974, 1976b), they are expressed by meaning postulates, while Dowty (1978b) and Bartsch (1978) use interpretation rules tied to lexical entries. We shall adopt a variant of the second approach.

In the next part of this section, we will discuss the way in which the difference between subject-controlled and object-controlled infinitives has been captured in categorial grammar, and show how the analysis can be reconstructed in the present framework.[13]

We will take as our examples a familiar pair of contrasting verbs, *persuade* and *promise*. Each of these verbs combines with an NP and an infinitival VP to form a VP. If we allow only binary branching in a categorial grammar, then the complement NP must either be added before or after the infinitive. Does this difference in the order of combination have any consequences? Consider the following claim:

(47)   The first NP argument to combine with a functor in which a VP occurs is the (semantic) controller of that VP.

Since *us* is the controller in *Kim persuaded us to leave*, the claim requires (48) to be the analysis tree for this sentence:

(48)

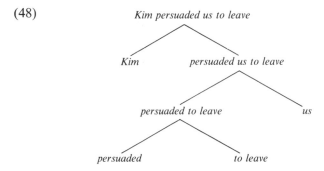

By contrast, in the sentence *Kim promised us to leave*, the controller of the infinitive is *Kim*. Consequently, (47) requires the analysis tree to be (49), where the complement NP *us* is added before the infinitive, so that the first NP to combine after the infinitive is the subject.

(49)

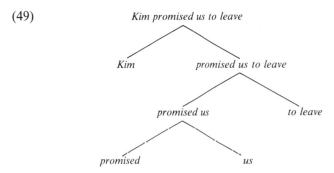

In order to achieve this result in a categorial grammar, these two classes of verbs have to be assigned to two different categories. Since *persuade* combines first with an infinitive (say, of category INF) and then with an NP, it will be of category (VP/NP)/INF, whereas *promise*, which combines first with an NP and then with an INF, will be of category (VP/INF)/NP.

Let us consider now whether this analysis can be transposed into our framework. The situation is parallel to the one that arose in relation to Dowty's treatment of grammatical relations. Put briefly, since the syntactic relationships in analysis trees (51) and (52) are echoed in the semantic translations which they induce, the claim expressed in (50) can also be expressed in terms of semantic relationships. One approach might be the following:

(50)   Let a, β and γ be constituents whose types are $\langle VP, \langle NP, a \rangle \rangle$, VP and NP respectively, and whose translations are a', β', and γ'. If $\phi = a' (\beta')(\gamma')$, then γ controls β.

Let us illustrate (50). The translations associated with the top nodes of (48) and (49) will be (51) and (52):

(51)   **persuade′ (leave′)(us*)(Kim*)**

(52)   **promise′ (us*)(leave′)(Kim*)**

Translation (51) contains a subexpression ϕ of the form required by (50), namely **persuade′ (leave′)(us*)**, in which **us*** controls **leave′**. However, (52) itself is the smallest expression which meets the requirement of (50), and so *Kim* is the controller of the infinitive. It can also be observed that, given the notions defined in the preceding section, **us*** is the 2-argument, i.e. the direct object, in (51), but the 3-argument, i.e. the indirect object, in (52).

Bartsch (1978) argues that there are independent reasons for regarding the NP complement after *promise* as an indirect object.

As we pointed out earlier, the syntactic realization of control involves agreement between the controller and some part of the controlled expression. Thus, there is the familiar contrast between the possibilities for reflexivization associated with *persuade* and *promise*:

(53)   They persuaded us to see ourselves/*themselves/*yourself.

(54)   They promised us to see themselves/*ourselves/*yourself.

The feature instantiation patterns that underlie such agreement processes are governed by the Control Agreement Principle (discussed in detail in chapter 5). The CAP says, in effect, that controlled constituents agree with their controllers. This expresses the claim that while the agreement relations associated with control are syntactic in nature, the terms of the relation are determined on semantic grounds, in line with (50). In fact, we offered a slightly different definition of control in chapter 5, which we repeat here.

> *Definition 1*: Control
> If ϕ is a projection of r, where $r = C_0 \rightarrow C_1, \ldots, C_n$, then a category $\phi(C_i)$ *controls* ϕ (C_j) in ϕ, $1 \leq i, j \leq n$, if and only if
> (i) $TYP(\chi(\phi(C_j))) = \langle TYP(\chi(\phi(C_i))), TYP(\chi(\phi(C_0))) \rangle$, or
> (ii) $TYP(\chi(\phi(C_j))) = TYP(VP)$ and one of the types associated with the head of r is $\langle TYP(VP), \langle TYP(\chi(\phi(C_i))), TYP(VP) \rangle \rangle$.

Note that the characterization of 'the head of r' in clause (ii) is the type-theoretical equivalent of the category (VP/NP)/INF, which as we pointed out earlier is the category assigned to verbs like *persuade* on the categorial analysis. Although the above definition does not claim that *Kim* controls *leave* in (52), it does claim that, by clause (i), *Kim* controls the whole VP *promise to leave*. This interacts with the other principles for feature distribution to ensure that there is syntactic agrmeent between *Kim* and *leave* of the appropriate sort, as we showed in chapter 5. The semantic entailments associated with control are not directly determined by a claim such as (47) in our analysis, but are instead determined by meaning postulates associated with control verbs. We return to this topic in chapter 10, section 4.

Notes

1 Strictly speaking, this ought to read 'members of *Den*(NP) are applied as functions to members of *Den*(VP) . . .', given that the range of *Den* is always a

set of denotations. For convenience, we will adopt the looser terminology used in the text.

2 In fact, D is a homomorphism from the algebra of types to the algebra of domains. The algebra of types can be represented as $(\{e, t\}, \{O, O'\})$, where O is the unary operator which forms intensional types, and O' is the binary operator which forms functional types. That is, for any types a and b.

$$O(a) = \langle s, a \rangle$$
$$O'(a, b) = \langle a, b \rangle$$

The algebra of domains is $(\{E, \{0, 1\}, W\}, \{Q\})$, where Q is the binary operator which forms functional domains. For any domains X and Y,

$$Q(X, Y) = Y^X.$$

Then D is a homomorphism which carries both O and O' over to Q:

$$D_{O(a)} = Q(D_a, W)$$
$$D_{O'(a, b)} = Q(D_a, D_b)$$

3 Let f and g be two functions such that $f: Y \to Z$ and $g: X \to Y$. Then $f \circ g$ is that function $h: X \to Z$ such that for any $x \in X$, $h(x) = f(g(x))$.

4 The work of Keenan and Faltz (1978) consistently adopts this position.

5 Bach (1979) also takes a step in this direction by developing a formalism in which the categories of categorial grammar are decomposed into (a) major class features, together with (b) the categorial index which determines the semantic type.

6 Although we there identified $Den(S)$ with $\{0, 1\}$, we will in fact treat sentences as denoting propositions. Hence, given our other assumptions, $TYP(S)$ will be $\langle s, t \rangle$.

7 Cf. Thomason (1976b), Klein (1978), Bach (1980b).

8 We henceforth adopt the familiar notational convention of abbreviating $[^\wedge \lambda PP(c)]$ as c^*, where c is any expression of type e.

9 To simplify displays of IL expression here and later in this section, we ignore the internal composition of the VP complement. Lambda reduction has been carried out in (14) for the same reason.

10 Cf. Dowty forthcoming, Keenan and Faltz 1978, Klein and Sag forthcoming, Sag and Klein 1982.

11 See Keenan 1974. A more detailed discussion of the topic of agreement in the present framework can be found above in chapter 5.

12 Recall that PP[PFORM *to*] will be of type NP.

13 The analysis we are about to sketch is developed in Thomason 1976a,b, Partee 1975, Bach 1979, and Dowty 1982c.

10

General principles of semantic interpretation

1 Introduction

Within current formal approaches to the semantic analysis of natural language, it has become commonplace to accept what Bach (1976) has termed the 'rule-to-rule hypothesis'. Recent proposals within Montague's general framework have virtually all adopted the position that for every syntactic rule within the grammar, a corresponding semantic rule must be stated which specifies how structures of the sort analyzed by that rule are to be interpreted. In this chapter, we shall explain how the rule-to-rule hypothesis is implemented in our grammar. To provide a basis for that discussion, we shall take the opportunity here to discuss the treatment of semantic rules in previous work in GPSG.

In Gazdar 1982, grammar-rules are pairs consisting of (a) a phrase structure rule, and (b) a semantic rule which specifies how the constituent analyzed by (a) is to be translated into an appropriate logical expression.[1] In (1) we give an example of such a rule pair (except that we have replaced the PS rule by an ID rule):

$$(1) \qquad \langle S \to NP, VP; VP' (NP') \rangle$$

In order to explain the translation rule, let us first of all compare (1) with the corresponding pair of rules in a fairly orthodox Montague grammar:

(2) a. If α is an NP and β is a VP, then $F_0(\alpha, \beta)$ is an S, where $F_0(\alpha, \beta) = \alpha \char`\^ \beta$.

  b. If α is an NP, β is a VP, and α, β translate into α', β', respectively, then $F_0(\alpha, \beta)$ translates into $\beta'(\alpha')$.

There is of course a difference in the ways in which the syntactic rules operate. The rule in (2a) simply constructs strings and does not assign any constituent structure. By contrast, we have interpreted the ID rule in (1) as admitting (in conjunction with other parts of the grammar) a local tree:

(3)

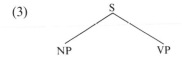

While the semantic rule (2b) shows how the strings defined by the syntactic rule (2a) induce a translation into IL, it seems reasonable to view the semantic component of (1) as part of an inductive definition for translating the trees generated by the grammar into appropriate expressions of IL. In order to show graphically how a translation is associated with a syntactic tree, we adopt the device of an *interpreted* tree. This is just like an ordinary constituent structure tree except that its nodes can be labeled by meaningful expressions of IL as well as syntactic categories. An IL expression accompanying a node label C is the translation of the string which is analyzed by the tree rooted in C. Suppose now that a translation has already been associated with the subtrees rooted in NP and VP in (3), and let us denote these translations by NP' and VP', respectively. Then the semantic rule above assigns to the S node a translation in which VP' is applied as a functor to NP'. That is, it will yield the following interpreted tree:

(4)

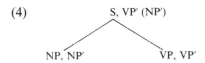

Of course, in practice we will be interested in the translations assigned to terminated trees. Terminal symbols are translated as constants of IL, and these will form the inductive basis for the translations of complex expressions. We adopt the usual convention in Montague semantics that the constants of IL which translate lexical items of English are referred to by primed (boldface) variants of those items. In addition, we assume that for each lexical aim a of category C, the grammar will admit a local tree of the form below:

(5)

A series of mappings similar to that from (3) to (4) will yield (7) as the interpreted tree associated with (6). In this case, the metavariables NP' and VP' are instantiated as **a'** (**man'**) and **walk'** respectively.

(6)

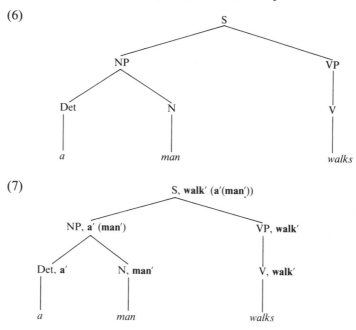

(7)

We introduce in this chapter two significant modifications of the standard rule-to-rule hypothesis. The first is that we will exhibit general principles that allow the form of most semantic rules to be determined automatically by the semantic type of the participating constituents. The second is that our translation rules will make essential reference to information that is present in local trees, but possibly absent from the licencing ID rules. We have just seen that a translation rule is plausibly viewed as a function which, given a local subtree where translations are associated with the daughter nodes, yields a new tree that has a translation associated with the mother. If the syntactic rules with which they are associated are rich enough, there is no need to explicitly introduce tree structures in the way we have done. The position is very different, however, when syntactic rules are radically impoverished in the manner we have proposed earlier in this book. Semantically significant properties which are absent from ID rules accrue in the transition to local trees. To take one key example, the **FOOT** features whose distribution is governed by the FFP play a crucial role in determining the semantics of unbounded dependencies. To take another example, we shall propose in the next section that linear order (which of course is absent from ID rules) helps to determine the grammatical functions assigned in double object constructions. All these matters will be taken up in greater detail in the following sections.

2 Functional realization

In the preceding section, we briefly sketched the rule-to-rule approach to semantic translation. The usual implementations of this approach within phrase structure grammar have tended to be highly redundant.[2] Consider for example the syntactic–semantic rule pairs in (8).

(8)   a. $\langle S \rightarrow NP, VP; VP' (NP') \rangle$
      b. $\langle VP \rightarrow V[2], NP; V' (NP') \rangle$
      c. $\langle NP \rightarrow Det, N^1; Det' (N^{1'}) \rangle$
      d. $\langle N^1 \rightarrow N[35], PP[of]; N' (PP') \rangle$

In each case, the semantic rule says simply that the functor should be applied to the argument in such a way as to build an expression of IL of the appropriate type, viz. the type of the mother category in the syntactic rule. All daughter translations must be used exactly once. Which translation is the functor and which is the argument is uniquely determined by the assignment of types in the grammar. For example, we saw in the previous chapter that Det and N^1 are associated with the following types:

(9) $TYP(Det) = \langle N^1, N^1 \rangle$
      $TYP(N^1), = \langle e, t \rangle$

Consequently, if Det' is the translation of a member of Det, and $N^{1'}$ is the translation of a member of N^1, then the only possible way of combining Det' and $N^{1'}$ in a translation rule is (10a). The expression in (10b) cannot be construed as a meaningful expression of IL.

(10)   a.   Det' $(N^{1'})$
      b. $N^{1'}$ (Det')

There is no way to apply a function of the N' sort to a function of the Det' sort to yield a value of the NP' sort. Given a type system like that of IL, rules such as those in (8) are predictable on the basis of a principle like the following:

(11)   Use functional application to combine the translations of the daughters of a node labeled C so as to yield an expression in $ME_{TYP(C)}$.

We hypothesize that, in a large proportion of cases, the translations of structures admitted by ID rules can be derived in the fashion of (11), given an assignment of semantic types to syntactic categories, rather than by reference to individual translation rules. Our first task is to define the important notion of *functional realization*. Loosely speaking, functional realization is a mapping which, given a multiset Σ of expressions of intensional logic, yields a set T_Σ of new expressions which can be built up out of Σ. When Σ contains the semantic translations of the daughters in a local tree, T_Σ will contain an appropriate semantic translation for the root node of the tree.

We pointed out earlier that the translation rules in Montague semantics have the property that the translation of each component of a complex expression occurs exactly once in the translation of the whole. This property must be preserved by functional realization. That is to say, we do not want the set T_Σ mentioned above to contain *all* well-formed expressions of IL which can be built up from the elements of Σ, but only those which use each element of Σ exactly once. For example, suppose that $\Sigma = \{\textbf{walk}', \textbf{quickly}'\}$, where **walk**$'$ is of type VP and **quickly**$'$ is of type $\langle$VP, VP$\rangle$. Then T_Σ should contain **quickly**$'$ (**walk**$'$), but not **quickly**$'$ (**quickly**$'$ (**walk**$'$)), or any other of the infinite number of expressions constructed in this way. Klein and Sag forthcoming suggest that what is required is the notion of the *bounded closure* of a set under a binary operation h. By contrast to the standard notion of the closure of a set under some operation, bounded closure obeys the restriction just discussed, namely that each element in the initial set is employed exactly once. The operation that we are interested in is functional application, but it is convenient to give a definition that is somewhat more general. We shall not go through all the technical details here, and the interested reader is referred to Klein and Sag forthcoming for the relevant definitions. Instead, taking h to be the operation of functional application, we will assume that

$$h[\Sigma]_\text{B}$$

is a well-defined set representing the bounded closure of a multiset Σ under h.

In fact, given our analysis of prenominal adjectives as functions which apply to the intensions of their arguments, functional realization should also include the semantic operation of intensional functional application. However, to simplify matters, we will ignore this extra consideration here. For a discussion of the possibility of developing a universal set of primitive semantic operations, see Partee 1979.

Next, we turn to the notion of functional realization. Recall that we wanted this to be a function which took the translations of daughters in a local tree, and yielded as output an appropriate translation for the root of the tree. In order for the translation to be appropriate, it must, among other things, be of a type which is appropriate. And this, of course, is the type which is associated with the category label at the root node of the local tree. Since this type is a vital parameter for functional realization, we take the latter to be a function FR of two arguments: a type, and a multiset of expressions of IL. Given as input a type a and a multiset Σ, therefore, the output of FR is a set of elements each of which (i) belongs to the bounded closure of Σ under the operation of functional application, and (ii) is a well-formed expression of IL of type a, that is, belongs to the set ME_a.

> *Definition 1*
> Let Σ be a multiset included in ME. For any type a, *the functional realization of Σ with respect to a is*
> $$FR(a, \Sigma) = \{a: a \in h[\Sigma]_B \cap ME_a\}$$

3   The Semantic Interpretation Schema

The Semantic Interpretation Schema provides an inductive definition of the set of interpreted trees allowed by the grammar. It basically consists of a compositional translation schema: given an interpreted tree in which translations have been assigned to the daughter nodes, the schema yields a new interpreted tree in which the root node has been assigned a translation that is a function of the translations of the daughters. The basis of the induction is the set of *terminated interpreted local trees*. A terminated local tree is a tree whose only daughter is a terminal symbol, i.e. a word in the language (or the lexical entry that is its representation in terms of our syntactic theory). As we remarked in chapter 5, we assume that the properties of a terminated local tree are determined by the lexicon, in particular by the lexical entry for the daughter in the tree. This will specify *inter alia* the category to which the item belongs and one or more translations into intensional logic.[3] Thus a *terminated interpreted local tree* is one in which the root node is labeled by a translation as well as a lexical category. Although it is not part of our definition, an obvious procedure for assigning a semantic translation to a nonlocal tree would be the following: start at the nodes labeled by lexical categories, and compute the translation of their mothers on the basis of the Semantic Interpretation Schema; continue this procedure at the next level up, and so on, until the root of the tree is reached.

(12)   Semantic Interpretation Schema (first formulation)

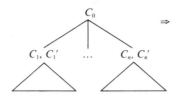

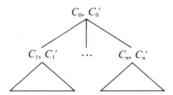

where C_0' is the unique member of
$FR(TYP(C_0), \{C_1', \ldots, C_n'\}_m)$.

The input to the schema is a tree in which translations have been associated with the daughter nodes $C_1, \ldots, C_n$, and the output is a new tree in which the Functional Realization of $C_1', \ldots, C_n'$ is the translation associated with the mother node. Notice that the schema only inspects a local subtree of its input. Because of this, it is convenient to talk of the Semantic Interpretation Schema as though it associated translations with local trees, and we shall in fact do so for the remainder of the chapter.

As an illustration, consider the ID rules in (13) (derived from the rule pairs in (8) above):

(13)   a.   S → XP, H[SUBJ−]
        b.   VP → H[2], NP
        c.   NP → Det, H¹
        d.   N¹ → H[35], PP[*of*]

Notice to begin with that given our treatment of heads, there is no way of determining what semantic type should be associated with the head of a rule like (13c). Without the vital information about major category features which is determined by the HFC, the association between categories and types cannot be invoked, and functional realization cannot be applied. Suppose, on the other hand, that local trees have been admitted from the rules, and that translations of the appropriate type have been assigned to the daughter nodes. Then in each case FR will yield a singleton set which is the desired semantic translation. Consequently, the Semantic Interpretation Schema will give rise to the interpreted local subtrees shown in (14)–(18). As a notational convenience, we have split the trees into two parts. The (a) part, as usual, consists of a local tree in list style, while the (b) part consists of the translation assigned to the root of the tree. The schematic translations associated with the daughter nodes are omitted, since these contain no unpredictable information.

(14)   a.   S
            NP
            VP
       b.   VP′ (NP′)

(15)   a.   VP
            V[2]
            NP
       b.   V′ (NP′)

(16)   a.   NP
            Det
            N¹
       b.   Det′ (N¹′)

(17)   a.   N¹
            N[35]
            PP[*of*]
       b.   N′ (PP′)

In the event that two daughters in a given structure have the same semantic type, FR will fail to produce a singleton set. In both (18a) and (18b), for example, there are two daughter categories of type NP.

(18)   a.   VP
            V[3]
            NP
            PP[*to*]
       b.   VP
            V[5]
            NP
            NP

Hence, assuming that the type of the lexical head in each structure is $\langle$NP, $\langle$NP, S$\rangle\rangle$, FR yields a set containing two elements. This is illustrated below.[4]

(19)   a.   FR(VP, {V[3]′, NP′, PP′ }$_m$) =
            {V[3]′ (NP′) (PP′), V[3]′ (PP′) (NP′)}
       b.   FR(VP, {V[5]′, NP$_1$′, NP$_2$′}$_m$) =
            {V[5]′ (NP$_1$′) (NP$_2$′), V[5]′ (NP$_2$′) (NP$_1$′)}

Unfortunately, this indeterminacy is pernicious. To allow both translations amounts to saying that a sentence like (20) is ambiguous according to whether it was Sandy who received Fido or vice versa.

(20)   We gave Fido to Sandy.

Our resolution of this problem builds on the characterization of grammatical relations that was presented in chapter 9. According to Dowty's (1982b,c) analysis, *Fido* is the direct object in (20), while *Sandy* is the direct object in (21).[5]

(21)   We gave Sandy Fido.

This suggests that the indeterminacy in translation can be resolved by appeal to the semantic relation between linear precedence and argument order. One way of accomplishing this is to impose the following language-particular condition on Functional Realization:[6]

(22)   Argument Order
In a local tree t, if
(i)   there are C_i, C_j such that $TYP(C_i) = TYP(C_j) = NP$, and
(ii) C_j immediately follows C_i in t, then
$C_0' \in FR(a_0, \{a_1, \ldots, a_n\}_m)$ only if C_i is the 2-argument in C_0'.

This principle correctly ensures that the only semantic translations derived for structures introducing ditransitive rules are those indicated in the interpreted structures in (23) and (24).

(23)   a.   VP
            V[3]
            NP
            PP
     b.   V' (PP')(NP')
(24)   a.   VP
            V[5]
            NP_1
            NP_2
     b.   V' (NP_2')(NP_1')

4   Lexical interpretation

We begin this section by introducing a minor, but important modification in the treatment of lexical translation mentioned in section 1. Certain lexical items, e.g. the verb *prefer* and the adjective *eager*, take complements which may be instantiated as either S[INF] or [VP[INF]]. Because these two kinds of complements are of distinct semantic types, it is necessary to associate the predicates in question with two distinct IL-translations; one will successfully combine with the VP complement, and the other with the S complement. As we shall see, the two translations of a verb like *prefer* will be of type $\langle S, \langle NP, S \rangle \rangle$ and $\langle VP, \langle NP, S \rangle \rangle$ respectively.

To accommodate this mode of analysis, we assume a principle stating that whenever a lexical item a of category C is associated with a set T of IL-translations, then for each $\tau \in T$, the grammar will admit an interpreted subtree of the form

This principle has two immediate consequences: first, it entails that the function TYP discussed in the previous chapter is a multi-valued function in that it may assign more than one type to a lexical category, and second, a choice of translation for a given lexical subtree may fail to produce any translation for the constituent containing it in virtue of type incompatability.[7]

As noted in the previous chapter, our approach to semantic analysis is similar to other work in 'extended Montague grammar' in that important semantic relations involving infinitival complements are expressed by meaning postulates, which constrain the interpretations of particular lexical items. Our semantic analysis of equi and raising predicates,[8] however, differs from familiar Montague-style analyses, e.g. those of Thomason (1976a,b) and Bach (1979), in that it makes use of two semantic combinators,[9] f_R and f_E, which induce (schematic) raising and equi semantics, respectively.

Consider the case of raising-to-object verbs first. On an approach like Thomason's there are two distinct constants of IL, e.g. **believe′** and **believe†**: one translates a verb when it combines with a *that* clause complement, and the other translates the same verb when it is subcategorized for an NP and infinitival VP complement. The interpretations of such pairs of translations are related by meaning postulates.

A slightly different approach is to postulate a single IL constant, e.g. **believe′**, that is used in constructing the lexical translations of both verbs.[10] We take the basic type of **believe′** to be $\langle S, \langle NP, S \rangle \rangle$, and list **believe′** as the lexical translation for V[40], the V that combines with a sentential complement. The lexical translation of V[17], the corresponding raising-to-object verb, is given as $f_R(\textbf{believe′})$, which is an IL expression of type $\langle VP, \langle NP, \langle NP, S \rangle \rangle \rangle$. In virtue of these type assignments, functional realization as defined in the preceding section will lead us to predict the semantic translations indicated in (25).

(25)   a.   VP

            V[40]
            S[FIN]]

      b.   V' (S')

      c.   VP

            V[17]
            NP
            VP[INF]

      d.   V' (VP')(NP')

The schematic meaning postulate for f_R which we discuss in a moment will ensure that such pairs as (26a) and (26b) are semantically equivalent.

(26)   a.   Terry believes Lou to be insane.
      b.   Terry believes (that) Lou is insane.

The analysis of equi predicates is similar. In the context of a sentential complement, the lexical translation of an equi predicate is simple, e.g. **prefer'**, which is of the type $\langle S, \langle NP, S \rangle \rangle$. When such a verb combines with a VP-type complement, its lexical translation employs f_E. For example, f_E (**prefer'**) is an IL expression of type $\langle VP, \langle NP, S \rangle \rangle$, which is exactly the type it must have in order to combine with an infinitival VP by function application to give a VP type ($= \langle NP, S \rangle$) expression.

We thus have the interpreted local trees shown in (27).

(27)   a.   VP

            V[14]
            S[INF]

      b.   V' (S')

      c.   VP

            V[14]
            VP[INF]

      d.   V' (VP')

The schematic meaning postulate for f_E will establish the appropriate semantic relations involving equi predicates in diverse syntactic contexts.

The combinatorics of f_R and f_E are given by the following principles, formulated here as syntactic formation ruls for IL:

(28)   If α is in $ME_{\langle S, a \rangle}$, where a is of the form
        $\langle NP_1, \langle \ldots NP_n, S \rangle \ldots \rangle \rangle$, then
      a. $f_R(\alpha) \in ME_{\langle VP, \langle NP, a \rangle \rangle}$, and
      b. $f_E(\alpha) \in ME_{\langle VP, a \rangle}$.

We exploit these operators in the lexical translations shown in (29).[11]

(29)

SUBCAT number	verb	translations	type
40	*believe*	**believe'**	$\langle S, \langle NP, S \rangle \rangle$
17	*believe*	$f_R(\textbf{believe}')$	$\langle VP, \langle NP, \langle NP, S \rangle \rangle \rangle$
14	*prefer*	**prefer'**	$\langle S, \langle NP, S \rangle \rangle$
		$f_E(\textbf{prefer}')$	$\langle VP, \langle NP, S \rangle \rangle$
13	*tend*	$f_R(\textbf{tend}')$	$\langle VP, \langle NP, S \rangle \rangle$
18	*persuade*	$f_F(\textbf{persuade}')$	$\langle VP, \langle NP, \langle NP, S \rangle \rangle \rangle$
19	*promise*	$\lambda \mathscr{P}[f_E(\textbf{promise}' \ (\mathscr{P}))]$	$\langle NP, \langle VP, \langle NP, S \rangle \rangle \rangle$

The Semantic Interpretation Schema yields interpreted local trees of the following kinds in addition to those in (27).

(30) a. VP
           V[40]
           S[FIN]
      b. V' (S')

(31) a. VP
           V[17]
           NP
           VP[INF]
      b. V' (VP')(NP')

(32) a. VP
           V[13]
           VP[INF]
      b. V' (VP')

(33) a. VP
           V[18]
           NP
           VP[INF]
      b. V' (VP')(NP')

(34) a. VP
           V[19]
           NP
           VP[INF]
      b. V' (NP')(VP')

The interpretations of f_R and f_E are constrained by schematic meaning postulates:

General principles of semantic interpretation

(35) $\forall V \forall \mathcal{P}_1 \ldots \mathcal{P}_n \square [f_R(\zeta)(V)(\mathcal{P}_1) \ldots (\mathcal{P}_n) \leftrightarrow \zeta(V(\mathcal{P}_1)) \ldots (\mathcal{P}_n)]$

(36) $\forall V \forall \mathcal{P}_1 \ldots \mathcal{P}_n \square [f_E(\zeta)(V)(\mathcal{P}_1) \ldots (\mathcal{P}_n) \leftrightarrow$
        $\mathcal{P}_1 \{\lambda x[\zeta(V(x^*))(x^*)(\mathcal{P}_2) \ldots (\mathcal{P}_n)]\}]$
        where $\mathcal{P}$ is of NP type and $n \geq 1$.

In particular, it is guaranteed that raising predicates allow certain readings that are systematically absent for analogous equi predicates. Our analysis correctly predicts for example that (37a) but not (37b) entails the existence of a cat.[12]

(37)   a.   A cat wants to be in the garden.
        b.   A cat appears to be in the garden.

It also provides a satisfactory account of the historically troublesome fact that (38a) and (38b) are not paraphrases.

(38)   a.   A Swede wants to sit in the garden.
        b.   A Swede wants a Swede to sit in the garden.

In addition, we treat correctly a wide variety of semantic entailment and synonymy relations involving equi and raising predicates.

The meaning postulates given in (35) and (36) yield equivalences of the following sort.

(39)   a.   Lee tends to go.
        a'. $f_R(\textbf{tend}')(\textbf{to-go}')(\textbf{Lee*})$
              $\Leftrightarrow \textbf{tend}' (\textbf{to-go}' (\textbf{Lee*}))$
        b.   Kim believes Lee to be ill.
        b.' $f_R(\textbf{believe}')(\textbf{to-be-ill}')(\textbf{Lee*})(\textbf{Kim*})$
              $\Leftrightarrow \textbf{believe}' (\textbf{to-be-ill}' (\textbf{Lee*}))(\textbf{Kim*})$

(40)   a.   Lee wants to go.
        a'. $f_E(\textbf{want}')(\textbf{to-go}')(\textbf{Lee*})$
              $\Leftrightarrow \textbf{Lee*}\{\lambda x[\textbf{want}' (\textbf{to-go}' (x^*))(x^*)]\}$
        b.   Kim persuades Lee to go.
        b'. $f_E(\textbf{persuade}')(\textbf{to-go}')(\textbf{Lee*})(\textbf{Kim*})$
              $\Leftrightarrow \textbf{Lee*}\{\lambda x[\textbf{persuade}' (\textbf{to-go}' (x^*))(x^*)(\textbf{Kim*})]\}$

Notice that the combinator f_R is equivalent to the standard function composition operator. That is, if f and g are the functions denoted by **tend'** and **to-go'**, respectively, then $f_R(\textbf{tend}')(\textbf{to-go}')$ denotes $f \circ g$, i.e. the composition of f and g.

We have adopted the position that the NP complement of *promise* is an oblique rather than a direct object (cf. Bach 1980a, Bartsch 1978 and Thomason 1976a,b). At the level of function-argument structure, this means that *promise* combines with the NP argument before its VP complement. The lexical type which is assigned to *promise* in (29) guarantees this result. This analysis correctly captures the fact that *Kim* is the semantic controller of *to go* in (41).

(41)   Kim promises Lee to go.

This example will be assigned the translation in (42a), which is equivalent to (42b), where the control binding is explicitly indicated.

(42)   a. f_E(**promise'** (**Lee***))(**to-go'**)(**Kim***)
         b.   **Kim***$\{\lambda x$[**promise'** (**Lee***)(**to-go**(x^*))$(x^*)]\}$

The analysis just sketched thus embodies Bach and Partee's (1980) generalization about control and function argument structure which we mentioned in the preceding chapter, repeated here:

(43)   The first NP argument to combine with a functor in which a VP occurs is the (semantic) controller of that VP.

This is in effect a semantic version of Rosenbaum's (1967) 'Minimal Distance Principle'.[13]

We are now in a position to consider the semantic analysis of passive verbs. The morphological and semantic regularities of passivization are predicted on our account by positing a lexical rule which we formulate as (44).

(44)   Lexical Rule for Passive Forms
         if   (i) a belongs to V[n] and
               (ii) a' is the translation of a, and
               (iii) $TYP(a') = \langle a_1, \langle \ldots \langle a_n, \langle \beta, \langle NP, S \rangle \rangle \rangle \ldots \rangle \rangle$,
                      where $\beta = $ NP or S,
         then (i) $F(a)$ belongs to V[n, PAS], where $F(a)$ is the past participial form of a and
               (ii) $F(a)' = f_P(a')$, and
               (iii) $TYP(f_P(a')) = \langle NP, \langle a_1, \langle \ldots \langle a_n, \langle \beta, S \rangle \rangle \ldots \rangle \rangle \rangle$.

This rule simply introduces the appropriate passive morphology[14] onto verb forms and assigns a lexical translation constructed by means of the operator f_P which has the effect of cyclically permuting the verb's arguments. We thus derive the passive forms in (45) with the indicated lexical translations.

(45)

SUBCAT	verb	translation	resulting type
2	*loved*	$f_P(\textbf{love}')$	$\langle \text{NP}, \langle \text{NP}, \text{S} \rangle \rangle$
40	*believed*	$f_P(\textbf{believe}')$	$\langle \text{NP}, \langle \text{S}, \text{S} \rangle \rangle$
17	*believed*	$f_P(f_R(\textbf{believe}'))$	$\langle \text{NP}, \langle \text{VP}, \langle \text{NP}, \text{S} \rangle \rangle \rangle$
18	*persuaded*	$f_P(f_E(\textbf{persuade}'))$	$\langle \text{NP}, \langle \text{VP}, \langle \text{NP}, \text{S} \rangle \rangle \rangle$

And these derived type assignments ensure that the translation mechanism will produce the following interpreted local trees, derived from outputs of the Passive Metarule.

(46) a. VP[PAS]
        V[2, PAS]
        PP[*by*]
  b. V' (PP')

(47) a. VP[PAS]
        V[40, PAS]
        PP[*by*]
  b. V' (PP')

(48) a. VP[PAS]
        V[17, PAS]
        VP[INF]
        PP[*by*]
  b. V' (PP')(VP')

(49) a. VP[PAS]
        V[18, PAS]
        VP[INF]
        PP[*by*]
  b. V' (PP')(VP')

The semantic interpretation of f_P is also given by meaning postulate:

(50) $\forall \mathscr{P}_1 \forall \mathscr{P}_2 \forall v_1 \ldots v_n \square [f_P(\zeta)(\mathscr{P}_1)(v_1) \ldots (v_n)(\mathscr{P}_2) \leftrightarrow$
$\zeta(v_1) \ldots (v_n)(\mathscr{P}_2)(\mathscr{P}_1)]$
where $\mathscr{P}_1$ and $\mathscr{P}_2$ are of NP type.

In virtue of this postulate we ensure the synonymy of such pairs of examples as the following, whose IL translations are as indicated.[15]

(51)   a.   Kim loves Sandy.
       a'. **love' (Sandy*)(Kim*)**
       b.   Sandy is loved by Kim
       b'. f_P(**love'**)(**Kim***)(**Sandy***)

(52)   a.   Lee believes that Pat is dead.
       a'. **believe' (dead' (Pat*))(Lee*)**
       b.   That Pat is dead is believed by Lee.
       b'. f_P(**believe'**)(**Lee***)(**dead' (Pat*)**)

(53)   a.   Lee believes Pat to be dead.
       a'. f_R(**believe'**)(**dead'**)(**Pat***)(**Lee***)
       b.   Pat is believed to be dead by Lee.
       b'. f_P(f_R(**believe'**))(**Lee***)(**dead'**)(**Pat***)

Note further that members of V[19], e.g. the *promise* that subcategorizes for an NP and a VP[INF], cannot undergo the passive lexical rule in (44). The type of the translation of these verbs is $\langle$NP, $\langle$VP, $\langle$NP, S$\rangle\rangle\rangle$, and this is not of the form required by the semantic part of the rule in (44). Since no translation is defined for V[19, PAS], it follows that there are no interpreted structures derived from the rule in (54), and hence no way to derive passive verb phrases like (55).

(54)   VP[PAS] → H[19], VP[INF], PP[*by*]

(55)   *promised to go to the store by Terry.

Note further that it is this same type assignment to V[19] that induces subject control of its infinitival complement, rather than the object control associated with V[17] and V[18], exemplified by *believe* and *persuade*, respectively. Hence a correlation is established between subject control and the failure of passivization in examples like these and others that have been discussed by Bresnan (1978), Wasow (1977, 1980), and Anderson (1977a), among others, under the rubric of 'Visser's Generalization'.

Consider now the lexical translations of predicate expressions which take sentential subjects. These are all of the type $\langle$S, S$\rangle$, e.g. **likely'** or else $\langle$NP, $\langle$S, S$\rangle\rangle$, e.g. **bother'**, depending on whether or not the predicate in question subcategorizes for extra arguments, e.g. an NP in the case of *bother* or an optional PP[*to*] in the case of *obvious*. Given such type assignments, functional realization works in the desired way.

The Extraposition Metarule introduced in chapter 6 gives new rules which introduce these same predicates marked as [AGR NP[*it*]] with S complements as their sisters. One such rule is given in (56).

(56)   a.   VP[AGR NP[*it*]] → H[20], NP, S
       b.   bother, amuse, . . .

We assume that the dummy NPs *it* and *there* translate as a distinguished constant Δ of the NP type. The denotation of Δ in any model is stipulated to be (the intension of) that function from sets of individuals to truth values that yields truth for every argument. The translations of VP[AGR NP[*it*]]s, therefore, which map such NP arguments into propositions, must be analyzed in such a way as to systematically discard the interpretation of the dummy translation and give as a value the proposition determined by the appropriate elements within the VP.

We shall adopt the strategy suggested by a number of authors (e.g. Dowty, forthcoming) of using vacuous lambda-abstraction.

(57)   Lexical Rule for Extraposition Verbs
    if   (i) a belongs to V[n] and
        (ii) a' is the translation of a, and
        (iii) $TYP(a') = \langle a_1, \langle \ldots \langle a_n, \langle S, S \rangle \rangle \ldots \rangle \rangle$,
    then (i) $F(a)$ belongs to V[n, AGR NP[*it*]], where $F(a) = a$ and
         (ii) $F(a)' = \lambda v_1 \ldots \lambda v_n \lambda \mathscr{P}[a(v_1) \ldots (v_n)]$, and
         (iii) $TYP(F(a)') = \langle a_1, \langle \ldots \langle a_n, \langle S, \langle NP, S \rangle \rangle \rangle \ldots \rangle \rangle$.

Thus the lexical translation of the *bother* belonging to V[20,[AGR NP[*it*]] is given as $\lambda \mathscr{P}_1 \lambda p \lambda \mathscr{P}_2[\textbf{bother}' \ (\mathscr{P}_1)(p)]$, which is an IL expression of type $\langle NP, \langle S, \langle NP, S \rangle \rangle \rangle$ (where p is a variable of type $\langle s, t \rangle$).[16] The Semantic Interpretation Schema yields interpreted local trees like (58) from the rule in (57) above, which in turn has the consequence that a sentence like (59) is translated as in (60).

(58)   a.   VP[AGR NP[*it*]]
                V[20, AGR NP[*it*]]
                NP
                S[FIN]
        b.   V' (NP')(S')

(59)   It bothers Kim that Sandy is short.

(60) $\lambda \mathscr{P}[\textbf{bother}' \ (\textbf{Kim}^*)(\textbf{short}' \ (\textbf{Sandy}^*))](\Delta)$

The translation in (60) is semantically equivalent to (61), which is in fact the IL translation of (62).

(61) $\textbf{bother}' \ (\textbf{Kim}^*)(\textbf{short}' \ (\textbf{Sandy}^*))$

(62)   That Sandy is short bothers Kim.

Thus fundamental paraphrase relations in this domain are correctly established.

The semantics of existential *there* sentences is analogous to that just sketched for *it* extraposition. The IL translation of dummy *there* is just the same as that of dummy *it*, and a V[AGR NP[*there*]] will likewise be analyzed by means of vacuous lambda-abstraction. The translation of the verb *be* has $\langle NP, S \rangle$ as its basic type, in fact we translate it in terms of the same semantic IL predicate we use to translate the verb *exist*. As an instance of V[22, AGR NP[*there*]], however, the lexical translation of *be* is specified as $\lambda \mathscr{P}_1 \lambda \mathscr{P}_2[\textbf{exist}'(\mathscr{P}_1)]$, which is of type $\langle NP, \langle NP, S \rangle \rangle$. We thus get interpreted structures like the one in (63).

(63)   a.   VP[AGR NP[*there*]]
                 V[22, AGR NP[*there*]]
                 NP
        b.   V' (NP')

And as a consequence, sentences like (64) are translated as in (65).

(64)   There is a unicorn.

(65) $\lambda \mathscr{P}[\textbf{exist}'\ (\textbf{a}'\ (\textbf{unicorn}'))](\varDelta)$

And this correctly renders (64) semantically equivalent to (66).

(66)   A unicorn exists.

5 Feature translation

The Semantic Interpretation Schema is extremely general. Yet given the type system of the grammar, it successfully assigns semantic translations to a wide variety of constructions that were previously dealt with on a case-by-case basis. Nevertheless, it must be modified if it is to accommodate constructions where minor features play a role in determining the interpretation. We saw in the previous chapter that minor features such as PFORM can affect the semantic type associated with a given category. But here we are concerned with something else. Carlson (1983b, p. 305) has recently focused attention on the fact that 'function items often appear "lower" in the tree than they should for grammatical and semantic purposes'. Familiar examples are the formatives that express tense, aspect, possession, and number. The distribution of such forms is determined in our grammar by **HEAD** features. Typically, these features are introduced into the tree at some phrasal node, and trickle down to the lexical level by virtue of the HFC. The introduction of **HEAD** features is usually motivated by grammatical considerations. So, for example, an embedded clause may be specified as [VFORM FIN] because it is the sister of a verb which is subcategorized for finite complements Ss. This syntactic restriction on the complement is imposed at the S level but only realized morphologically at the level of the lexical V head. Nevertheless, it is clear that many features also contribute to the semantic interpretation of the structures in which they occur. Plausible candidates are ADV, CONJ, PAST, PLU, POSS, PRD and WH. Let us stipulate that some such set of features are *semantical*. The question arises as to where in the tree such features should make their contribution to the interpretation.[17] Our answer is: at the highest point of occurrence. More precisely, we have the following definition.

> *Definition 2*
> Let f be a semantical feature. Then a feature specification $\langle f, a \rangle$ is *semantically potent* on a daughter node labeled C in a local subtree t if and only if
> (i) $\langle f, a \rangle \in C$, and
> (ii) it is not the case that $\langle f, a \rangle \in C_0$.

This idea is illustrated with respect to the feature specification [+PAST] in the following two trees.

(67) a.

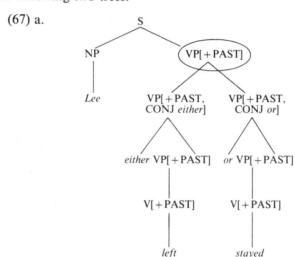

b.

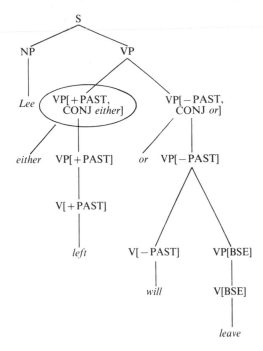

The nodes at which [+PAST] is semantically potent have been circled. In (67a), this is the VP node immediately dominated by the S. This is so because we assume the FCR in (68) which prevents the specification [+PAST] from ever being inherited up to an S-node by the HFC.[18]

(68)   FCR 5: [+PAST] ⊃ [FIN, −SUBJ]

By contrast, the node at which [+PAST] is potent in (67b) is the highest VP within the left conjunct of the coordinate structure. Notice that, by the HFC, there is no PAST specification on the mother VP in the coordinate structure, since the two heads have distinct specifications. This seems to be correct from the semantic point of view. If tense were associated with constituents at the S level, there would be no plausible way of interpreting structures like (67b).

Let us suppose that for each semantically potent feature specification $\langle f, v \rangle$ there is a corresponding constant a in IL. Thus, we might take PAST′ to be a constant of type $\langle VP, VP \rangle$. We do not have any special views on how tense is to be semantically interpreted; but following Bach (1980b), PAST′ could be assigned an interpretation of the following sort, relative to a world w and time t.

(69)   PAST′ denotes that function h such that for any NP extension a and VP extension β, $h(\beta)(a)(\langle w, t \rangle) = 1$ if and only if $\exists t'$ such that $t' < t$ and $\beta(a)(\langle w, t' \rangle) = 1$.

So that operators of this sort can be introduced into the translation, we must modify the Semantic Interpretation Schema. The modification we shall suggest, which is sketched in (71), makes use of the ancillary notion of a translation subfunction (notated *Tr*) defined in (70).

(70)   Given a node C in a local subtree t,
        (i) If f is a semantically potent feature specification in C and f' is the translation of f, then $Tr(C) = f'(C')$,
        (ii) otherwise, $Tr(C) = C'$

(71)   Semantic Interpretation Schema (second formulation)[19]

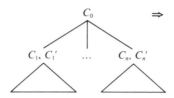

$$C_0' = \mathrm{FR}(TYP(C_0), \{Tr(C_1), \ldots, Tr(C_n)\}_m).$$

The tree in (72) illustrates the kind of mapping we envisage.

(72)   a.   S
               NP
               VP[+PAST]
        b.   PAST' (VP')(NP')

Constituent questions might also be analyzed by semantically interpreting syntactic features. The interpretation of **FOOT** features that we present in the following section will treat constituent questions in the same way as relative clauses. If nothing further is said, a string like (73) will receive the same translation into IL, namely (74), whether it is analyzed as a constituent question or a relative clause.

(73)   who Lee sees

(74) $\lambda\mathscr{P}[\textbf{see}' (\mathscr{P})(\textbf{Lee*})]$

A semantics for questions modeled on that of Karttunen (1977) might be provided by introducing an operator **WHQ** which converts expressions like the one in (74) to expressions with question denotations. Since the category S[WH NP] is of type $\langle$NP, S$\rangle$, while question denotations are taken to be sets of true propositions, **WHQ** is of type $\langle\langle$NP, S$\rangle, \langle$S, $t\rangle\rangle$. The introduction of this operator will be licenced when the specification [WH NP[WHMOR Q]] is semantically potent on a node. In (75) we illustrate the translation that will be induced when a verb takes a constituent question as its complement.

(75) a. VP

         V

        S[WH NP[WHMOR Q]]

    b. V′ (**WHQ**(S′))

Meaning postulates would guarantee the equivalence in (76).[20]

(76) a. Kim wonders who walks.

    b. wonder′ (**WHQ**(**walk**′))(**Kim***)

    c. wonder′ ($\lambda p[\exists x[^\lor p \land p = $ **walk**′ $(x^*)]])$(**Kim***)

The proper semantic treatment of interrogative structures is of course a controversial current issue within formal semantic research. There are a number of other currently available proposals that seem quite harmonious with the general program being outlined here.[21]

As another example of the semantic interpretation of syntactic features, we consider the case of postnominal modifiers such as those italicized in (77).

(77) a. someone *standing by the door*

    b. a chair *by the door*

    c. a responsibility *given to the chairman*

    d. a house *more comfortable than this one*

    e. a box *which I sat on*

The possible categories of postnominal modifiers consist of VP, S[WH NP[WHMOR R]], PP or AP. Although this is an apparently disparate set, it is not unreasonable to suppose that each of these categories can be associated with a common type, namely *TYP*(VP).[22] Yet a problem remains. The semantic type of the N¹ sister of such modifiers is ⟨e, t⟩. Under our assumptions there is no way for functional realization to combine an N¹ with an expression of VP-type to produce an N¹-type expression.

One solution to this dilemma is to introduce a semantical feature **MOD** onto postnominal modifiers. This will give rise to translations like (78).[23]

(78)

Suppose, in addition, that we define MOD′ as shown below:

(79) $\text{MOD}' = \lambda v^{VP} \lambda P \lambda x [P(x) \land \ ^\lor v^{VP}(x^*)]$

Then these rules will induce (80b) as the translation of (80a).

(80)   a.

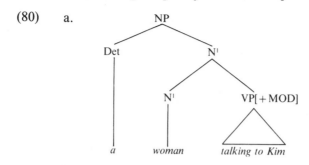

b.   **a′** $(\lambda x[\textbf{woman}' \, (x) \, \wedge \, {}^{\vee}\textbf{talking}' \, (\textbf{Kim*})(x*)])$

The coordination schemata presented in chapter 3 may also be treated by associating a translation schema with the feature CONJ. The benefit of so doing is that this provides a solution to a difficulty pointed out in Carlson 1983a. In certain instantiations of the iterating coordination schema, there is more than one occurrence of the conjunction:

(81)

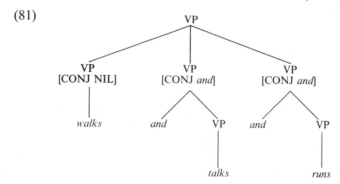

Despite multiple occurrences of *and*, the interpretation of such structures involves just a single *and* interpretation. It is difficult to see how any approach which interprets each *and* individually can deal with structures of this sort.[24]

Assuming conjunctions translate into IL as one of a family of Boolean operators (i.e. one for each relevant type), we can remove this difficulty by modifying our translation schema in the following way.

(82)   Semantic Interpretation Schema (third formulation)

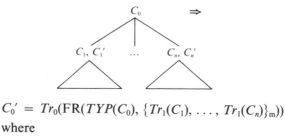

$C_0' = Tr_0(\text{FR}(TYP(C_0), \{Tr_1(C_1), \ldots, Tr_1(C_n)\}_m))$
where

    (i)   If f is a semantically potent feature specification in C, then
           $Tr_1(C) = f'(C')$, otherwise, $Tr_1(C) = C'$.
    (ii) If [CONJ a] is in some daughter but absent from C_0, where
           $a \in \{and, or, \ldots\}$, then $Tr_0(\phi) = a' \, (\phi)$,
           otherwise, $Tr_0(\phi) = \phi$.

The result will be interpreted structures such as the following.

(83)   a.   VP
               VP_1[CONJ NIL, $+$PAST]
               VP_2[CONJ *and*, $-$PAST]
               VP_3[CONJ *and*, $-$PAST]
      b.   **and'** (PAST' (VP_1'), VP_2', VP_3')

(84)   a.   NP
               NP_1[CONJ *either*]
               NP_2[CONJ *or*]
      b.   **or'** (NP_1', NP_2')

The general approach to the semantics of coordination outlined in Gazdar 1980 is thus rendered compatible with the syntax of coordination we have put forward.

None of the analyses discussed in this section should be taken as definitive. Our purpose here has been rather to illustrate how the mechanism of functional realization outlined in section 1 can be incorporated in translation schemas that allow syntactic features to be semantically interpreted, and to show that this method provides a framework for developing solutions to difficult problems of semantic analysis.[25]

6 Unbounded dependency semantics

When we discussed the syntax of unbounded dependency constructions in chapter 7, we pointed out that it is useful to think of the structure of such constructions as consisting of three parts: a top, where the dependency is introduced, a middle, where the information that there is a missing constituent is passed down the tree by means of the feature SLASH, and the bottom, where the SLASH information is terminated. The same tripartite distinction turns out to be useful in discussing the semantics of UDCs, and we shall again start in the middle.

A distinctive property of our treatment concerns the semantic type of 'slash categories'. On the analysis presented in Gazdar 1981, the type associated with a category a/β is identical to the type associated with the category a. Expressions of the latter category differ from those of the former only in containing a free occurrence of a distinguished β type variable. On the present approach the type associated with a category α/β is $\langle TYP(\beta),\ TYP(\alpha)\rangle$, i.e. the category whose members denote functions from β type denotations to α type denotations.[26] The kind of translations that we assign to local trees involved in UDCs are illustrated in (85)–(88).

(85) a. S/NP
            NP
            VP/NP
       b. $\lambda\mathscr{P}[\text{VP/NP}'\ (\mathscr{P})(\text{NP}')]$

(86) a. VP/NP
            V[2]
            NP/NP
       b. $\lambda\mathscr{P}[\text{V}'\ (\text{NP/NP}'\ (\mathscr{P}))]$

(87) a. S/AP
            NP
            VP/AP
       b. $\lambda v^{\text{AP}}[\text{VP/AP}'\ (v^{\text{AP}})(\text{NP})]$

(88) a. VP/VP
            V[13]
            VP[INF]/VP
       b. $\lambda v^{\text{VP}}[\text{V}'\ (\text{VP/VP}'\ (v^{\text{VP}}))]$

Each of these local trees is the result of instantiating [SLASH XP] (for some value of XP) on a daughter and the mother according to the conditions imposed by the FFP. Each semantic translation is constructed by forming a lambda abstract in which a variable v^{XP} is bound. The body of the lambda abstract consists of the functional realization of the daughters, given one proviso: the translation of any daughter α_i which contains an instantiated feature specification [SLASH XP] is taken to be $\alpha_i'(v^{\text{XP}})$, rather than simply α_i'.

We now introduce a translation schema that allows these interpreted structures to be derived.

(89) Semantic Interpretation Schema (final formulation)

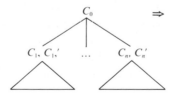

$C_0' = Tr_0(Tr_1(\text{FR}((C_0 - \textbf{FOOT}),\ \{Tr_2(C_1'),\ \ldots,\ Tr_2(C_n')\}_{\text{m}})))$
where

(i) if $\exists f \in$ **FOOT** such that $\langle f, a \rangle \in C_0$, then $Tr_0(\phi) = \lambda v^a \phi$, otherwise $Tr_0(\phi) = \phi$.

(ii) if [CONJ a] is in some daughter but absent from C_0, where $a \in \{and, or, \ldots\}$, then $Tr_1(\phi) = a'(\phi)$ otherwise $Tr_1(\phi) = \phi$

(iii) if $\exists f \in$ **FOOT** such that $\langle f, a \rangle \in C_0$, then $Tr_2(C_i') = Tr_3(C_i')(v^a)$ or $Tr_2(C_i') = Tr_3(C_i')$, otherwise $Tr_2(C_i') = Tr_3(C_i')$.

(iv) if $\exists \sigma$ such that σ is a semantically potent feature specification in C_i, then $Tr_3(C_i') = \sigma'(C_i)$, otherwise $Tr_3(C_i') = C_i'$.

When applied to local trees, this will yield the results indicated in (85)–(88). Let us now look at a larger tree fragment in which the slash information is passed through two local subtrees. The Semantic Interpretation Schema will induce the following result:[27]

(90)

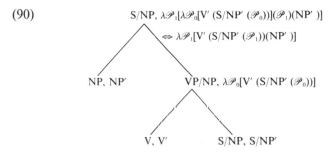

$$S/NP, \lambda \mathscr{P}_1[\lambda \mathscr{P}_0[V'\ (S/NP'\ (\mathscr{P}_0))](\mathscr{P}_1)(NP'\ )]$$
$$\Leftrightarrow \lambda \mathscr{P}_1[V'\ (S/NP'\ (\mathscr{P}_1))(NP'\ )]$$

NP, NP'

$$VP/NP, \lambda \mathscr{P}_0[V'\ (S/NP'\ (\mathscr{P}_0))]$$

V, V'   S/NP, S/NP'

Recall that the local trees which terminate UDCs are admitted from rules produced by the Slash Termination Metarules. Because the lexical translations of $X^?[+NULL]$ constituents are identity functions on the semantic domain of X^2 constituents, our translation schema gives us such translations as the following:

(91)

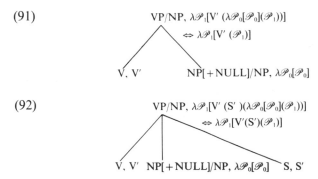

$$VP/NP, \lambda \mathscr{P}_1[V'\ (\lambda \mathscr{P}_0[\mathscr{P}_0](\mathscr{P}_1))]$$
$$\Leftrightarrow \lambda \mathscr{P}_1[V'\ (\mathscr{P}_1)]$$

V, V' $NP[+NULL]/NP, \lambda \mathscr{P}_0[\mathscr{P}_0]$

(92)

$$VP/NP, \lambda \mathscr{P}_1[V'\ (S'\ )(\lambda \mathscr{P}_0[\mathscr{P}_0](\mathscr{P}_1))]$$
$$\Leftrightarrow \lambda \mathscr{P}_1[V'(S')(\mathscr{P}_1)]$$

V, V' $NP[+NULL]/NP, \lambda \mathscr{P}_0[\mathscr{P}_0]$ S, S'

By putting various of these translations together and performing relevant reductions, we have S/NP translations like the one in (93).

(93)   a.   Sandy says Kim likes *e*.

        b. $\lambda\mathscr{P}_4[(\textbf{say}' \ (\textbf{like}' \ (\mathscr{P}_4))(\textbf{Kim*}))(\textbf{Sandy*})]$

In the translations produced by our schema, it is in general the case that a daughter's translation will include an occurrence of the variable bound by the λ-operator only if that daughter contains an instantiation of the relevant **FOOT** feature specification, as in the examples just illustrated. However clause (iii) of (89) does not require that this be so. In some cases, such as the following structure admitted from an output of the second Slash Termination Metarule discussed in chapter 7 (where no daughter contains the relevant **FOOT** feature specification), the only possible translation is the one indicated.

(94)   a.   VP/NP
             V[40]
             VP[FIN, +PAST]

        b. $\lambda\mathscr{P}_0[V' \ (\textbf{PAST}' \ (VP')(\mathscr{P}_0))]$

The analysis we have sketched thus provides a semantic analysis of phrases which occur in UDCs without using unbound distinguished variables. The reduced lambda abstract in (94b) is in fact the same one employed in Gazdar's (1981b) analysis of this sentential constituent. The difference is that on our analysis, the lambda expression has been built up as the translation of the S/NP by compositional rules, rather than by capturing a distinguished variable that happens to occur freely within the translation of a daughter constituent.

Let us now turn our attention to the tops of UDCs. The topicalization rule is distinguished from the rules we have been considering in virtue of the fact that it specifies [SLASH X^2] on the S daughter. (By constrast, the [SLASH NP] specifications which occur on categories in UDC middles get there by feature instantiation.) Hence there is no [SLASH X^2] instantiated on the mother in structures admitted from this rule. We take UDC constructions to be semantically extensional in nature[28] and predict this observation by assuming that [SLASH NP] is a semantically significant feature specification. Let us call the translation of this feature specification **EXT** and define it semantically as in (95).

(95) $\textbf{EXT} = \lambda v^{\text{VP}}\lambda\mathscr{P}[^\frown\mathscr{P}\{\lambda x[v^{\text{VP}}(x*)]\}]$

Because [SLASH NP] is semantically potent at the top of UDCs the topicalization rule will give rise to translations of the type shown in (96)

(96) a. S

       NP
       S/NP

  b. **EXT**(S/NP′)(NP′)

This correctly ensures that such pairs of sentences as (97) are rendered truth-conditionally equivalent.

(97) a. Kim loved Sandy.
    b. Sandy, Kim loved.

And when SLASH has been instantiated on more than one daughter, as is possible in the case of the rules responsible for parasitic gaps discussed in chapter 7, translations like the one in (98) are derived.

(98) a. VP/NP

       VP/NP
       PP/NP

  b. $\lambda\mathscr{P}[\text{PP}'\ (\mathscr{P})(\text{VP}'\ (\mathscr{P}))]$

Here the translation has the effect of semantically associating the filler in a UDC with the position of both gaps in examples like (99).

(99)

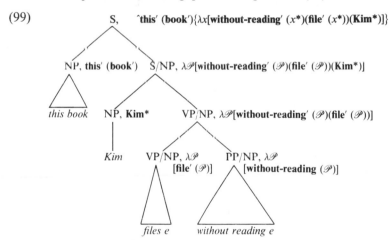

And in the case of coordinate structures, where we also find [SLASH NP] specified on more than one daughter, our analysis predicts translations like the one shown in (100).

(100) a. S[SLASH NP]

       S[SLASH NP, CONJ NIL]
       S[SLASH NP, CONJ *and*]

  b. $\lambda\mathscr{P}[\mathbf{and}'\ (\text{S[SLASH NP, CONJ NIL]}'\ (\mathscr{P}),$
     (S[SLASH NP, CONJ *and*]′ $(\mathscr{P}))]$

The semantic facts of coordinate structures in UDCs are thus properly systematized.

The semantic analysis sketched for SLASH inheritance extends to the inheritance of the other **FOOT** features. We assume that interrogative and relative lexical items designate identity functions on the semantic categories they are customarily associated with, as illustrated in (101).

(101)

α	syntactic category	$Tr(\alpha)$	$TYP(Tr(\alpha))$
what	NP[WH NP[WHMOR Q]].	$\lambda\mathscr{P}[\mathscr{P}]$	$\langle$NP, NP$\rangle$
who	NP[WH NP[WHMOR Q]]	$\lambda\mathscr{P}[\mathscr{P}]$	$\langle$NP, NP$\rangle$
who	NP[WH NP[WHMOR R]]	$\lambda\mathscr{P}[\mathscr{P}]$	$\langle$NP, NP$\rangle$
when	AP[+ADV, WH ADV[WHMOR Q]]	$\lambda v^{\text{ADV}}[v^{\text{ADV}}]$	$\langle$ADV, ADV$\rangle$
whose	NP[POSS, WH NP[WHMOR Q]]	$\lambda\mathscr{P}[\mathscr{P}]$	$\langle$NP, NP$\rangle$
whose	NP[POSS, WH NP[WHMOR R]]	$\lambda\mathscr{P}[\mathscr{P}]$	$\langle$NP, NP$\rangle$

This being the case, we can establish the semantic connection between these items and the environments higher in the tree where binding will take place. We assume a semantics of the same general sort for the inheritance of these features, but because of FCRs, far fewer structures will be involved. Some of those that are are listed in (102)–(105).

(102) a.   NP[WH NP[WHMOR R]]
            DET
            N¹[WH NP[WHMOR R]]
       b. $\lambda\mathscr{P}[\text{DET}' \ (\text{N}^{1\prime} \ (\mathscr{P}))]$

(103) a.   N¹[WH NP[WHMOR R]]
            N[35]
            PP[*of*,[WH NP[WHMOR R]]]
       b. $\lambda\mathscr{P}[\text{N}^1 \ (\text{PP}' \ (\mathscr{P}))]$

(104) a.   NP[WH NP[WHMOR R]]
            NP[POSS,[WH NP[WHMOR R]]]
            N¹[AGR NP]
       b. $\lambda\mathscr{P}[\text{N}^{1\prime} \ (\text{NP}' \ (\mathscr{P}))]$

(105) a.   S[WH NP[WHMOR R]]
            NP[WH NP[WHMOR R]]
            VP[FIN]
       b. $\lambda\mathscr{P}[\text{VP}' \ (\text{NP}' \ (\mathscr{P}))]$

These schematic phrasal translations and the lexical translations given above interact to assign relative clauses translations of VP type, as illustrated in (106).[29]

(106)

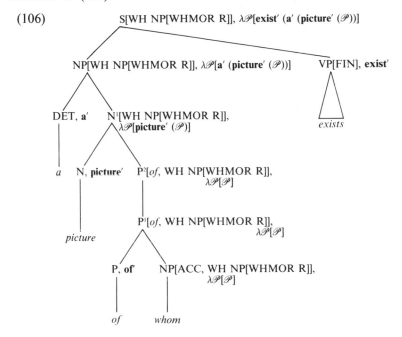

The grammar for relative clauses presented in chapter 7 also makes use of the rule for topicalized clauses. This gives rise to the trickling of [WH NP[WHMOR R]] specifications in local trees like the following:

(107)   a.   S[WH NP[WHMOR R]]
            NP[WH NP[WHMOR R]]
            S/NP
     b. $\lambda \mathscr{P}[\mathbf{EXT}(S/NP') (NP' (\mathscr{P}))]$

(107) interacts with the treatment of SLASH categories just outlined to treat the bulk of the familiar cases of relative clauses introduced by 'dislocated' constituents. This is illustrated in (108).

(108)

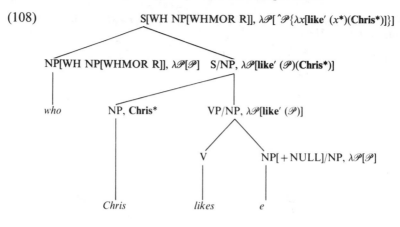

7 Idioms

'Fixed expressions', or phrasal idioms, have played an important role in linguistic argumentation. For example, the co-occurrence dependencies between *keep*, *tabs*, and *on* illustrated in (109) are commonly thought to be syntactic in nature.[30]

(109) a.
$$\text{Pat} \left\{ \begin{array}{l} \text{kept} \\ \#\,\text{maintained} \\ \#\,\text{held} \end{array} \right\} \text{tabs on Terry.}$$

 b.
$$\text{Pat kept tabs} \left\{ \begin{array}{l} \text{on} \\ \#\,\text{against} \\ \#\,\text{for} \end{array} \right\} \text{Terry.}$$

Similar claims have been made for other fixed expressions like the following:

(110) a.
$$\text{Hilary} \left\{ \begin{array}{l} \text{pulled} \\ \#\,\text{yanked} \\ \#\,\text{tugged at} \end{array} \right\} \text{strings to get the job.}$$

 b.
$$\#\,\text{Hilary pulled} \left\{ \begin{array}{l} \text{twine} \\ \text{rope} \end{array} \right\} \text{to get the job.}$$

(111) a.
$$\text{Robin} \left\{ \begin{array}{l} \text{took} \\ \#\,\text{obtained} \\ \#\,\text{extracted} \end{array} \right\} \text{advantage of Lee.}$$

 b.
$$\#\,\text{Robin took advantage} \left\{ \begin{array}{l} \text{on} \\ \text{from} \\ \text{over} \end{array} \right\} \text{Lee.}$$

Parts of fixed expressions, so-called 'idiom chunks', may appear *inter alia* in passive and raising constructions, as illustrated below, and hence whatever account is given of the restricted distribution of these elements must interface smoothly with the analysis of those constructions that we have given.

(112)   (Close) tabs were kept on Terry by the KGB.

(113)   Hilary believed strings to have been pulled in Sandy's getting the job.

(114)   (Unfair) advantage appeared to have been taken of Lee by almost everyone.

Traditional wisdom dictates that an idiom is by definition a constituent or series of constituents whose semantic interpretation is not a compositional function of the interpretations of its parts. In most analyses in generative grammar, idioms are treated as elements which are possibly assigned internal syntactic structure, but no internal semantic structure.[31] This view leaves unexplained many fundamental facts about those idioms whose parts are at all syntactically mobile (i.e. which appear in raising or passive constructions).

There are a number of reasons to believe that the parts of such idioms should be assigned interpretations:
(i)   Parts of idioms may be modified by either adjectives or relative clauses as in (115).

(115)   a.   leave no legal stone unturned
        b.   take unfair advantage
        c.   kick the filthy habit
        d.   Pat got the job by pulling strings that weren't available to anyone else.

Note that these are examples of what Ernst (1980) has termed *internal modification*, that is modification of only *part* of the meaning of the idiom. (115a) for example, means (roughly) that all legal methods were used.
(ii)   Parts of idioms may be quantified, viz.

(116)   a.   pull a string or two
        b.   touch a couple of nerves
        c.   take as much advantage of the situation as you can
        d.   That's the third gift horse she's looked in the mouth this year.

The fact that we can coherently collocate quantifiers with the idiomatic elements like *nerves* and *strings* indicates minimally that some interpretation is being assigned to those idiom chunks. Presumably, these idiomatic nouns have extensions that can be quantified over.

(iii)   Parts of idioms may be emphasized through topicalization (see chapter 7), as in (117).

(117)   a.   Those strings, he wouldn't pull for you.
        b.   They might keep tabs on us, but close tabs, they'll never keep on us
        c.   His closets, you can find skeletons in.

It would not make sense to make a topic out of an idiom part in this way unless these parts have identifiable meanings.

(iv)   Finally, parts of idioms can be omitted in VP-Ellipsis.

(118)   a.   My goose is cooked, but yours isn't.
        b.   We had expected that excellent care would be taken of the orphans, and it was.
        c.   I said close tabs would be kept on Sandy, but they weren't.

It has been shown (Sag 1976, 1981; Williams 1977) that the antecedents of the missing elements in such constructions must be semantic units. From this it follows that the VPs in these examples, which are composed of *parts* of idiomatic expressions, must have identifiable semantic interpretations.

Our proposal for accommodating these observations, following Wasow, Nunberg, and Sag (1982), is to view the dependency between the syntactically versatile parts of an idiomatic expression as being purely semantic in nature. The account they suggest for this makes essential use of the notion of partial function. To illustrate, the verb *spill* might be assigned two senses (perhaps by the same mechanism introduced in section 4 for multiple lexical translations), which we can represent as two distinct expressions of intensional logic: **spill′** (representing the literal sense) and **spill″** (representing the idiomatic sense – roughly (but not exactly) the sense of *divulge*). Similarly, *beans* is assigned two senses: **beans′** and **beans″**, the latter of which has roughly (but not exactly) the sense of *information*.

The normal principles of compositional semantics will thus assign an idiomatic interpretation to *the beans* (we will represent this interpretation informally as **the-beans″**), which serves as the argument of **spill″**, but nothing else. By treating the translations of transitive verbs as partial functions from NP-type intensions to VP-type denotations (instead of total functions, as is customary), we have a purely semantic mechanism for ensuring this.[32] Such a function may be defined at only one argument, e.g., the sense of **the-beans″**, or it may be defined at a family of such senses. This is just what partial functions allow one to do.

All syntactically active idiomatic expressions have a metaphorical basis. Speakers know this, but they may no longer know the actual basis of the metaphor. In the example at hand, for example, speakers know that there is some function f such that

(119) $f(\textbf{spill}' \ (\textbf{the-beans}')) = \textbf{spill}''(\textbf{the-beans}'')$

The existence of such functions, at the 'phrasal' level, so to speak, constrains the particular interpretations assigned to individual parts of an idiomatic expression. The parts, nonetheless, have isolatable interpretations.

This approach to the semantics of idioms requires a fine-grained theory of word meaning, one quite in the spirit of Goodman (1949), and Bolinger (1965), which in general eschews complete synonymy. Thus it is assumed that however close in meaning such pairs as *tabs* and *surveillance* may be, they have distinct senses. The function denoted by idiomatic *keep* is defined only for the sense of the former:

(120) a.   keep tabs on
       b.   # keep surveillance on

Consequently, our approach is incompatible with accounts of word meaning which seek to characterize word meanings in terms of a fixed set of atomic semantic features. Such theories would be hard-pressed to provide the necessary fine-grained distinctions of lexical and phrasal meaning.

The partialness of verb denotation functions will of course permeate the entire lexicon, as the intension of *tabs*, for instance, must be outside the domain of the function denoted by a verb like *maintain*.

(121) Kim maintained tabs on Pat.

This presents no problem of principle, but leaves many details of description unexplored. On this view, however, one would expect to find idioms where more than one chunk was available in a given position, as any subset of the set of NP-intensions is a possible domain for the function denoted by a verb. This prediction appears to be correct, since we find idiom variants like the following:

(122) a.   hit the sack/hay
       b.   pack a punch/wallop
       c.   get off one's ass/butt/rear/fanny/duff/tuchus …

Similarly, there may be a family of function-denoting expressions which produce idiomatic interpretations when supplied with a given idiomatic argument:

(123) a.   stretch/strain/push a point
       b.   stop/turn on a dime
       c.   pick/punch/poke/shoot holes in an argument
       d.   lay/throw/place/put one's cards on the table

These observations are utterly surprising on standard, purely syntactic views of idiomaticity. They are to be expected given the semantic theory just outlined.

The approach sketched above also allows one to begin to explain the observations cited earlier. Since idiom chunks have interpretations, they may in principle be modified and quantified, though there are severe restrictions on these processes which are not yet well understood. VPs within the relevant idioms have interpretations, and hence may undergo VP-Ellipsis in a fashion consistent with current theories. Similarly, it makes sense to topicalize certain idiom chunks, as certain sentences may well be 'about' (if that is the correct pragmatic notion to associate with the topicalization construction) the denotation of the dislocated chunk.

This approach to the analysis of idioms fits nicely with the basic proposals we have advanced. A VP like *pull strings*, for example, can be treated in just the same way as other transitive VPs. Our account of passive and raising immediately provides an account of the fact that NP idiom chunks can be spread about in those constructions. The semantic interpretation of sentences containing passive and subject-raising VPs is directly related by meaning postulate to sentential expressions where the idiomatic functors take the appropriate idiomatic NPs as arguments. Hence the partial domains of idiomatic functors are inherited by the appropriate 'passivized' and 'raised' expressions that contain them. So a passive VP like *kept on Kim* (and by the same argument a larger VP containing it, like *were kept on Kim*) denotes a function that preserves exactly the partialness of the function denoted by *keep* in *keep tabs on Kim*. That function is defined only at the appropriate arguments, i.e. those provided by the NPs *tabs*, *close tabs*, *unusually close tabs*, etc. We thus have a straightforward semantic account of the following familiar sorts of facts.

(124) $\left\{\begin{array}{l} \text{Tabs} \\ \#\text{Surveillance patrols} \\ \#\text{Investigations} \end{array}\right\}$ were kept on Kim by the FBI.

(125) We believed close $\left\{\begin{array}{l} \text{tabs} \\ \#\text{surveillance patrols} \\ \#\text{investigations} \end{array}\right\}$ $\begin{array}{l} \text{to have been} \\ \text{kept on Kim.} \end{array}$

(126) Close $\left\{\begin{array}{l} \text{tabs} \\ \#\text{surveillance patrols} \\ \#\text{investigations} \end{array}\right\}$ appear to have been kept on Kim.

In addition, it follows that idiom chunks whose interpretations are outside the domain of the functions denoted by active transitive verbs are also outside the domains of the functions denoted by the corresponding passive VP. Thus our semantic analysis allows us to unify the account of contrasts like these:

(127)   a.   #Kim found tabs on Sandy.
        b.   #Tabs were found on Sandy by Kim.
(128)   a.   #Pat tugged strings to get the job.
        b.   #Strings were tugged by Pat to get the job.

Arbitrarily complex examples involving nesting of passive and raising are explained in like fashion.

(129)   Close $\left\{ \begin{array}{l} \text{tabs} \\ \#\text{surveillance patrols} \\ \#\text{investigations} \end{array} \right\}$ are believed to have been kept on Kim by the FBI.

(130)   Numerous strings continue to appear to have been $\left\{ \begin{array}{l} \text{pulled} \\ \#\text{tugged} \end{array} \right\}$

in getting Leslie the job.

The relevant NP-arguments in equi constructions on the other hand are related (also by meaning postulate) to property sets of individuals, more specifically to property sets of *volitional* agents, and objects that are able to hope, want, or promise things, or that are capable of being persuaded of things, promised things or of being compelled to do things. It is a fact that virtually all idiom chunks in English have intensions which determine nonanimate extensions, and this fact suffices to explain the commonly made observation that idiom chunks may not be distributed in equi constructions:

(131)   a.   #Strings tried to be pulled to get the job.
        b.   #We persuaded/promised unfair advantage to be taken of Sandy.

However, this mode of explanation leads one to search for idioms whose parts do denote (property sets of) animate objects. *Pay the piper* appears to be one such example, and (although the appropriate example may be somewhat strained for other reasons), it seems that *the piper* can indeed occur in the relevant NP-positions, if, for example, the user of such sentences in uttering *the piper* indeed intends to make reference to a given person who is exacting his or her due:

(132)   The piper wants to be paid.

This semantic approach to the analysis of idioms thus meshes well with the analyses of this chapter which have been motivated entirely on independent grounds. No additional devices need be added to the syntax in accounting for the peculiarities of fixed expressions.[33]

Notes

1 In fact, the rules also included a rule index as third element. Since this has been dispensed with, we are ignoring it here.

2 This redundancy can be reduced in a categorial grammar by schematizing the translation rules. So, for example, the grammar can contain a general principle that for every syntactic rule of the form (ia), there is an associated translation rule of the form (ib) (cf. Bach 1983).

    (i)   a. $A \rightarrow A/B\ B$
           b. $A/B'\ (B')$

3 The reason for allowing the lexicon to associate a *set* of translations with a single item is discussed in section 4.

4 Subscripts have been placed on the NPs as a means of distinguishing them, and have no other significance. Note also that the first argument of FR, designated 'VP', stands for $TYP(\text{VP})$.

5 The two *give*s can be treated via distinct IL expressions related by a meaning postulate like (i):

    (i) $\forall \mathscr{P}_1 \forall \mathscr{P}_2 \forall \mathscr{P}_3 \ \Box \ [V[3]'\ (\mathscr{P}_1)(\mathscr{P}_2)(\mathscr{P}_3) \leftrightarrow V[5]'(\mathscr{P}_2)(\mathscr{P}_1)(\mathscr{P}_3)]$

Alternatively, one *give*-translation can be derived from the other in the manner proposed by Dowty (1978b).

6 The notion of 2-argument was defined in the preceding chapter.

7 Note that this second consequence does *not* mean that the semantics is being used as a filter on the syntax. Every well-formed syntactic structure is assigned a nonempty set of semantic translations. The type incompatabilities merely restrict the size of that set. Some related ideas on type interaction are explored in Partee 1984, Partee and Rooth 1983, and Rooth and Partee 1982.

8 We are here using the term 'predicate' to cover verbs and adjectives.

9 These have a certain resemblance to the combinators used by Schoenfinkel (1924) and subsequent work in combinatorial logic. However, Schoenfinkel was interested in showing that a logic whose only logical constants were the combinators I, C, and S was expressively complete, i.e. equivalent to first order logic. We are interested in trying to isolate those combinators which appear to have a central role in natural language semantics.

10 In this respect our analysis is somewhat similar to that proposed by Dowty (1978b), though see also Dowty forthcoming.

11 Note that there are no verbs whose translations are **tend'**, **persuade'**, or **promise'**. Our use of these expressions is motivated by the systematic account of entailments and other meaning relations that result from the assumption that all control verbs are analyzed in terms of basic expressions which take propositional arguments. It might be thought that the *persuade* that takes clausal complements should be translated as *persuade'*. However the semantic

relation between *persuade that* sentences and *persuade to* sentences is more distant than generally supposed. Hence we posit a separate IL expression (which is also of type $\langle S, \langle NP, VP \rangle \rangle$) as the translation of the *persuade* which subcategorizes for a clausal complement. Similarly, we treat the *promise* which takes a clausal complement in terms of a separate IL expression of type $\langle S, \langle NP, VP \rangle \rangle$.

12 The Semantic Interpretation Schema, taken together with the meaning postulates restricting the interpretations of f_R and f_E, assigns narrow scope to the subjects in examples like (37b). We assume that wide-scope readings, those which do, for example, carry existential import, are to be derived by some version of 'Cooper storage' (Cooper 1975, 1983).

13 This account of control seems superior to configurational accounts stated in terms of c-command, the defects of which are discussed in Bresnan 1982a. Our treatment differs from that offered by Bresnan in that it is restricted to cases of obligatory control. We thus draw a sharp distinction between cases of the sort discussed in the text and examples like (i), discussed by Bresnan.

   (i)   Contradicting the teacher will bother Leslie.

The semantic argument (the missing subject) of the gerunds in examples like these can in principle always be supplied from the discourse context. Hence nothing more need be said to allow for the possibility that the missing subject is supplied on the basis of an element present within the same sentence.

14 We leave unresolved the matter of how best to formulate a mechanism for dealing with morphological irregularities.

15 There remain a number of interesting issues concerning the interaction of passivization and scope assignment which we will not address here. For some discussion and proposed treatments, see Keenan 1980 and Pollard 1984, which contain specific proposals for the proper semantic treatment of optional *by*-phrases as well.

16 We leave open the precise formulation of the process by which these lexical translations are derived.

17 This problem is also discussed in Cann 1984, p. 358.

18 We note that this proposed analysis poses difficulties for the semantic interpretation of inverted sentences if these are treated by means of the Subject–Auxiliary Inversion Metarule presented in chapter 4. An alternative proposal, consistent with the semantic analysis we have put forth, is discussed in Pollard 1984.

19 Here and henceforth we adopt a more concise notation for translation schemata.

20 We are assuming here that **WHQ** is the IL-translation of the specification [WH NP[WHMOR Q]] and omit any discussion of how this proposal could be extended to deal with embedded constituent questions introduced by adjectival or adverbial phrases.

21 One proposal in fact is to say nothing special about the semantics of interrogatives (cf. Hausser 1978, Main and Benson 1983). This would assign to questions like *Who walks* a function from NP-type meanings to S-type meanings.

22 Notice that both AP and PP can play a predicative role. General considerations in favor of assigning relative clauses the same type as VP will be suggested in the next section.

23 We use the notation v^c to indicate a variable of type $TYP(C)$, where C is a category.

24 As Carlson points out, this problem manifests itself in the coordination systems of many of the world's languages.

25 There is an interesting issue concerning the proper formulation of the 'Optional Argument Convention' employed in earlier work within GPSG. We leave this matter to future research.

26 In this respect, we come close to the treatment of UDCs within categorial grammar which is developed in Ades and Steedman 1982 and Steedman 1983. The main discrepancies between our approach and theirs involve issues of analysis rather than theoretical framework. Most crucially, Ades and Steedman take subject NPs to be functors on VPs, while we adopt the position that they are arguments to the VP, for reasons of the sort presented in chapter 9.

27 For convenience, we assume a convention whereby, proceeding bottom-up, right-to-left, the least unused integer is employed as the index for a variable being newly introduced.

28 That is, we assume that sentences like (i) have only one possible scope assignment – where the existential quantifier takes wide scope.

      (i)   A friend of mine, everyone in the office wanted to meet.

29 In the previous section we showed how an analysis of this sort might be reconciled with a system wherein N's are of type $\langle e, t \rangle$.

30 The # prefixes in these examples and those throughout this section indicate a lack of the relevant idiomatic interpretation.

31 Essentially this position is held by Fraser (1970), Katz (1973), Heringer (1976), and Chomsky (1980), among others.

32 To carry out such an analysis properly, it is necessary to modify the model theory of intensional logic so as to accommodate partial functions. Presumably, a modification of this kind would also be required by a semantics for sortal incorrectness, following the suggestions of Thomason (1972). Indeed, it could be argued that idiomatic interpretation, as we have presented it, is just a special case of sortal restriction. In fact, we will not attempt such a modification here, since it raises certain problems which, while nontrivial, are not central to our analysis. For proposals involving partial models of intensional logic, see Kutschera (1975).

33 Certain idioms are of course semantically unanalyzable, e.g. *kick the bucket* and *trip the light fantastic*. These are to be analyzed as syntactically complex lexical items associated with a single, undecomposable semantic interpretation. From this it follows that their parts are never distributed in complex syntactic constructions:

      (i)   # The bucket was kicked by Sandy.
      (ii)   # The light was tripped fantastic.

See Wasow et al. 1983 for a discussion of several other types of idioms.

APPENDIX

List of features and rules

Features and feature values

CAT = {C | C is a category}

feature	value range
CASE	{ACC, NOM}
COMP	{*for, that, whether, if*, NIL}
CONJ	{*and, both, but, neither, either, nor, or*, NIL}
GER	{+, −}
NEG	{+, −}
NFORM	{*there, it*, NORM}
NULL	{+, −}
POSS	{+, −}
REMOR	{RECP, REFL}
WHMOR	{R, Q, FR, EX}

Head features

feature	value range
AGR	*CAT*
ADV	{+, −}
AUX	{+, −}
BAR	{0, 1, 2}
INV	{+, −}
LOC	{+, −}
N	{+, −}
PAST	{+, −}
PER	{1, 2, 3}
PFORM	{*to, by, for,* ...}
PLU	{+, −}
PRD	{+, −}
SLASH	*CAT*

SUBCAT $\{1, \ldots, n\}$ $\cup$
                 $\{for, that, \ldots, and, both, ..\}$
SUBJ $\{+, -\}$
V $\{+, -\}$
VFORM $\{$BSE, FIN, INF, PAS, PRP, PSP$\}$

Foot features

feature	value range
RE	*CAT*
SLASH	*CAT*
WH	*CAT*

Feature co-occurrence restrictions

FCR 1: $[+\text{INV}] \supset [+\text{AUX, FIN}]$
FCR 2: $[\text{VFORM}] \supset [+\text{V}, -\text{N}]$
FCR 3: $[\text{NFORM}] \supset [-\text{V}, +\text{N}]$
FCR 4: $[\text{PFORM}] \supset [-\text{V}, -\text{N}]$
FCR 5: $[\text{PAST}] \supset [\text{FIN}, -\text{SUBJ}]$
FCR 6: $[\text{SUBCAT}] \supset \sim[\text{SLASH}]$
FCR 7: $[\text{BAR } 0] \equiv [\text{N}] \,\&\, [\text{V}] \,\&\, [\text{SUBCAT}[$
FCR 8: $[\text{BAR } 1] \supset \sim[\text{SUBCAT}]$
FCR 9: $[\text{BAR } 2] \supset \sim[\text{SUBCAT}]$
FCR 10: $[+\text{INV, BAR } 2] \supset [+\text{SUBJ}]$
FCR 11: $[+\text{SUBJ}] \supset [+\text{V}, -\text{N, BAR } 2]$
FCR 12: $[\text{AGR}] \supset [-\text{N}, +\text{V}]$
FCR 13: $[\text{FIN, AGR NP}] \supset [\text{AGR NP[NOM]}]$
FCR 14: $([+\text{PRD}] \,\&\, [\text{VFORM}]) \supset ([\text{PAS}] \lor [\text{PRP}])$
FCR 15: $[\text{COMP}] \equiv [+\text{SUBJ}]$
FCR 16: $[\text{WH}, +\text{SUBJ}] \supset [\text{COMP NIL}]$
FCR 17: $[\text{COMP } \textit{that}] \supset ([\text{FIN}] \lor [\text{BSE}])$
FCR 18: $[\text{COMP } \textit{for}] \supset [\text{INF}]$
FCR 19: $[+\text{NULL}] \supset [\text{SLASH}]$
FCR 20: $\sim([\text{SLASH}] \,\&\, [\text{WH}])$
FCR 21: $A^1 \supset \sim[\text{WH}]$
FCR 22: $\text{VP} \supset \sim[\text{WH}]$

Feature specification defaults

FSD 1: $[-\text{INV}]$
FSD 2: $\sim[\text{CONJ}]$
FSD 3: $\sim[\text{NULL}]$
FSD 4: $\sim[\text{NOM}]$
FSD 5: $[\text{PFORM}] \supset [\text{BAR } 0]$

FSD 6:   [+ADV] ⊃ [BAR 0]
FSD 7:   [BAR 0] ⊃ ~[PAS]
FSD 8:   [NFORM] ⊃ [NFORM NORM]
FSD 9:   [INF, +SUBJ] ⊃ [COMP *for*]
FSD 10:   [+N, −V, BAR 2] ≡ [ACC]
FSD 11:   [+V, BAR 0] ⊃ [AGR NP[NFORM NORM]]

Immediate dominance rules

VP → H[1]   (*die*)
VP → H[2], NP   (*love*)
VP → H[3], NP, PP[*to*]   (*give*)
VP → H[4], NP, PP[*for*]   (*buy*)
VP → H[5], NP, NP   (*spare*)
VP → H[6], NP, PP[+LOC]   (*put*)
VP[+AUX] → H[7], XP[+PRD]   (*be*)
VP → H[8], NP, S[FIN]   (*persuade*)
VP → H[9], (PP[to]), S[FIN]   (*concede*)
VP → H[10], S[BSE]   (*prefer*)
VP → H[11], (PP[*of*]), S[BSE]   (*require*)
VP[INF, +AUX] → H[12], VP[BSE]   (*to*)
VP → H[13], VP[INF]   (*tend*)
VP → H[14], V²[INF, +NORM]   (*prefer*)
VP → H[15], VP[INF, +NORM]   (*try*)
VP → H[16], (PP[*to*]), VP[INF]   (*seem*)
VP → H[17], NP, VP[INF]   (*believe*)
VP → H[18], NP, VP[INF, +NORM]   (*persuade*)
VP → H[19], (NP), VP[INF, +NORM]   (*promise*)
VP[AGR S] → H[20], NP   (*bother*)
VP[+*it*] → H[21], (PP[*to*]), S[FIN]   (*seem*)
VP[AGR NP[*there*, αPLU]] → H[22], NP[αPLU]   (*be*)

AP → ({⟨SUBCAT, 23⟩}), H¹
A¹ → H[24], PP[*about*]   (*angry*)
A¹[AGR S] → H[25], PP[*to*]   (*apparent*)
A¹ → H[26], S[FIN]   (*afraid*)
A¹ → H[27], S[BSE]   (*insistent*)
A¹ → H[28], VP[INF]   (*likely*)
A¹ → H[29], V²[INF, +NORM]   (*eager*)

N¹ → H[30]   (*death*)
N¹ → H[31], PP[*with*], PP[*about*]   (*argument*)
N¹ → H[32], S[COMP *that*]   (*belief*)
N¹ → H[33], S[BSE, COMP *that*]   (*request*)
N¹ → H[34], V²[INF]   (*plan*)
N¹ → H[35], PP[*of*]   (*love*)
N¹ → H[36], PP[*of*], PP[*to*]   (*gift*)

$N^1 \rightarrow H[37], PP[of, GER]$ *(dislike)*

$P^1 \rightarrow H[38], NP$ *(in)*
$P^1 \rightarrow H[39], PP[of]$ *(out)*
$VP \rightarrow H[40], S[FIN$ *(believe)*
$P^1[+POSS] \rightarrow H[41], NP[+POSS]$ *(of)*
$A^1 \rightarrow H[42], V^2[INF]/NP[-NOM]$ *(easy)*
$VP \rightarrow H[43], S[+Q]$ *(inquire)*
$VP[+it] \rightarrow H[44], NP, S[+R]$ *(be)*
$VP[+it] \rightarrow H[44], X^2, S[FIN]/X^2$ *(be)*
$VP \rightarrow H[45], PP[of]$ *(approve)*
$VP[+AUX] \rightarrow H[46], VP[-AUX, BSE]$ *(do)*
$VP \rightarrow H[47], PP[to], PP[about]$ *(talk)*
$VP \rightarrow H[48], H[CONJ \ and]$ *(go)*

Nonlexical ID rules

$S \rightarrow X^2, H[-SUBJ]$
$S[COMP \ \alpha] \rightarrow \{[SUBCAT \ \alpha]\}, H[COMP \ NIL]$
where α is in $\{that, for, whether, if\}$
$S \rightarrow X^2, H/X^2$
$VP \rightarrow H, ADVP$
$NP \rightarrow NP[+POSS], H^1$
$N^1 \rightarrow H, PP[+POSS]$
$N^1 \rightarrow H, S[+R]$
$AP \rightarrow (A^2[+ADV]), H^1$
$X[CONJ \ NIL] \rightarrow H$
$X[CONJ \ \alpha] \rightarrow \{[SUBCAT \ \alpha]\}, H$

Iterating coordination scheme (CS^+)

$X \rightarrow H[CONJ \ \alpha_0], H[CONJ \ \alpha_1]^+$
where α is in $\{\langle and, NIL \rangle, \langle NIL, and \rangle, \langle neither, nor \rangle,$
$\langle or, NIL \rangle, \langle NIL, or \rangle\}$

Binary coordination schema (CS^2)

$X \rightarrow H[CONJ \ \alpha_0], H[CONJ \ \alpha_1]$
where α is in $\{\langle both, and \rangle, \langle either, or \rangle, \langle NIL, but \rangle\}$

Linear precedence statements

$[SUBCAT] \prec \sim[SUBCAT]$
$[+N] \prec P^2 \prec V^2$
$[CONJ \ \alpha_0] \prec [CONJ \ \alpha_1]$
where α_0 is in $\{both, either, neither, NIL\}$
and α_1 is in $\{and, but, nor, or\}$.

Metarules

Passive Metarule

$$VP \rightarrow W, NP$$
$$\Downarrow$$
$$VP[PAS] \rightarrow W, (PP[by])$$

'Subject–Aux Inversion' (SAI) Metarule

$$V^2[-SUBJ] \rightarrow W$$
$$\Downarrow$$
$$V^2[+INV, +SUBJ] \rightarrow W, NP$$

Extraposition Metarule

$$X^2[AGR\ S] \rightarrow W$$
$$\Downarrow$$
$$X^2[AGR\ NP[it]] \rightarrow W, S$$

Complement Omission Metarule

$$[+N, BAR\ 1] \rightarrow H, W$$
$$\Downarrow$$
$$[+N, BAR\ 1] \rightarrow H$$

Slash Termination Metarule 1 (STM1)

$$X \rightarrow W, X^2$$
$$\Downarrow$$
$$X \rightarrow W, X^2[+NULL]$$

Slash Termination Metarule 2 (STM2)

$$X \rightarrow W, V^2[+SUBJ, FIN]$$
$$\Downarrow$$
$$X/NP \rightarrow W, V^2[-SUBJ]$$

Bibliography

Abraham, R. C. 1941. *A Modern Grammar of Spoken Hausa*. London: Crown Agents for the Colonies.

Ades, Anthony E. and Mark J. Steedman 1982. On the order of words. *Linguistics and Philosophy*, 4, 517–58.

Aho, Alfred V. and Jeffrey D. Ullman 1972. *The Theory of Parsing, Translation, and Compiling*. Englewood Cliffs, New Jersey: Prentice-Hall.

Akmajian, Adrian and Frank Heny 1975. *Introduction to the Principles of Transformational Syntax*. Cambridge, Massachusetts: MIT Press.

Anderson, Carol 1984. Coordinate structure and asymmetric gaps. Unpublished paper, Pennsylvania State University.

Anderson, Stephen R. 1977a. Comments on the paper by Wasow. In Peter W. Culicover, Thomas Wasow and Adrian Akmajian (eds), *Formal Syntax*. New York: Academic Press, 361–77.

Anderson, Stephen R. 1977b. On the formal description of inflection. In Woodford A. Beach, Samuel E. Fox and Shulamith E. Philosoph (eds), *Papers from the 13th Regional Meeting, Chicago Linguistic Society*, 15–44.

Anderson, Stephen R. 1981. Why phonology isn't 'natural'. *Linguistic Inquiry*, 12, 493–539.

Andrews, Avery D. III 1983. A note on the constituent structure of modifiers. *Linguistic Inquiry*, 14, 695–7.

Anward, Jan 1982. Basic Swedish. In Elisabet Engdahl and Eva Ejerhed (eds), *Readings on Unbounded Dependencies in Scandinavian Languages. Acta Universitatis Umensis, Umea Studies in the Humanities*, 43. Stockholm: Almqvist & Wiksell, 47–75.

Bach, Emmon 1976. An extension of classical transformational grammar. *Problems in Linguistic Metatheory, Proceedings of the 1976 Conference at Michigan State University*, 183–224.

Bach, Emmon 1979. Control in Montague Grammar. *Linguistic Inquiry*, 10, 515–31.

Bach, Emmon 1980a. In defense of Passive. *Linguistics and Philosophy*; 3, 297–341.

Bach, Emmon 1980b. Tenses and aspects as functions on verb-phrases. In

Christian Rohrer (ed.), *Time, Tense and Quantifiers*. Tubingen: Max Niemeyer, 19–37.

Bach, Emmon 1981. Discontinuous constituents in generalized categorial grammars. In Victoria A. Burke and James Pustejovsky (eds), *Proceedings of the 11th Annual Meeting of the North Eastern Linguistic Society*, 1–12. Department of Linguistics, University of Massachusetts at Amherst.

Bach, Emmon 1983. On the relationship between word-grammar and phrase-grammar. *Natural Language and Linguistic Theory*, 1, 65–89.

Bach, Emmon and Barbara H. Partee 1980. Anaphora and semantic structure. In Jody Kreiman and Almerindo E. Ojeda (eds), *Papers from the Parasession on Pronouns and Anaphora*, Chicago: Chicago Linguistic Society, 1–28.

Barlow, Michael 1983. A defense of phrase structure grammar. Paper presented at the Spring Meeting of the Linguistics Association of Great Britain, University of Sheffield, March 23–25, 1983.

Barlow, Michael 1984. Control agreement and syntax. Paper presented to the Spring Meeting of the Linguistics Association of Great Britain, University of Hull, March 28–30, 1984.

Bartsch, Renate 1976. The role of categorial syntax in grammatical theory. In Asa Kasher (ed.), *Language in Focus: Foundations, Methods and Systems*. Dordrecht: D. Reidel, 503–40.

Bartsch, Renate 1978. Infinitives and the control problem in categorial grammar. *Theoretical Linguistics*, 5, 217–50.

Barwise, Jon and Robin Cooper 1981. Generalized quantifiers and natural language. *Linguistics and Philosophy*, 4, 159–219.

Barwise, Jon and John Perry 1983. *Situations and Attitudes*. Cambridge, Massachusetts: MIT Press.

Bear, John 1981. Gaps as syntactic features. MA dissertation, University of Texas at Austin.

Beesley, Kenneth R. 1982. Evaluative adjectives as one-place predicates in Montague grammar. *Journal of Semantics*, 1, 195–249.

Bolinger, Dwight L. 1965. The atomization of meaning. *Language*, 41, 555–73.

Borsley, Robert 1983a. A Welsh agreement process and the status of VP and S. In Gerald Gazdar, Ewan H. Klein, and Geoffrey K. Pullum (eds), *Order, Concord and Constituency*. Dordrecht: Foris, 57–74.

Borsley, Robert 1983b. Mobile inflections in Polish. Paper presented to the Autumn Meeting of the Linguistics Association of Great Britain, University of Newcastle, September 21–23, 1983.

Borsley, Robert 1984a. On the nonexistence of VP's. In Willem de Geest and Yvan Putseys (eds), *Sentential Complementation*, Dordrecht: Foris, 55–65.

Borsley, Robert 1984b. Welsh subjects and agreement. Paper presented to the Spring Meeting of the Linguistics Association of Great Britain, University of Hull, March 28–30, 1984.

Brame, Michael K. 1976. *Conjectures and Refutations in Syntax and Semantics*. New York: Elsevier North-Holland.

Brame, Michael K. 1978. *Base-Generated Syntax*. Seattle: Noit Amrofer.

Brame, Michael K. 1981. Trace theory with filters vs. lexically based syntax without. *Linguistic Inquiry*, 12, 275–93.

Bresnan, Joan W. 1976. On the form and functioning of transformations. *Linguistic Inquiry*, 7, 3–40.

Bresnan, Joan W. 1977. Transformations and categories in syntax. In R. F. Butts and J. Hintikka, (eds), *Basic Problems in Methodology and Linguistics*. Dordrecht: D. Reidel, 261–82.

Bresnan, Joan W. 1978. A realistic transformational grammar. In Morris Halle, Joan W. Bresnan and G. A. Miller (eds), *Linguistic Theory and Psychological Reality*. Cambridge, Massachusetts: MIT Press, 1–59.

Bresnan, Joan W. 1982a. Control and Complementation. *Linguistic Inquiry*, 13, 343–434.

Bresnan, Joan W. 1982b. Polyadicity. In Joan W. Bresnan (ed.), *The Mental Representation of Grammatical Relations*. Cambridge, Massachusetts: MIT Press, 149–72.

Bresnan, Joan W. and Jane Grimshaw 1978. The syntax of free relatives in English. *Linguistic Inquiry*, 9, 331–91.

Brys, Becky 1984. Tag questions in GPSG: The theory is adequate, isn't it? Unpublished paper, University of Wisconsin at Madison.

Cann, Ronald 1983a. An approach to the Latin accusative and infinitive. In Gerald Gazdar, Ewan H. Klein, and Geoffrey K. Pullum (eds), *Order, Concord and Constituency*. Dordrecht: Foris, 113–37.

Cann, Ronald 1983b. Agreement in Greek. Paper presented at the Spring Meeting of the Linguistics Association of Great Britain, University of Sheffield, March 23–25, 1983.

Cann, Ronald 1984. Features and morphology in generalized phrase structure grammar. Unpublished PhD thesis, University of Sussex.

Capell, A. 1971. *Arosi Grammar*. Pacific Linguistics, Series B, No. 20, Canberra: Australian National University.

Carlson, Greg 1983a. Marking constituents. In Frank Heny and Barry Richards (eds), *Linguistic Categories: Auxiliaries and Related Puzzles*, Vol. 1. Dordrecht: D. Reidel. 69–98.

Carlson, Greg 1983b. Logical form: types of evidence. *Linguistics and Philosophy*, 6, 295–317.

Chierchia, Gennaro 1984. Anaphoric properties of infinitives and gerunds. In Mark Cobler, Susannah MacKaye and Michael Wescoat, (eds), *Proceedings of the Third West Coast Conference on Formal Linguistics*. Stanford, California: Stanford University Linguistics Department, 28–39.

Chomsky, Noam 1957. *Syntactic Structures*. The Hague: Mouton.

Chomsky, Noam 1965. *Aspects of the Theory of Syntax*. Cambridge, Massachusetts: MIT Press.

Chomsky, Noam 1970. Remarks on nominalization. In Roderick A. Jacobs and Peter S. Rosenbaum (eds), *Readings in English Transformational Grammar*. Waltham, Massachusetts: Ginn and Company, 184–221.

Chomsky, Noam 1973. Conditions on transformations. In Stephen R. Anderson and Paul Kiparsky (eds), *A Festschrift for Morris Halle*. New York: Holt, Rinehart and Winston, 232–86.

Chomsky, Noam 1977. On *wh*-movement. In Peter W. Culicover, Thomas Wasow and Adrian Akmajian (eds), *Formal Syntax*. New York: Academic Press, 71–132.

Chomsky, Noam 1980. On binding. *Linguistic Inquiry*, 11, 1–46.

Chomsky, Noam 1981. *Lectures on Government and Binding*. Dordrecht: Foris.

Chomsky, Noam and Morris Halle 1968. *The Sound Pattern of English*. New York: Harper and Row, 400–35.

Chung, Sandra and James McCloskey 1983. On the interpretation of certain island facts in GPSG. *Linguistic Inquiry*. 14, 704–13.

Cleaveland, J. and R. Uzgalis 1975. *Grammars for programming language: what every programmer should know about grammar*. New York: Elsevier.

Comrie, Bernard 1984. Language universals and linguistic argumentation: a reply to Coopmans. *Journal of Linguistics*, 20, 155–63.

Cooper, Robin 1975. *Montague's semantic theory and transformational syntax*. PhD dissertation, University of Massachusetts at Amherst.

Cooper, Robin 1979. Model theory for a fragment of English. Unpublished paper, University of Wisconsin at Madison.

Cooper, Robin 1981. Swedish noun phrases and context-free grammar. Paper presented at the Fifty-Sixth Annual Meeting of the Linguistic Society of America, New York, December 27–30, 1981.

Cooper, Robin 1982. Swedish and the head-feature convention. Paper presented at the Workshop on Scandinavian Syntax and Theory of Grammar, University of Trondheim, June 3–5, 1982.

Cooper, Robin 1983. *Quantification and syntactic theory*. Dordrecht: D. Reidel.

Corbett, Greville 1983a. Resolution rules: agreement in person, number, and gender. In Gerald Gazdar, Ewan Klein, and Geoffrey K. Pullum (eds), *Order, Concord and Constituency*. Dordrecht: Foris, 175–206.

Corbett, Greville 1983b. *Hierarchies, Targets and Controllers: Agreement Patterns in Slavic*. London: Croom Helm.

Crain, Stephen and Janet D. Fodor in press. How can grammars help parsers? In David Dowty, Lauri Karttunen, and Arnold M. Zwicky (eds), *Natural Language Processing: Psycholinguistic, Computational, and Theoretical Perspectives*. New York: Cambridge University Press.

Cullen, Constance 1982. Two aspects of Mandarin Chinese. Paper presented at the Spring Meeting of the Linguistics Association of Great Britain, University of Reading, March 24–26, 1982.

Culy, Christopher 1983. An extension of phrase structure rules and its application to natural language. MA thesis, Stanford University.

Culy, Christopher forthcoming. The complexity of the vocabulary of Bambara. To appear in *Linguistics and Philosophy*.

Curry, H. B. 1961. Some logical aspects of grammatical structure. *Structure of Language and its Grammatical Aspects: Proceedings of the 12th Symposium in Applied Mathematics*, American Mathematical Society, 56–68.

Dahl, Östen 1974. Operational grammars. Gothenburg: Logical Grammar Report 8.

Dalrymple, Mary 1984. Verb agreement in Hindi. Unpublished paper, University of Texas at Austin.

Derbyshire, Desmond C. and Geoffrey K. Pullum (eds), forthcoming. *Handbook of Amazonian Languages*, Volume 1.

Dixon, Robert M. W. 1972. *The Dyirbal language of North Queensland*. Cambridge Studies in Linguistics, 9. London: Cambridge University Press.

Dowty, David R. 1978a. Applying Montague's views on linguistic metatheory to the structure of the lexicon. In Donka Farkas, W. M. Jacobsen and K. W. Todrys (eds), *Papers from the Parasession on the Lexicon*. Chicago: Chicago Linguistic Society, 97–137.

Dowty, David R. 1978b. Governed transformations as lexical rules in a Montague Grammar. *Linguistic Inquiry*, 9, 393–426.

Dowty, David R. 1979a. Dative 'movement' and Thomason's extensions of Montague Grammar. In Steven Davis and Marianne Mithun (eds), *Linguistics, Philosophy, and Montague Grammar*. Austin: University of Texas Press, 153–222.

Dowty, David R. 1979b. *Word Meaning and Montague Grammar*. Dordrecht: D. Reidel.

Dowty, David R. 1980. Comments on the paper by Bach and Partee. In Jody Kreiman and Almerindo E. Ojeda (eds), *Papers from the Parasession on Pronouns and Anaphora*. Chicago: Chicago Linguistic Society, 29–40.

Dowty, David R. 1982a. A simple analysis of non-constituent conjunction. Unpublished paper, Ohio State University.

Dowty, David R. 1982b. Grammatical relations and Montague Grammar. In Pauline Jacobson and Geoffrey K. Pullum (eds), *The Nature of Syntactic Representation*. Dordrecht: D. Reidel, 79–130.

Dowty, David R. 1982c. More on the categorial analysis of grammatical relations. In *Working Papers in Linguistics* (Ohio State University), 26, 102–33. Also in Annie Zaenen (ed.), *Subjects and Other Subjects: Proceedings of the Harvard Conference on Grammatical Relations*. Bloomington: Indiana University Linguistics Club.

Dowty, David R. 1982d. Tenses, time adverbs, and compositional semantic theory. *Linguistics and Philosophy*, 5, 23–55.

Dowty, David R. forthcoming. On recent treatments of 'control': Solutions in search of a problem? To appear in *Linguistics and Philosophy*.

Dowty, David R., Robert Wall and Stanley Peters 1981. *Introduction to Montague Semantics*. Dordrecht: D. Reidel.

Edwards, Malcolm 1983. Relative clauses in Egyptian Arabic. Paper presented to the Autumn Meeting of the Linguistics Association of Great Britain, University of Newcastle, September 21–23, 1983.

Emonds, Joseph E. 1976. *A Transformational Approach to English Syntax: Root, Structure-preserving and Local Transformations*. New York: Academic Press.

Engdahl, Elisabet 1980. *The syntax and semantics of questions in Swedish*. PhD dissertation, University of Massachusetts at Amherst.

Engdahl, Elisabet 1983. Parasitic gaps. In *Linguistics and Philosophy*, 6, 5–34.

Ernst, T. 1980. Grist for the linguistics mill: idioms and 'extra' adjectives. Paper presented at the Fifty-Fifth Annual Meeting of the Linguistic Society of America, San Antonio, Texas.

Espinal i Farre, Maria Teresa 1981. The auxiliary in Catalan. MA Dissertation, University of London.

Espinal i Farre, Maria Teresa 1983. *Els Verbs Auxiliars en Catala. Monografies de Quaderns de Traduccio i Interpretacio, 1*. Bellaterra: Universitat Autonoma de Barcelona.

Evans, Roger 1982. A model of English verbs. Unpublished paper, University of Sussex.

Evans, Roger and Gerald Gazdar 1984. *The ProGram Manual.* University of Sussex, *Cognitive Science Research Paper,* 35 (CSRP 035).

Falk, Yehuda 1983. Constituency, word order, and phrase structure rules. *Linguistic Analysis* 11, 331–60.

Farkas, Donka 1984a. The status of VP in Hungarian. To appear in *Papers from the 20th Regional Meeting of the Chicago Linguistics Society.*

Farkas, Donka 1984b. The syntactic position of focus in Hungarian. Unpublished paper, Pennsylvania State University.

Farkas, Donka, Daniel Flickinger, Gerald Gazdar, William Ladusaw, Almerindo Ojeda, Jessie Pinkham, Geoffrey K. Pullum and Peter Sells 1983. Some revisions to the theory of features and feature instantiation. Mimeo, UCLA. Also in *Proceedings of the ICOT Workshop on Non-Transformational Grammars.* Tokyo: Institute for New Generation Computer Technology, 11–13.

Farkas, Donka and Almerindo Ojeda forthcoming: Agreement and coordinate NPs. To appear in *Linguistics.*

Finer, Daniel 1981. French causatives in a context-free grammar. Paper presented at the Fifty-Sixth Annual Meeting of the Linguistic Society of America, New York, December 27–30, 1981.

Finer, Daniel 1982. A non-transformational relation between causatives and non-causatives in French. In Daniel Flickinger, Marlys Macken, and Nancy Wiegand (eds), *Proceedings of the First West Coast Conference on Formal Linguistics.* Stanford: Stanford Linguistics Department, 47–59.

Flickinger, Daniel 1981. Indirect objects in Spanish: a case for NP's. Paper presented at the Fifty-Sixth Annual Meeting of the Linguistic Society of America, New York, December 27–30, 1981.

Flickinger, Daniel 1983. Lexical heads and phrasal gaps. In Michael Barlow, Daniel Flickinger, and Michael Wescoat (eds), *Proceedings of the Second West Coast Conference on Formal Linguistics.* Stanford: Stanford Linguistics Department, 89–101.

Flynn, Michael 1983. A categorial theory of structure building. In Gerald Gazdar, Ewan H. Klein, and Geoffrey K. Pullum (eds), *Order, Concord and Constituency.* Dordrecht: Foris, 138–174.

Fodor, Janet D. 1980. Parsing, constraints and the freedom of expression. Mimeo, Storrs: University of Connecticut.

Fodor, Janet D. 1983a. Constraints on gaps: is the parser a significant influence? *Linguistics,* 21, 9–34.

Fodor, Janet D. 1983b. Phrase structure parsing and the island constraints. *Linguistics and Philosophy,* 6, 163–223.

Fraser, B. 1970. Idioms within a transformational grammar. *Foundations of Language,* 6, 22–42.

Gazdar, Gerald 1980. A cross-categorial semantics for coordination. *Linguistics and Philosophy,* 3, 407–9.

Gazdar, Gerald 1981a. On syntactic categories. *Philosophical Transactions (Series B) of the Royal Society,* 295, 267–83.

Gazdar, Gerald 1981b. Unbounded dependencies and coordinate structure. *Linguistic Inquiry,* 12, 155–84.

Gazdar, Gerald 1982. Phrase structure grammar. In Pauline Jacobson and Geoffrey K. Pullum (eds), *The Nature of Syntactic Representation*. Dordrecht: D. Reidel, 131–186.

Gazdar, Gerald, Ewan Klein, Geoffrey K. Pullum and Ivan A. Sag 1982. Coordinate structure and unbounded dependencies. In Michael Barlow, Daniel Flickinger and Ivan A. Sag (eds), *Developments in Generalized Phrase Structure Grammar: Stanford Working Papers in Grammatical Theory*, Volume 2. Bloomington, Indiana: Indiana University Linguistics Club, 38–68.

Gazdar, Gerald and Geoffrey K. Pullum 1976. Truth-functional connectives in natural language. In Salikoko S. Mufwene, Carol A. Walker and Sanford B. Seever (eds), *Papers from the 12th Regional Meeting, Chicago Linguistic Society*, 220–34.

Gazdar, Gerald and Geoffrey K. Pullum 1981. Subcategorization, constituent order and the notion 'head'. In M. Moortgat, H.v.d. Hulst and T. Hoekstra (eds), *The Scope of Lexical Rules*. Dordrecht: Foris, 107–23.

Gazdar, Gerald and Geoffrey K. Pullum 1982. Generalized phrase structure grammar: a theoretical synopsis. Bloomington, Indiana: Indiana University Linguistics Club, August 1982.

Gazdar, Gerald, Geoffrey K. Pullum and Ivan A. Sag 1982. Auxiliaries and related phenomena in a restrictive theory of grammar. *Language*, 58, 591–638. [Earlier drafts appeared as an IULC mimeo 1981, and in *Stanford Working Papers in Grammatical Theory*, *Volume 1*, 1980.]

Gazdar, Gerald, Geoffrey K. Pullum, Ivan A. Sag and Thomas Wasow 1982. Coordination and transformational grammar. *Linguistic Inquiry*, 13, 663–76.

Gazdar, Gerald and Ivan A. Sag 1981. Passive and reflexives in phrase structure grammar. In Jeroen A. G. Groenendijk, Theo Janssen, and Martin Stokhof (eds), *Formal Methods in the Study of Language*. Amsterdam: Mathematical Centre Tracts, 131–52. Also in *Stanford Working Papers in Grammatical Theory*, Volume 1, 1980.

Geggus, Jana 1983. GPSG and the typology of NP-internal agreement. Paper presented at the 2nd Workshop on Scandinavian Syntax and Theory of Grammar, Biskops-Arno, June 4–6, 1983.

George, Leland 1980. *Analogical generalizations of natural language syntax*. PhD dissertation, MIT.

Georgopoulos, Carol 1983. Trace and resumptive pronouns in Palauan. In Amy Chukerman, Mitchell Marks and John F. Richardson (eds), *Papers from the 19th Regional Meeting of the Chicago Linguistic Society*, 134–45.

Goodall, Grant 1983. A three-dimensional analysis of coordination. In Amy Chukerman, Mitchell Marks and John F. Richardson (eds), *Papers from the 19th Regional Meeting of the Chicago Linguistic Society*, 146–54.

Goodman, Nelson 1949. On the likeness of meaning. *Analysis*, 10, 1–7.

Greenberg, Joseph H. 1963. Some universals of grammar with particular reference to the order of meaningful elements. In Joseph H. Greenberg (ed.), *Universals of Language*. Cambridge, Massachusetts: MIT Press, 73–113.

Grimshaw, Jane 1982. Subcategorization and grammatical relations. In Annie Zaenen (ed.), *Subjects and Other Subjects: Proceedings of the Harvard Conference on the Representation of Grammatical Relations*. Bloomington: IULC.

Grinder, John and Suzette Elgin 1973. *Guide to Transformational Grammar*. New York: Holt, Rinehart and Winston.

Grosu, Alexander 1974. On the nature of the left branch condition. *Linguistic Inquiry*, 5, 308–19.

Gunji, Takao 1981. A phrase structural analysis of the Japanese language. MA dissertation, Ohio State University.

Gunji, Takao 1982. Apparent object control of reflexives in a restrictive theory of grammar. *Papers in Japanese Linguistics*, 8, 63–78.

Gunji, Takao 1983a. Control of gaps and reflexives in Japanese. In *Proceedings of the Second Japanese–Korean Joint Workshop on Formal Grammar*, 151–86 (Logico-Linguistic Society of Japan).

Gunji, Takao 1983b. Generalized phrase structure grammar and Japanese reflexivization. *Linguistics and Philosophy*, 6, 115–56.

Gunji, Takao 1983c. *Introduction to Linguistics for Computer Scientists, Volume 2: Generalized Phrase Structure Grammar* (in Japanese). Tokyo: Information Technology Promotion Agency.

Gunji, Takao 1983d. Topicalization in Japanese. In *Proceedings of the ICOT Workshop on Non-Transformational Grammars*. Tokyo: Institute for New Generation Computer Technology, 21–7.

Halle, Morris 1969. How not to measure length of lexical representations and other matters. *Journal of Linguistics*, 5, 305–8.

Halvorsen, Per-Kristian and William A. Ladusaw 1979. Montague's 'Universal Grammar': An introduction for the linguist. *Linguistics and Philosophy*, 3, 185–223.

Harlow, Stephen 1981. The Head Feature Convention, clause types and morphology in Welsh. Unpublished paper, University of York.

Harlow, Stephen 1983. Celtic relatives. *York Papers in Linguistics*, 10, 77–121.

Harman, Gilbert 1963. Generative grammars without transformation rules: a defense of phrase structure. *Language*, 39, 597–616.

Harris, Zellig S. 1946. From morpheme to utterance. *Language*, 22, 162–83.

Harris, Zellig S. 1951. *Methods in Structural Linguistics*. Chicago: University of Chicago Press.

Hausser, Roland 1978. Surface compositionality and the semantics of mood. In Jeroen A. G. Groenendijk and Martin Stokhof (eds), *Amsterdam Papers in Formal Grammar*, Volume 2, 174–93.

Hellan, Lars 1980. *Toward an Integrated Theory of Noun Phrases*. Trondheim: University of Trondheim.

Hendrick, Randall 1978. The phrase structure of adjectives and comparatives. *Linguistic Analysis*, 4, 255–99.

Hendrick, Randall 1981. Subcategorization: its form and its functioning. *Linguistics*, 19, 871–910.

Heny, Frank 1979. Review of Noam Chomsky, Logical structure of linguistic theory (1975). *Synthese*, 40, 317–52.

Heringer, J. 1976. Idioms and lexicalization in English. In Masayoshi Shibatani (ed.), *Syntax and Semantics 6: The Grammar of Causative Constructions*. New York: Academic Press, 205–16.

Higgins, F. R. 1976. The Pseudo-cleft construction in English. PhD dissertation:

MIT (1973), Bloomington: Indiana University Linguistics Club.

Hinrichs, Erhard 1984. Attachment of articles and prepositions in German: simple cliticization of inflected prepositions. *Working Papers in Linguistics* (Ohio State University), 29, 127–38.

Hopcroft, John and Jeffrey Ullman 1979. *Introduction to Automata Theory, Languages, and Computation.* Reading, Massachusetts: Addison-Wesley.

Horrocks, Geoffrey 1983. The order of constituents in Modern Greek. In Gerald Gazdar, Ewan H. Klein, and Geoffrey K. Pullum (eds), *Order, Concord and Constituency.* Dordrecht: Foris, 95–112.

Horrocks, Geoffrey 1984. The lexical head constraint, X-Bar theory and the 'pro-drop' parameter. In Willem de Geest and Yvan Putseys (eds), *Sentential Complementation.* Dordrecht: Foris, 117–25.

Horrocks, Geoffrey and Gerald Gazdar 1981. Greek relatives revisited. Paper presented to the Spring Meeting of the Linguistics Association of Great Britain, Manchester, April 1981.

Huang, Chu-Ren 1983. Reduplication reanalysed: A fragment of Chinese PS rules. Unpublished paper, Cornell University.

Hudson, Grover 1972. Is deep structure linear? *UCLA Papers in Syntax*, 2, 51–77.

Hudson, Richard 1977. The power of morphological rules. *Lingua*, 42, 73–89.

Ikeya, Akira 1983. Japanese honorific systems in generalized phrase structure grammar. In *Proceedings of the ICOT Workshop on Non-Transformational Grammars.* Tokyo: Institute for New Generation Computer Technology, 17–20.

Iwakura, Kunihiro 1980. On *wh*-movement and constraints on rules. *Linguistic Analysis*, 6, 53–95.

Jackendoff, Ray S. 1973. The base rules for prepositional phrases. In Stephen R. Anderson and P. Kiparsky (eds), *A Festschrift for Morris Halle.* New York: Holt, Rinehart, and Winston, 345–56.

Jackendoff, Ray S. 1977. *X-bar Syntax: A Study of Phrase Structure.* Cambridge, Massachusetts: MIT Press.

Jacobson, Pauline 1984. Connectivity in generalized phrase structure grammar. *Natural Language and Linguistic Theory*, 1, 535–81.

Jakobson, Roman C., Gunnar M. Fant and Morris Halle 1951. *Preliminaries to Speech Analysis.* Cambridge, Massachusetts: MIT Press.

Janssen, Theo 1980. On problems concerning the quantification rules in Montague Grammar. In Christian Rohrer (ed.), *Time, Tense and Quantifiers.* Tübingen: Max Niemeyer, 113–34.

Janssen, Theo 1983. *Foundations and Applications of Montague Grammar.* Amsterdam: Mathematisch Centrum.

Jenkins, L. 1975. *The English Existential.* Tubingen: Niemeyer.

Johnson, David E. and Paul M. Postal 1980. *Arc Pair Grammar.* Princeton, N.J.: Princeton University Press.

Johnson, Mark 1983. A GPSG account of VP fronting in German. Unpublished paper, University of California at San Diego.

Jones, Michael A. 1983. Getting 'tough' with *wh*- movement. *Journal of Linguistics*, 19, 129–59.

Kameshima, Nanako 1984. CNPC violations in Japanese: A GPSG account. Unpublished paper.

Kamp, J. A. W. 1981. A theory of truth and semantic representation. In Jeroen A. G. Groenendijk, Theo Janssen, and Martin Stokhof (eds), *Formal Methods in the Study of Language*. Amsterdam: Mathematical Centre Tracts, 277–322.

Karttunen, Lauri 1977. Syntax and semantics of questions. *Linguistics and Philosophy*, 1, 3–44.

Karttunen, Lauri 1984. Features and values. In *Proceedings of Coling84*, Menlo Park: Association for Computational Linguistics, 28–33.

Katz, Jerrold 1973. Compositionality, idiomaticity, and lexical substitution. In Steven R. Anderson and Paul Kiparsky (eds), *A Festschrift for Morris Halle*. New York: Holt, Rinehart and Winston, 357–76.

Katz, Jerrold 1981. *Language and Other Abstract Objects*. Oxford: Blackwell.

Kay, Martin 1979. Functional Grammar. In Christina Chiarello et al. (eds), *Proceedings of the Fifth Annual Meeting of the Berkeley Linguistic Society*, 142–58.

Kay, Martin 1983. When meta-rules are not meta-rules. In Karen Sparck-Jones and Yorick Wilks (eds), *Automatic Natural Language Parsing*. Chichester: Ellis Horwood.

Keenan, Edward L. 1974. The functional principle: generalizing the notion of 'subject of'. In Michael W. La Galy, Robert A. Fox and Anthony Bruck (eds), *Papers from the 10th Regional Meeting of the Chicago Linguistics Society*, 298–309.

Keenan, Edward L. 1980. Passive is phrasal (not sentential or lexical). In T. Hoekstra, H. v.d. Hulst and M. Moortgat (eds), *Lexical Grammar*. Dordrecht: Foris, 181–213.

Keenan, Edward L. 1983. Boolean algebra for linguists. In Susan Mordechay (ed.), *UCLA Working Papers in Semantics*. Los Angeles, California: UCLA Department of Linguistics, 1–75.

Keenan, Edward L. and Leonard Faltz 1978. Logical types for natural language. *UCLA Occasional Papers in Linguistics*, 3. Los Angeles: UCLA Department of Linguistics.

Keenan, Edward L. and Leonard Faltz 1984. *Logical Types for Natural Language*. Dordrecht: D. Reidel.

Kim, Yang Soon 1984. Korean topicalization in GPSG. Unpublished paper.

Klein, Ewan H. 1978. *On sentences which report beliefs, desires, and other mental attitudes*. PhD dissertation, University of Cambridge.

Klein, Ewan H. and Ivan A. Sag forthcoming. Type-driven translation. To appear in *Linguistics and Philosophy*.

Knuth, Donald E. 1969. *The Art of Computer Programming*, Volume 2. Reading, Massachusetts: Addison-Wesley.

Kraft, Charles H. and Kraft, Marguerite G. 1973. *Introductory Hausa*. Berkeley: University of California Press.

Kuno, Susumo 1973. Constraints on internal clauses and sentential subjects. *Linguistic Inquiry*, 4, 363–85.

Kutschera, F. V. 1975. Partial interpretations. In Edward L. Keenan (ed.), *Formal Semantics of Natural Language*. Cambridge, Massachusetts: Cambridge University Press, 156–74.

Lakoff, George P. 1970. *Irregularity in Syntax*. New York: Holt, Rinehart, and Winston.

Langendoen, D. Terence 1976. On the weak generative capacity of infinite grammars. *CUNYForum*, 1, City University of New York, 13–24.

Langendoen, D. Terence 1981. The generative capacity of word-formation components. *Linguistic Inquiry*, 12, 320–2.

Langendoen, D. Terence and Paul M. Postal 1984. *The Vastness of Natural Languages*. Oxford: Blackwell.

Lapointe, Steven G. 1979. *A theory of grammatical agreement*. PhD Dissertation, University of Massachusetts at Amherst.

Lapointe, Steven G. 1980. A lexical analysis of the English auxiliary verb system. In Teun Hoekstra, Harry van der Hulst and Michael Moortgat (eds), *Lexical Grammar*. Dordrecht: Foris, 215–54.

Lapointe, Steven G. 1981. General and restricted agreement phenomena. In Michael Moortgat, Harry van der Hulst, and Teun Hoekstra (eds), *The Scope of Lexical Rules*. Dordrecht: Foris, 125–59.

Lasnik, Howard and Joseph J. Kupin 1977. A restrictive theory of transformational grammar. *Theoretical Linguistics*, 4, 173–96.

Lyons, John 1968. *Introduction to Theoretical Linguistics*. Cambridge: Cambridge University Press.

MacKaye, Susannah 1982. The coordination of relative clauses: A problem for the UDCS analysis. Paper presented to the Summer Meeting of the LSA, University of Maryland, July 1982.

Main, M. G. and D. B. Benson 1983. Denotational semantics for 'natural language' question-answering programs. *American Journal of Computational Linguistics*, 9, 11–21.

Maling, Joan 1983. Transitive adjectives: a case of categorial reanalysis. In Frank Heny and Barry Richards (eds), *Linguistic Categories: Auxiliaries and Related Puzzles*. Dordrecht: Reidel, 253–89.

Maling, Joan and Annie Zaenen 1982. A phrase structure account of Scandinavian extraction phenomena. In Pauline Jacobson and Geoffrey K. Pullum (eds), *The Nature of Syntactic Representation*. Dordrecht: D. Reidel, 229–82.

Milsark, Gary L. 1974. Existential sentences in English. PhD dissertation, MIT.

Milsark, Gary L. 1977. Toward an explanation of certain peculiarities of the existential construction in English. *Linguistic Analysis*, 3, 1–29.

Montague, Richard 1970. Universal Grammar. *Theoria*, 36, 373–98. [Reprinted in Richmond H. Thomason (ed.) *Formal Philosophy: Selected Papers of Richard Montague*. New Haven: Yale University Press (1974), 222–46.]

Montague, Richard 1974. *Formal Philosophy*. New Haven: Yale University Press.

Monzon, Christina 1979. A constituent structure rule grammar of the Spanish clitic positioning in complex and simple sentences. MA Dissertation, University of Texas at Austin.

Moortgat, Michael 1984. A Fregean restriction on metarules. In Charles Jones and Peter Sells (eds), *Proceedings of the Fourteenth Annual Meeting of the North Eastern Linguistic Society*, 306–25.

Morgan, Jerry L. 1972. Verb agreement as a rule of English. In Paul M. Peranteau, Judith N. Levi and Gloria C. Phares (eds), Papers from the 8th Regional Meeting, Chicago Linguistic Society, 278–86.

Nanni, Deborah L. 1978. *The EASY class of adjectives in English*. Amherst, Massachusetts: Graduate Linguistic Students' Association.

262 *Bibliography*

Nanni, Deborah L. 1980. On the surface syntax of constructions with *easy*-type adjectives. *Language*, 56, 568–81.

Nerbonne, John 1982. 'Phantoms' in German fronting: poltergeist constituents? Paper presented at the Fifty-Seventh Annual Meeting of the Linguistic Society of America, San Diego, December 1982.

Nerbonne, John 1984. German temporal semantics: three-dimensional tense logic and a GPSG fragment. *Working Papers in Linguistics* (Ohio State University), 30.

Ojeda, Almerindo 1984. On the ambivalence of the Spanish infinitive. Unpublished paper, University of Wisconsin at Madison.

Partee, Barbara H. 1975. Montague grammar and transformational grammar. *Linguistic Inquiry*, 6, 203–300.

Partee, Barbara H. 1979. Montague grammar and the well-formedness constraint. In Frank W. Heny and Helmut S. Schnelle (eds), *Syntax and Semantics 10: Selections from the Third Groningen Round Table.* New York: Academic Press, 275–313.

Partee, Barbara H. 1982. Belief-sentences and the limits of semantics. In Stanley Peters and E. Saarinen (eds), *Processes, Beliefs, and Questions.* Dordrecht: D. Reidel, 87–106.

Partee, Barbara H. 1984. Noun phrase interpretation and polymorphic types. Presented to 4th Amsterdam Colloquium on Formal Semantics, August 28–31, 1984.

Partee, Barbara H. in press. Compositionality. In Fred Landman and Frank Veltman (eds), *Varieties of Formal Syntax, Proceedings of the 4th Amsterdam Colloquium,* September 1982, Dordrecht: Foris.

Partee, Barbara H. and Mats Rooth 1983. Generalized conjunction and type ambiguity. In Rainer Bauerle, Ch. Schwarze and Arnim von Stechow (eds), *Meaning, Use and Interpretation of Language.* Berlin: de Gruyter, 361–383.

Pereira, Fernando C. N. and Stuart M. Shieber 1984. The semantics of grammar formalisms seen as computer languages. In *Proceedings of Coling84,* Menlo Park: Association for Computational Linguistics, 123–9.

Perlmutter, David M. (ed.), 1983. *Studies in Relational Grammar 1.* Chicago: University of Chicago Press.

Perlmutter, David M. (ed.), 1984. *Studies in Relational Grammar 2.* Chicago: University of Chicago Press.

Peters, P. Stanley Jr. and R. W. Ritchie 1973. Context-sensitive immediate constituent analysis: context-free languages revisited. In *Mathematical Systems Theory,* 6, 324–33 [Also in *ACM Symposium on Theory of Computing,* ACM (1969) 1–8].

Peters, P. Stanley Jr. and Hans Uszkoreit 1982. Essential variables in metarules. Paper presented at the Fifty-Seventh Annual Meeting of the Linguistic Society of America, San Diego, December 1982.

Peterson, Thomas H. 1971. Multi-ordered base structures in generative grammar. In *Papers from the 7th Regional Meeting, Chicago Linguistic Society,* 181–92.

Pinkham, Jessie 1983. A phrase structure analysis of parallel phrasal comparatives in French. Paper presented to the Southern California Conference on Romance Linguistics, UCLA, July 16–17, 1983.

Pollard, Carl 1982. Generalized grammar: toward the formalization of some concepts on the syntax–semantics frontier. Unpublished paper, Stanford University.

Pollard, Carl J. 1984. Generalized phrase structure grammars, head grammars, and natural languages. PhD dissertation, Stanford University.

Pollard, Carl and Ivan A. Sag 1983. Reflexives and reciprocals in English: an alternative to the binding theory. In Michael Barlow, Daniel Flickinger, and Michael Wescoat (eds), *Proceedings of the Second West Coast Conference on Formal Linguistics*. Stanford: Stanford Linguistics Department, 189–203.

Postal, Paul 1964. Limitations of phrase structure grammars. In Jerry A. Fodor and Jerrold J. Katz (eds), *The Structure of Language: Readings in the Philosophy of Language*. Englewood Cliffs: Prentice-Hall, 137–51.

Pullum, Geoffrey K. 1982. Free word order and phrase structure rules. In James Pustejovsky and Peter Sells (eds), *Proceedings of the Twelfth Annual Meeting of the North Eastern Linguistic Society*, 209–220. Graduate Linguistics Student Association, University of Massachusetts at Amherst.

Pullum, Geoffrey K. and Gerald Gazdar 1982. Natural languages and context free languages. *Linguistics and Philosophy*, 4, 471–504.

Quine, Willard Van Orman 1960. *Word and Object*. Cambridge, Massachusetts: MIT Press.

van Riemsdijk, Henk C. 1978. *A Case Study in Syntactic Markedness*. Lisse: The Peter de Ridder Press.

van Riemsdijk, Henk C. 1982. Derivational grammar vs. representational grammar in syntax and phonology. In Linguistic Society of Korea (ed.), *Linguistics in the Morning Calm*. Seoul: Hanshin Publishing Company, 211–31.

Rooth, Mats and Barbara Partee H. 1982. Conjunction, type ambiguity, and wide scope 'or'. In Daniel Flickinger, Marlys Macken, and Nancy Wiegand (eds), *Proceedings of the First West Coast Conference on Formal Linguistics*, Stanford: Stanford Linguistics Department, 353–62.

Rosenbaum, Peter S. 1967. *The Grammar of English Predicate Complement Constructions*. Cambridge, Massachusetts: MIT Press.

Ross, John R. 1967. *Constraints on variables in syntax*. PhD thesis, MIT. Bloomington, Indiana: Indiana University Linguistics Club.

Russell, Graham 1983. Compound verbs and constituent order in German. Unpublished paper, University of Sussex.

Russell, Graham 1984. Auxiliary ellipsis in Swedish. Paper presented to the Spring Meeting of the Linguistics Association of Great Britain, University of Hull, March 28–30, 1984.

Sag, Ivan A. 1976. *Deletion and logical form*. PhD dissertation, MIT. Also published by Garland Publishing Inc., New York, 1980.

Sag, Ivan A. 1981. Partial variable assignment functions, verb phrase ellipsis, and the dispensability of logical form. Unpublished paper, Stanford University.

Sag, Ivan A. 1983. On parasitic gaps. *Linguistics and Philosophy*, 6, 35–45. Also in Daniel Flickinger, Marlys Macken, and Nancy Wiegand (eds), *Proceedings of the First West Coast Conference on Formal Linguistics*. Stanford: Stanford Linguistics Department, 35–46, 1982.

Sag, Ivan A. and Ewan H. Klein 1982. The syntax and semantics of English expletive pronoun constructions. In Michael Barlow, Daniel Flickinger, and Ivan A. Sag (eds), *Developments in Generalized Phrase Structure Grammar: Stanford Working Papers in Grammatical Theory*, Volume 2. Bloomington, Indiana: Indiana University Linguistics Club, 92–136.

Sag, Ivan A., Thomas Wasow, Gerald Gazdar and Steven Weisler forthcoming. Coordination and how to distinguish categories. To appear in *Natural Language and Linguistic Theory*.

Saito, Mamoru 1980. An analysis of the 'tough' construction in Japanese. MA Dissertation, Stanford University.

Sanders, G. A. 1970. Invariant order. Mimeo, Indiana University Linguistics Club.

Schachter, Paul 1981. Lovely to look at. *Linguistic Analysis*, 8, 431–48.

Schachter, Paul 1984. Auxiliary reduction: An argument for GPSG. *Linguistic Inquiry*, 15, 514–23.

Schoenfinkel, Moses 1924. Über die Bausteine der mathematische Logik. In *Mathematische Annalen*, 92, 305–31.

Sells, Peter 1982a. A phrase structure grammar for Irish relative clauses. Unpublished paper, University of Massachusetts at Amherst.

Sells, Peter 1982b. Control in Modern Irish. Unpublished paper, University of Massachusetts at Amherst.

Sells, Peter 1983b. Relative clauses in Irish and Welsh. *York Papers in Linguistics*, 10, 159–72.

Sells, Peter 1983c. Thinking about foot features. Unpublished paper, University of Massachusetts at Amherst.

Sells, Peter 1984. *Syntax and semantics of resumptive pronouns*. PhD dissertation, University of Massachusetts at Amherst, distributed by the Graduate Linguistics Student Association.

Šaumjan, S. K. and P. A. Soboleva 1963. *Applikativnaja poroždajuščaja model' i isčislenie transformacij v russkom jazyke*. Moscow: Izdatel'stvo Akademii Nauk, SSSR.

Shieber, Stuart M. 1984. Direct parsing of ID/LP grammars. *Linguistics and Philosophy*, 7, 135–54.

Shieber, Stuart M. forthcoming. Evidence against the non-context-freeness of natural language. To appear in *Linguistics and Philosophy*.

Shieber, Stuart M., Susan Stucky, Hans Uszkoreit and Jane Robinson 1983. Formal constraints on metarules. Technical Note 283, SRI International. Also in *Proceedings of the 21st Annual Meeting of the Association for Computational Linguistics*, 22–7.

Soames, Scott 1984. Linguistics and psychology. *Linguistics and Philosophy*, 7, 155–79.

Staal, J. F. 1967. *Word order in Sanskrit and universal grammar*. Dordrecht: D. Reidel.

Steedman, Mark 1983. A categorial syntax for subject and tense in English and some related languages. Unpublished paper, University of Warwick.

Stockwell, Robert P., Paul Schachter and Barbara H. Partee 1973. *The Major Syntactic Structures of English*. New York: Holt, Rinehart and Winston.

Stucky, Susan 1981a. Free word order languages, free constituent order languages, and the gray area in between. In Victoria A. Burke and James Pustejovsky (eds), *Proceedings of the 11th Annual Meeting of the North Eastern Linguistic Society*. Department of Linguistics, University of Massachusetts at Amherst, 364–76.

Stucky, Susan 1981b. Linear order and case marking. Paper presented at the Fifty-Sixth Annual Meeting of the Linguistic Society of America, New York, December 27–30, 1981.

Stucky, Susan 1981c. *Word order variation in Makua: a phrase structure grammar analysis*. PhD dissertation, University of Illinois at Urbana-Champaign.

Stucky, Susan 1982. Linearization rules and typology. In Daniel Flickinger, Marlys Macken, and Nancy Wiegand (eds), *Proceedings of the First West Coast Conference on Formal Linguistics*. Stanford: Stanford Linguistics Department, 60–70.

Stucky, Susan 1983. Verb phrase constituency and linear order in Makua. In Gerald Gazdar, Ewan H. Klein, and Geoffrey K. Pullum (eds), *Order, Concord and Constituency*. Dordrecht: Foris, 75–94.

Thomason, Richmond H. 1972. A semantic theory of sortal incorrectness. *Journal of Philosophical Logic*, 1, 209–58.

Thomason, Richmond H. (ed.) 1974. *Formal Philosophy: Selected Papers of Richard Montague*. New Haven: Yale University Press.

Thomason, Richmond H. 1976a. On the semantic interpretation of the Thomason 1972 fragment. Mimeo, Indiana University Linguistics Club.

Thomason, Richmond H. 1976b. Some Extensions of Montague Grammar. In Barbara H. Partee (ed.), *Montague Grammar*. New York: Academic Press, 75–117

Thompson, Henry 1982. Handling metarules in a parser for GPSG. *Edinburgh D.A.I. Research Paper No. 175*. Also in Michael Barlow, Daniel Flickinger, and Ivan A. Sag (eds), *Developments in Generalized Phrase Structure Grammar: Stanford Working Papers in Grammatical Theory*, Volume 2. Bloomington: Indiana University Linguistics Club, 26–37. Also in *Proceedings of the 21st Annual Meeting of the Association for Computational Linguistics*, 26–37.

Thompson, Henry and John Phillips 1984. An implementation of GPSG within the MCHART chart parsing framework. Mimeo, University of Edinburgh, Department of Artificial Intelligence.

Trask, Larry 1983. The feature [TRANSITIVE] in GPSG. Paper presented at the Spring Meeting of the Linguistics Association of Great Britain, University of Sheffield, March 23–25, 1983.

Udo, Mariko 1982. The Japanese VP system. MA thesis, University College, London.

Uszkoreit, Hans 1982a. German word order in GPSG. In Daniel Flickinger, Marlys Macken, and Nancy Wiegand (eds), *Proceedings of the First West Coast Conference on Formal Linguistics*. Stanford: Stanford Linguistics Department, 137–48.

Uszkoreit, Hans 1982b. Topicalization in Standard German. Paper presented at the Fifty-Seventh Annual Meeting of the Linguistic Society of America, San Diego, December 1982.

Uszkoreit, Hans 1983. A framework for processing partially free word order. In *Proceedings of the 21st Annual Meeting of the Association for Computational Linguistics*, 106–12.

Vamling, Karina 1983. Adyge simple sentences: structure and agreement. Unpublished paper, Lund University.

Wall, Robert 1972. *Introduction to Mathematical Linguistics*. Englewood Cliffs, New Jersey: Prentice-Hall.

Warner, Anthony forthcoming. *English Auxiliaries: Structure and History*. Cambridge: Cambridge University Press.

Wasow, Thomas 1972. Anaphoric Relations in English. PhD dissertation, MIT. (Published in 1979 under the title *Anaphora in Generative Grammar*, Studies In Generative Linguistic Analysis (SIGLA) Vol. 2. Ghent: Story-Scientia.)

Wasow, Thomas 1977. Transformations and the lexicon. In Peter W. Culicover, Thomas Wasow and Adrian Akmajian (eds), *Formal Syntax*. New York: Academic Press, 327–60.

Wasow, Thomas 1980. Major and minor rules in lexical grammar. In Teun Hoekstra, Harry van der Hulst and Michael Moortgat (eds), *Lexical Grammar*. Dordrecht: Foris, 285–312.

Wasow, Thomas, Ivan A. Sag and Geoffrey Nunberg 1983. Idioms: an interim report. In Shiro Hattori and Kazuko Inoue (eds), *Proceedings of the XIIIth International Congress of Linguists*. Tokyo: CIPL, 102–15. (Also in *Preprints of the Plenary Session Papers, The XIIIth International Congress of Linguists, August 29–September 4, 1982*. Tokyo: CIPL.)

Weeda, Donald 1981. Tenseless *that*-clauses in generalized phrase structure grammar. In Roberta A. Hendrick, Carrie S. Masek and Mary Frances Miller (eds), *Papers from the 17th Regional Meeting, Chicago Linguistic Society*, 404–10.

van Wijngaarden, A. 1969. Report on the algorithmic language ALGOL68. *Numerische Mathematik*, 14, 79–218.

Williams, Edwin 1977. Discourse and logical form. *Linguistic Inquiry*, 8, 101–39.

Williams, Edwin 1978. Across-the-board rule application. *Linguistic Inquiry*, 9, 31–43.

Williams, Edwin 1981. On the notions 'lexically related' and 'head of a word'. *Linguistic Inquiry*, 12, 245–74.

Williams, Edwin 1984. *There*-insertion. *Linguistic Inquiry*, 15, 131–53.

Zubizaretta, Maria-Luisa and Jean-Roger Vergnaud 1981. On virtual categories. Unpublished paper, University of Massachusetts at Amherst/CNRS, Paris.

Zwicky, Arnold M. 1984. German adjective agreement in GPSG. *Working Papers in Linguistics* (Ohio State University), 31.

Name index

Abraham 179
Ades 73, 244
Aho 55
Akmajian 18, 19
Anderson, C. x, 73, 178
Anderson, S. 21, 221
Andrews 126
Anward x, 15

Bach x, 8, 84, 106, 189, 205, 206, 215, 218, 219, 225, 242
Barlow x, xi, 15, 107
Bartsch 195, 202, 203, 218
Barwise 135, 183
Bear 79
Benson 243
Bolinger 239
Borsley x, 15, 61, 106
Brame 1, 41, 67, 200
Bresnan xi, 6, 21, 41, 128, 135, 195, 200, 221, 243

Cann x, 15, 106, 107, 243
Capell 107
Carlson x, 223, 228, 244
Chierchia 201
Chomsky 6, 17, 18, 20, 21, 28, 29, 34, 35, 41, 42, 55, 64, 126, 147, 167, 195, 244
Chung 167
Cleaveland 65
Comrie 6
Cooper x, 15, 108, 135, 171, 243
Corbett x, 106
Crain 5
Cullen x, 15

Culy x, 15, 16, 55, 66
Curry 55

Dahl xi, 55
Dalrymple x, 15
Derbyshire 108
Dixon 179
Dowty xi, 3, 9, 55, 111, 129, 135, 167, 179, 183, 188, 193, 195 f., 201, 202, 203, 205, 222, 242

Edwards 15
Elgin 83
Emonds 19, 56, 64
Engdahl x, xi, 81, 164 f., 168
Ernst 237
Espinal i Farre 15
Evans x, 21, 61, 74

Falk 55
Faltz x, 84, 171, 183, 189, 193, 205
Fant 17
Farkas x, 15, 174, 179
Finer 15
Flickinger x, xi, 15, 24, 41, 59, 73, 106, 167
Flynn 55
Fodor xi, 5, 142, 167
Fraser 244
Frege 8

Gazdar 15, 16, 21, 39, 50, 55, 61, 64, 65, 66, 69, 73, 79, 106, 108, 125, 135, 139, 150, 167, 169, 171, 178, 179, 206, 229, 232
George 179

Subject index